Microsoft® Project For Dummies®

W9-BEY-566

 Cheat Sheet

Planning Your Project

1. Determine the project's scope. What are you going to do? What's the product?

2. Identify stakeholders. Who has a vested interest in the project, either in work to perform or in project outcomes? Plan how you'll report to them.

3. Determine standards. What equals quality for your project? Is there universal agreement about this?

4. List constraints. What unavoidable limitations exist in regards to time and the availability of resources?

5. Assess your muscle. How much support do you have for this project? Are there built-in organizational snafus? Is so, what will you do about them?

6. Face risks. How will you develop the necessary contingencies?

7. Set goals. Set achievable goals consistent with the project's scope.

8. Create categories or phases. What are the groups of functions (later called summary tasks)?

9. Break the project down into tasks. Identify the individual planned activities of the project.

10. Define task durations. Set a realistic length of time for each task.

11. Set milestones. Determine key points throughout the project that represent significant stages of completion.

12. Identify resources. Assign individuals or groups to perform the tasks.

13. Determine the critical path. What must be accomplished and in what order to keep the project on schedule?

14. Refine your project plan. Double-check each of these steps to ensure that they're consistent with the project's scope and goals.

15. Enter data into Microsoft Project.

16. Take a very long break. You can use this step as a recurring task throughout your project.

Creating a Schedule

1. Enter the project tasks by typing in the entry box.

2. Enter task durations (m — minutes, h — hours, d — days, w — weeks, 0 — milestones).

3. Link tasks by selecting them and then clicking the Link button on the Standard toolbar.

4. Change predecessors and successors using the Task form in split view (Window⇨Split).

5. Add resources using the Task form.

6. If necessary, change constraints using the Task Details form (View⇨More Views⇨Task Details Form).

7. Set the baseline by choosing Tools⇨Tracking⇨Save Baseline.

Six Ways to Correct Overallocated Resources

✔ Set overtime rates. In a resource view, choose Insert⇨Resource Information.

✔ Change the work calendar. Choose Tools⇨Change Working Time.

✔ Get assistance. Click the Resource Assignment button on the Standard toolbar. Either assign an additional existing resource or add a new one.

✔ Relieve some of the duty. Highlight a task and press Delete.

✔ Extend deadlines. Choose Tools⇨Resource Leveling.

✔ Take your project home and work evenings and weekends. Nah!

...For Dummies: #1 Computer Book Series for Beginners

Microsoft® Project For Dummies®

Cheat Sheet

Where'd You Say That Was?

Here are some helpful hints for your hunt.

How Do I . . .	*Answer*
Know if a project file is a template?	Its extension is .MPT.
Identify a workspace file?	Its extension is .MPW.
Temporarily hide a project?	Place it under your desk or make it the inactive window by choosing Window⇨Hide.
Make a consolidated project?	Choose Tools⇨Multiple Projects⇨ Consolidate Projects.
Create an outline?	Select the tasks and click the Indent button. The preceding task becomes a Summary task.
Make a split view?	Choose Window⇨Split.
Change a form in split view?	Highlight the lower pane, choose View⇨More Views, and select a form.
Make a highlighted filter instead of an isolated filter?	Holding down the Shift key, choose Tools⇨Filtered For:, and then choose a filter.
Change the timescale on the Gantt chart?	Double-click the date area. Choose major and minor scales.
Change the font style of items in the Gantt chart?	Choose Format⇨Text Styles. Select the Item to Change, and have at it.
Draw on the Gantt chart?	Use washable crayons on the monitor or choose Insert⇨Drawing to display a floating drawing toolbar. (The crayons work better.)
Put a movie in the Gantt chart?	Choose Insert⇨Object. From the list box, select Media Player. Open an AVI or an MOV file. A movie object appears on the screen. Double-click it to run the movie. Get out the popcorn.
Find project statistics?	Choose File⇨Project Info⇨Statistics.
Update tasks as completed to the present date?	Highlight the tasks, and then choose Tools⇨Tracking⇨Update Tasks.

...For Dummies: #1 Computer Book Series for Beginners

®

References for the Rest of Us! ®

COMPUTER BOOK SERIES FROM IDG

Are you intimidated and confused by computers? Do you find that traditional manuals are overloaded with technical details you'll never use? Do your friends and family always call you to fix simple problems on their PCs? Then the *...For Dummies*® computer book series from IDG Books Worldwide is for you.

...For Dummies books are written for those frustrated computer users who know they aren't really dumb but find that PC hardware, software, and indeed the unique vocabulary of computing make them feel helpless. *...For Dummies* books use a lighthearted approach, a down-to-earth style, and even cartoons and humorous icons to diffuse computer novices' fears and build their confidence. Lighthearted but not lightweight, these books are a perfect survival guide for anyone forced to use a computer.

> *"I like my copy so much I told friends; now they bought copies."*
>
> **Irene C., Orwell, Ohio**

> *"Quick, concise, nontechnical, and humorous."*
>
> **Jay A., Elburn, Illinois**

> *"Thanks, I needed this book. Now I can sleep at night."*
>
> **Robin F., British Columbia, Canada**

Already, hundreds of thousands of satisfied readers agree. They have made *...For Dummies* books the #1 introductory level computer book series and have written asking for more. So, if you're looking for the most fun and easy way to learn about computers, look to *...For Dummies* books to give you a helping hand.

MICROSOFT®
PROJECT
FOR
DUMMIES®

MICROSOFT® PROJECT FOR DUMMIES®

by Martin Doucette

Foreword
by Al Zeitoun

IDG Books Worldwide, Inc.
An International Data Group Company

Foster City, CA ♦ Chicago, IL ♦ Indianapolis, IN ♦ Southlake, TX

Microsoft® Project For Dummies®

Published by
IDG Books Worldwide, Inc.
An International Data Group Company
919 E. Hillsdale Blvd.
Suite 400
Foster City, CA 94404
www.idgbooks.com (IDG Books Worldwide Web site)
www.dummies.com (Dummies Press Web site)

Library of Congress Catalog Card No.: 96-80238

ISBN: 0-7645-0084-8

Printed in the United States of America

10 9 8 7 6 5 4 3 2

1E/QR/QY/ZX/IN

Distributed in the United States by IDG Books Worldwide, Inc.

Distributed by Macmillan Canada for Canada; by Transworld Publishers Limited in the United Kingdom; by IDG Norge Books for Norway; by IDG Sweden Books for Sweden; by Woodslane Pty. Ltd. for Australia; by Woodslane Enterprises Ltd. for New Zealand; by Longman Singapore Publishers Ltd. for Singapore, Malaysia, Thailand, and Indonesia; by Simron Pty. Ltd. for South Africa; by Toppan Company Ltd. for Japan; by Distribuidora Cuspide for Argentina; by Livraria Cultura for Brazil; by Ediciencia S.A. for Ecuador; by Addison-Wesley Publishing Company for Korea; by Ediciones ZETA S.C.R. Ltda. for Peru; by WS Computer Publishing Corporation, Inc., for the Philippines; by Unalis Corporation for Taiwan; by Contemporanea de Ediciones for Venezuela; by Computer Book & Magazine Store for Puerto Rico; by Express Computer Distributors for the Caribbean and West Indies. Authorized Sales Agent: Anthony Rudkin Associates for the Middle East and North Africa.

For general information on IDG Books Worldwide's books in the U.S., please call our Consumer Customer Service department at 800-762-2974. For reseller information, including discounts and premium sales, please call our Reseller Customer Service department at 800-434-3422.

For information on where to purchase IDG Books Worldwide's books outside the U.S., please contact our International Sales department at 415-655-3200 or fax 415-655-3295.

For information on foreign language translations, please contact our Foreign & Subsidiary Rights department at 415-655-3021 or fax 415-655-3281.

For sales inquiries and special prices for bulk quantities, please contact our Sales department at 415-655-3200 or write to the address above.

For information on using IDG Books Worldwide's books in the classroom or for ordering examination copies, please contact our Educational Sales department at 800-434-2086 or fax 817-251-8174.

For press review copies, author interviews, or other publicity information, please contact our Public Relations department at 415-655-3000 or fax 415-655-3299.

For authorization to photocopy items for corporate, personal, or educational use, please contact Copyright Clearance Center, 222 Rosewood Drive, Danvers, MA 01923, or fax 508-750-4470.

 is a trademark under exclusive license to IDG Books Worldwide, Inc., from International Data Group, Inc.

About the Author

Marty Doucette is president of Company of Pilgrims, Inc., of Indianapolis, Indiana, developers of interactive educational and marketing programs. In the past few years, he has developed and managed technical and managerial training programs for and with the State of Indiana, the Department of Justice, FEMA, the American Institute of Architects, Johnson Controls, the International Conference of Building Officials, and other Indianapolis area firms. Marty was introduced to project management in 1991 while producing a series of teleconferences with the Public Broadcasting Service. He is a member of the Project Management Institute and its Central Indiana Chapter.

Marty resides with his beautiful wife Lorita and their four children, Nicole, Ariel, Lindsay, and Eve, in Indianapolis. You can e-mail Marty at pilgrims@iquest.net.

ABOUT IDG BOOKS WORLDWIDE

Welcome to the world of IDG Books Worldwide.

IDG Books Worldwide, Inc., is a subsidiary of International Data Group, the world's largest publisher of computer-related information and the leading global provider of information services on information technology. IDG was founded more than 25 years ago and now employs more than 8,500 people worldwide. IDG publishes more than 275 computer publications in over 75 countries (see listing below). More than 60 million people read one or more IDG publications each month.

Launched in 1990, IDG Books Worldwide is today the #1 publisher of best-selling computer books in the United States. We are proud to have received eight awards from the Computer Press Association in recognition of editorial excellence and three from *Computer Currents'* First Annual Readers' Choice Awards. Our best-selling *...For Dummies®* series has more than 30 million copies in print with translations in 30 languages. IDG Books Worldwide, through a joint venture with IDG's Hi-Tech Beijing, became the first U.S. publisher to publish a computer book in the People's Republic of China. In record time, IDG Books Worldwide has become the first choice for millions of readers around the world who want to learn how to better manage their businesses.

Our mission is simple: Every one of our books is designed to bring extra value and skill-building instructions to the reader. Our books are written by experts who understand and care about our readers. The knowledge base of our editorial staff comes from years of experience in publishing, education, and journalism — experience we use to produce books for the '90s. In short, we care about books, so we attract the best people. We devote special attention to details such as audience, interior design, use of icons, and illustrations. And because we use an efficient process of authoring, editing, and desktop publishing our books electronically, we can spend more time ensuring superior content and spend less time on the technicalities of making books.

You can count on our commitment to deliver high-quality books at competitive prices on topics you want to read about. At IDG Books Worldwide, we continue in the IDG tradition of delivering quality for more than 25 years. You'll find no better book on a subject than one from IDG Books Worldwide.

John Kilcullen
CEO
IDG Books Worldwide, Inc.

Steven Berkowitz
President and Publisher
IDG Books Worldwide, Inc.

WINNER

*Eighth Annual
Computer Press
Awards ≥1992*

WINNER

*Ninth Annual
Computer Press
Awards ≥1993*

WINNER

*Tenth Annual
Computer Press
Awards ≥1994*

WINNER

*Eleventh Annual
Computer Press
Awards ≥1995*

IDG Books Worldwide, Inc., is a subsidiary of International Data Group, the world's largest publisher of computer-related information and the leading global provider of information services on information technology. International Data Group publishes over 275 computer publications in over 75 countries. Sixty million people read one or more International Data Group publications each month. International Data Group's publications include: **ARGENTINA:** Buyer's Guide, Computerworld Argentina, PC World Argentina; **AUSTRALIA:** Australian Macworld, Australian PC World, Australian Reseller News, Computerworld, IT Casebook, Network World, Publish, Webmaster; **AUSTRIA:** Computerwelt Osterreich, Networks Austria, PC Tip Austria; **BANGLADESH:** PC World Bangladesh; **BELARUS:** PC World Belarus; **BELGIUM:** Data News; **BRAZIL:** Annuário de Informática, Computerworld, Connections, Macworld, PC Player, PC World, Publish, Reseller News, Supergamepower; **BULGARIA:** Computerworld Bulgaria, Network World Bulgaria, PC & MacWorld Bulgaria; **CANADA:** CIO Canada, Client/Server World, ComputerWorld Canada, InfoWorld Canada, NetworkWorld Canada, WebWorld; **CHILE:** Computerworld Chile, PC World Chile; **COLOMBIA:** Computerworld Colombia, PC World Colombia; **COSTA RICA:** PC World Centro America; **THE CZECH AND SLOVAK REPUBLICS:** Computerworld Czechoslovakia, Macworld Czech Republic, PC World Czechoslovakia; **DENMARK:** Communications World Danmark, Computerworld Danmark, Macworld Danmark, PC World Danmark, Techworld Denmark; **DOMINICAN REPUBLIC:** PC World Republica Dominicana; **ECUADOR:** PC World Ecuador; **EGYPT:** Computerworld Middle East, PC World Middle East; **EL SALVADOR:** PC World Centro America; **FINLAND:** MikroPC, Tietoverkko, Tietoviikko; **FRANCE:** Distributique, Hebdo, Info PC, Le Monde Informatique, Macworld, Reseaux & Telecoms, WebMaster France; **GERMANY:** Computer Partner, Computerwoche, Computerwoche Extra, Computerwoche FOCUS, Global Online, Macwelt, PC Welt; **GREECE:** Amiga Computing, GamePro Greece, Multimedia World; **GUATEMALA:** PC World Centro America; **HONDURAS:** PC World Centro America; **HONG KONG:** Computerworld Hong Kong, PC World Hong Kong, Publish in Asia; **HUNGARY:** ABCD CD-ROM, Computerworld Szamitastechnika, Internetto online Magazine, PC World Hungary, PC-X Magazin Hungary; **ICELAND:** Tolvuheimur PC World Island; **INDIA:** Information Communications World, Information Systems Computerworld, PC World India, Publish in Asia; **INDONESIA:** InfoKomputer PC World, Komputek Computerworld, Publish in Asia; **IRELAND:** ComputerScope, PC Live!; **ISRAEL:** Macworld Israel, People & Computers/Computerworld; **ITALY:** Computerworld Italia, Macworld Italia, Networking Italia, PC World Italia; **JAPAN:** DTP World, Macworld Japan, Nikkei Personal Computing, OS/2 World Japan, SunWorld Japan, Windows NT World, Windows World Japan; **KENYA:** PC World East African, PC World Kenya; **KOREA:** Hi-Tech Information, Macworld Korea, PC World Korea; **MACEDONIA:** PC World Macedonia; **MALAYSIA:** Computerworld Malaysia, PC World Malaysia, Publish in Asia; **MALTA:** PC World Malta; **MEXICO:** Computerworld Mexico, PC World Mexico; **MYANMAR:** PC World Myanmar; **NETHERLANDS:** Computer! Totaal, LAN Internetworking Magazine, LAN World Buyers Guide, Macworld Netherlands, Net, WebWereld; **NEW ZEALAND:** Absolute Beginners Guide and Plain & Simple Series, Computer Buyer, Computer Industry Directory, Computerworld New Zealand, MTB, Network World, PC World New Zealand; **NICARAGUA:** PC World Centro America; **NORWAY:** Computerworld Norge, CW Rapport, Datamagasinet, Financial Rapport, Kursguide Norge, Macworld Norge, Multimediaworld Norge, PC World Ekspress Norge, PC World Nettverk, PC World Norge, PC World ProduktGuide Norge; **PAKISTAN:** Computerworld Pakistan; **PANAMA:** PC World Panama; **PEOPLE'S REPUBLIC OF CHINA:** China Computer Users, China Computerworld, China InfoWorld, China Telecom World Weekly, Computer & Communication, Electronic Design China, Electronics Today, Electronics Weekly, Game Software, PC World China, Popular Computer Week, Software Weekly, Software World, Telecom World; **PERU:** Computerworld Peru, PC World Profesional Peru, PC World SoHo Peru; **PHILIPPINES:** Click!, Computerworld Philippines, PC World Philippines, Publish in Asia; **POLAND:** Computerworld Poland, Computerworld Special Report Poland, Cyber, Macworld Poland, Networld Poland, PC World Komputer; **PORTUGAL:** Cerebro/PC World, Computerworld/Correio Informático, Dealer World Portugal, Mac*In/PC*In Portugal, Multimedia World; **PUERTO RICO:** PC World Puerto Rico; **ROMANIA:** Computerworld Romania, PC World Romania, Telecom Romania; **RUSSIA:** Computerworld Russia, Mir PK, Publish, Seti; **SINGAPORE:** Computerworld Singapore, PC World Singapore, Publish in Asia; **SLOVENIA:** Monitor; **SOUTH AFRICA:** Computing SA, Network World SA, Software World SA; **SPAIN:** Communicaciones World España, Computerworld España, Dealer World España, Macworld España, PC World España; **SRI LANKA:** Infolink PC World; **SWEDEN:** CAP&Design, Computer Sweden, Corporate Computing Sweden, Internetworld Sweden, it.branschen, Macworld Sweden, MaxiData Sweden, MikroDatorn, Nätverk & Kommunikation, PC World Sweden, PCaktiv, Windows World Sweden; **SWITZERLAND:** Computerworld Schweiz, Macworld Schweiz, PCtip; **TAIWAN:** Computerworld Taiwan, Macworld Taiwan, NEW ViSiON/Publish, PC World Taiwan, Windows World Taiwan; **THAILAND:** Publish in Asia, Thai Computerworld; **TURKEY:** Computerworld Turkiye, Macworld Turkiye, Network World Turkiye, PC World Turkiye; **UKRAINE:** Computerworld Kiev, Multimedia World Ukraine, PC World Ukraine; **UNITED KINGDOM:** Acorn User UK, Amiga Action UK, Amiga Computing UK, Apple Talk UK, Computing, Macworld, Parents and Computers UK, PC Advisor, PC Home, PSX Pro, The WEB; **UNITED STATES:** Cable in the Classroom, CIO Magazine, Computerworld, DOS World, Federal Computer Week, GamePro Magazine, InfoWorld, I-Way, Macworld, Network World, PC Games, PC World, Publish, Video Event, THE WEB Magazine, and WebMaster; online webzines: JavaWorld, NetscapeWorld, and SunWorld Online; **URUGUAY:** InfoWorld Uruguay; **VENEZUELA:** Computerworld Venezuela, PC World Venezuela; and **VIETNAM:** PC World Vietnam.   3/24/97

Author's Acknowledgments

Although this book has a single author, many people have put long hours into its creation. This is an acknowledgment of just a few.

My first acknowledgment is to my project editor, Susan Pink. Susan, you are one of the pickiest, most demanding people I have ever met. In other words, you were great. You care about your work and you care about the reader. Thank you.

And thank you Gareth Hancock, my acquisitions editor. Gareth, you believed I was the person to write the book and you encouraged me throughout the process. Every phone call began with "Are you still having fun?" Gareth, it was fun throughout.

Thank you to Darlene Wong for all your administrative help. And thank you Diane Steele and Mary Corder for turning all this into an actual book.

Last, thank you Lorita. Twenty-seven years (not counting the courting) have come and gone, and you are more beautiful, more kind, more spiritual, and more fun today than on our first date — and that was some first date. I love you.

Dedication

To Jim Weaver because all environments can be made sacred, and to Jon Bereman because miracles happen when someone extends a hand to a friend.

Publisher's Acknowledgments

We're proud of this book; please send us your comments about it by using the Reader Response Card at the back of the book or by e-mailing us at feedback/dummies@idgbooks.com. Some of the people who helped bring this book to market include the following:

Acquisitions, Development, and Editorial

Project Editor: Susan Pink

Acquisitions Editor: Gareth Hancock

Product Development Director: Mary Bednarek

Media Development Manager: Joyce Pepple

Technical Editor: Garrett Pease, Discovery Computing, Inc.

Editorial Manager: Mary C. Corder

Editorial Assistants: Constance Carlisle, Michael D. Sullivan

Production

Project Coordinator: Debbie Stailey

Layout and Graphics: Theresa Ball, Cameron Booker, Angela F. Hunckler, Ruth Loiacano, Jane Martin, Anna Rohrer, Theresa Sánchez-Baker, Brent Savage

Proofreaders: Kathy McGuinnes, Christine D. Berman, Melissa D. Buddendeck, Dwight Ramsey, Robert Springer, Carrie Voorhis, Karen York

Indexer: Ty Koontz

Special Help: Suzanne Packer, Lead Copy Editor; Stephanie Koutek, Proof Editor; Kevin Spencer, Associate Technical Editor

General and Administrative

IDG Books Worldwide, Inc.: John Kilcullen, CEO; Steven Berkowitz, President and Publisher

IDG Books Technology Publishing: Brenda McLaughlin, Senior Vice President and Group Publisher

Dummies Technology Press and Dummies Editorial: Diane Graves Steele, Vice President and Associate Publisher; Judith A. Taylor, Brand Manager; Kristin A. Cocks, Editorial Director

Dummies Trade Press: Kathleen A. Welton, Vice President and Publisher; Stacy S. Collins, Brand Manager

IDG Books Production for Dummies Press: Beth Jenkins, Production Director; Cindy L. Phipps, Supervisor of Project Coordination, Production Proofreading and Indexing; Kathie S. Schutte, Supervisor of Page Layout; Shelley Lea, Supervisor of Graphics and Design; Debbie J. Gates, Production Systems Specialist; Tony Augsburger, Supervisor of Reprints and Bluelines; Leslie Popplewell, Media Archive Coordinator

Dummies Packaging and Book Design: Patti Sandez, Packaging Specialist; Kavish+Kavish, Cover Design

◆

The publisher would like to give special thanks to Patrick J. McGovern, without whom this book would not have been possible.

◆

Contents at a Glance

Cartoons at a Glance

By Rich Tennant • Fax: 508-546-7747 • E-mail: the5wave@tiac.net

page 259

page 7

page 47

page 305

page 215

page 319

page 283

page 125

Table of Contents

· ·

Foreword

● ●

*T*he art of orchestrating an organization's resources for a period of time to achieve certain deliverables that end with some form of a final product is called project management. And *Microsoft Project For Dummies* can help you figure out what that definition means.

Our expectations and view of project management and project managers keeps changing. Consequently, project management continues to evolve. For example, organizations are reforming their business processes to direct their efforts to the use of project teams. These teams get together for a specific project and are disbanded at the end of their assignment. Then new teams are formed for the next task or another project. An integral part of this business trend is the skillful management of organizations by projects.

Microsoft Project can provide great support for project managers, project team members, and other project stakeholders. It is simple enough to be understood by the average computer user in a reasonable amount of time. It is also sophisticated enough that it ventures into some of the upper-end bells and whistles of advanced project management software.

Microsoft Project For Dummies provides a basic view of a valuable software product. It helps you discover how to best use Microsoft Project for managing project work. The book provides insight into key project management challenges and how to overcome some of these challenges. It makes this boring process of planning and executing a project more of a hobby than a chore.

Maturity in project management is like a journey. To enjoy this journey, you need to have the right attitude and the openness for changes in the course of the journey. I wish you a lot of fun in your journey of reading and using this book. I wish you equal fun in your implementation of project management so that it becomes more of a planned effort than just pure luck!

Al Zeitoun, Ph.D., PMP

President, Central Indiana Chapter
Project Management Institute

Al Zeitoun is a curriculum developer of graduate-level programs in project management and is Vice President of Global Project Management Services, International Institute of Learning.

Introduction

● ●

*H*ere's a scary picture. At this very moment, thousands of people are busily managing projects without knowing anything about the professional discipline of project management. This is a humongous crisis, folks! Well, actually, you know it isn't a crisis at all. You've been doing it for years.

You've probably performed a layperson's version of project management many times and muddled along just fine. You organized the plan, created a schedule, made assignments, and mothered the project to completion, sometimes even on time and under budget.

So why put yourself through all the trouble of figuring out a project management software program? Even more basic, why find out about project management? The answer is self-evident. Because you've managed projects before, you know that there has to be a better way. You're ready to discover what all this project management hoopla is about, and you'd like to use Microsoft Project to do the job. You've just made two good management decisions.

Confidentially Speaking

Deep down, the first question you'd like answered is whether or not this is going to hurt. Between us, finding out about Microsoft Project is straightforward and kind of fun. You don't have to know anything special about computers or project management to begin. As you'll see in the upcoming chapters, a simple wisdom is evident throughout the software program. You're going to look very good throwing all those Gantt charts and reports around at the office. And what's really neat is that you can let people assume that it took grueling labor and a steel will to figure out the program. It's our secret.

Using This Book

As this book's title so subtly implies, the following chapters show you how to use Microsoft Project. But what the title doesn't say is that this book also gives you a basic explanation of project management. Two for the price of one. You are some manager!

So how should you read it? You can read this book in three ways. First, if you want to check out the basics of project management and then figure out Microsoft Project step by glorious step, start at the very beginning and read the book to completion.

As a second approach, you can skip the basics of project management. Start in Chapter 3, where the Microsoft Project stuff begins, and progress from there.

Third, if you're like many managers, you don't have the time for a full-course meal. You're lucky to get fast-food carryout. You can use this book strictly as a reference tool. If it's possible, though, Chapters 4 through 7 are best read in sequence. Other than that, smorgasbord to your heart's content.

As you read this book, you may notice that, whenever I specifically tell you to choose a command, button, or dialog box option, certain letters are underlined. These underlined letters are known as hot keys. If you press Alt plus the underlined letter, you quickly activate the command, button, or option.

About the Disk

In the book, I assume that you have the Windows 95 version of Microsoft Project and that you can use it as you read the chapters. The book is written in a way that lets you master your project management skills by practice. I've also provided a sample disk with a number of project files so that you can read the material and do some practicing. (I tell you exactly when you can use the files from the disk.) At any time, you can use information in your own project instead of practicing with the sample files.

See Appendix C for installation instructions.

How This Book Is Organized

This book has eight parts. Each part is a logical grouping of chapters, with each chapter focusing on a major point about project management or Microsoft Project. The chapters are kept as brief as possible without sacrificing important details.

In each chapter, individual sections describe a specific function. Navigating the chapters' headings, you can easily find an explanation or specific information you need.

Part I: Basic Project Stuff

Starting at the beginning is often the right place for most of us. Quite frankly, there's nothing embarrassing about asking a question like "What's a project?" Most people might be surprised by the answer.

To go anywhere with project management, you must have a plan, know some basic project management principles, and know how to get around in Microsoft Project. In this part, you check out your knowledge of project planning, you find out about the three basic ingredients of project management, and you see how Microsoft Project works to provide you with information.

Part II: Putting Your Project Together

Part I shows you what you need to know to begin a project. Part II shows you how to enter the information into Microsoft Project. In this part, you create tasks and set their duration. You customize the work calendar or make multiple work calendars for different groups. You create a schedule of events and define the relationships of the tasks in the schedule. You create deadlines and determine where you can permit slack. You identify who is going to do what for how much and when. Your project manager muscles start to show a little tone. You're ready to strut around in Microsoft Project.

Part III: Viewing Your Project

The place where your work starts to pay dividends is the use of project views. How much work is assigned to each resource? Which tasks are critical? How can you find a specific piece or group of information and exclude unrelated information? In Part III, you become familiar with the multitude of ways that Microsoft Project can organize and calculate your information. Searching and sorting information is surprisingly simple after you get the hang of it, and it's where you start realizing how smart you're getting to be with this project management stuff.

Part IV: Making Project 4.1 Work for You

After you enter the project information and find out how to view tables, charts, and forms, you're ready to trim the fat and build up areas of weakness. Is anything overbudgeted? How can costs be reduced? Is the schedule tight? Are resources being used in the best manner? In Part IV, you get to tweak and poke and test and mold till you're satisfied that you have a project that's ready to fly.

Part V: Project Management

When the project is off the ground, you keep it on course with Microsoft Project's tracking tools. Compare the actual course of events against the original plan. Update the project with up-to-the-moment status reports. Analyze variances in cost or work or time. Create interim plans. Customize your work environment to better suit your style and needs.

Part VI: Telling the World How It's Going

Ready to flaunt your expertise a little? Microsoft Project provides all kinds of nifty ways to communicate project status. In Part VI, you print views and reports. You find out how to isolate specific resource information. You turn your information into graphs and charts. And you say it all in different kinds of reports. What's more, if you don't like the options available to you, you can customize your presentation. You're wearing your project manager status well—it looks good on you.

Part VII: The Part of Tens

Part VII takes you out on the highways and byways. You take templates off the Internet. You search and find new resources for your project. And you discover various services for your continuing growth as a project manager. If you're interested, this could even be a new career path.

Part VIII: Appendixes

The final part provides some basics about using Microsoft Project in workgroups and using data from other applications. I also show you how to load the sample project files.

Icons Used in This Book

This icon signals something technically wild and wonderful (if you're into technospeak). It may be interesting and useful to you, but it's not essential to doing business in Microsoft Project.

Here's a friendly little shortcut on your road to project management success. This icon usually tells you a way to do your work more easily or more quickly.

This icon tells you that the information is worth committing to one of your memory banks. Otherwise, if you don't recall it, you'll have egg on your face and on the keyboard. Don't worry, the book doesn't have many of these icons.

In some parts of Microsoft Project, a keystroke or a mouse click can take you to a point of no return. This icon warns you when you're approaching one of those places.

This icon is like an information sign on a highway. You don't have to know the information, but it can make your journey more enjoyable. This icon also indicates relevant project management information that you can find in another part of the book.

This icon tells you about other ...*For Dummies* books that could serve you in your understanding about a particular function of Microsoft Project.

Where to Go from Here

Project managers are decision makers. Here's your first one in this book. You can begin with Chapter 1 or Chapter 3. Or you can smorgasbord. In any case, have fun.

Part I
Basic Project Stuff

The 5th Wave   By Rich Tennant

"IT'S A SOFTWARE PROGRAM THAT MORE FULLY RE-FLECTS AN ACTUAL OFFICE ENVIRONMENT. IT MULTI-TASKS WITH OTHER USERS, INTEGRATES SHARED DATA, AND THEN USES THAT INFORMATION TO NETWORK VICIOUS RUMORS THROUGH AN INTER-OFFICE LINK-UP."

In this part . . .

Basic project management knowledge and skills are important. They're especially important if you're going to do project management. That may not be as dumb as it first sounds.

Part I covers three kinds of information you should know to use Microsoft Project successfully. First, you need to have a workable plan. Simple, you say. Well, maybe so. But then again, maybe not. You need a project plan that can face reality eyeball to eyeball. You need contingencies for the unforeseen. You need also to assess the strength of the support you have for carrying this project to completion. Okay, I'll lighten up. The point is, using Chapter 1 to define your project's scope and clarify your goals might be worth your while.

Second, some technical terms and skills are common to project management but aren't the type of thing you pick up around the water cooler. You might want to double-check your understanding of these terms and your ability to perform the tasks they define. This part prepares you for things such as project phases and tasks, durations and task relationships, and resources and work.

Third, make sure that you understand some of the inner workings of Windows 95, how to run Microsoft Project, the use of the keyboard and the mouse, and the overall Microsoft Project environment.

Chapter 1

Basic Project Management

- -

In This Chapter

▶ Defining a project

▶ Defining project management

▶ Projects have phases

▶ Discovering the seven steps of an effective project plan

▶ Understanding commonsense project management concepts

- -

*T*his chapter gives you some important background information, definitions, and explanations about project management. Hey! Don't break out the caffeine! A lot of this is actually interesting — and all of it is useful. My first exposure to the basics of project management showed me things I could do right away to improve my performance as a manager. All it took was embracing the discipline and putting the principles into practice.

Projects are as old as Noah's first shipbuilding contract. But project management is a dynamic, relatively young field — as in post-World War II. It's been around long enough, however, to have some proven, widely applied terms and practices. As you'll see, they're insightful and logical. And, perhaps most importantly, Microsoft Project is based on them.

As Complicated as You Need

If you're new to project management, you may be wondering just how complicated this is going to be. The answer may seem odd at first. Project management (and Microsoft Project) is as complicated as you need it to be. If you want to use Microsoft Project to plan and manage a snipe hunt, it's not complicated at all. If you need Microsoft Project to organize and manage an expedition to find the Sasquatch, you'll find it can handle the complexities of even the largest quest.

This chapter is called "Basic Project Management" because it helps you with the fundamentals. For those who want to make project management a career, I include references to organizations dedicated to helping you do just that. (See Chapter 22.) But this chapter and this book aim at another goal: to help you understand how to use Microsoft Project to successfully manage your projects.

Garbage in, a Big Mess Out

Microsoft Project is a powerful project management software program — but it's just a software program. It can make you shine like the genius you are, but only if you feed it the right stuff in the right way and at the right times. Microsoft Project wants a bunch of information from you. The better the information, the better it will perform project management functions to organize and assist you in your responsibilities.

It's not etched in granite somewhere that you have to know all I'm about to tell you. But if you give yourself the gift of some quality up-front planning, Microsoft Project will make you look like a gourmet chef among side-order cooks. So take a walk, do fifty jumping jacks, feed the dog, and clear your mind for a few minutes. Then get going on planning your project and your role in that project. The first thing you need to know is what makes up a project.

Defining a Project

Maybe the easiest way to define a project is to begin by saying what it isn't. A project isn't something you normally do. Project managers call the work you normally do *operations*. Work you don't normally do is often called a *project*.

For example, I usually spend my time sitting at a computer workstation performing my normal work operations — writing letters, sending invoices, receiving phone calls, and so forth. That's normal operation. Today is different. I'm sitting at the same workstation, doing what appears to be the same things, but I'm performing a project. I'm writing a book.

For work to be considered a project, it must meet four criteria. A project is *temporary*, *unique*, and the *creation* of a *product*.

Temporary

A project is temporary. It has a beginning and an end. It is not a place where you can hang your hat until the golden years.

Continuing with the book example, my project began with the submittal of the proposal to the publisher. There was a definite beginning. This book project will end for me when it's approved in its final version for publication by or before the deadline.

A project is temporary also in that it usually involves a project team that exists for the sole purpose of the project.

Throughout this chapter, I ask some questions that will help you define your project. If you want, answer them in your head or, better yet, write them down. Your answers to many of these questions will have a direct effect on the outcome of your project.

Questions:

Can you define your project's beginning and end?

When does your responsibility start and what are the conditions that mark completion?

Who will you temporarily need for your project team?

Unique

A project is *unique*. Its characteristics and outcome are one of a kind.

Every project's product is different in some way from other products or services. If you're managing a project, you're developing something that hasn't existed before in just this way. It doesn't matter whether the project is engineering a Mars landing, planning a party, or researching a new strain of garbanzo beans. If it's a project, it's unique.

And so, using my book example, Dummies Press publishes oodles of fascinating and worthwhile books. But the Microsoft Project For Dummies project has its own focus, deadlines, project team, marketing strategies, and so on. The product of this project is unique. And, carrying this further, books by other authors and publishers about the same subject are each unique in some way.

Questions:

What's unique about your project?

What have others accomplished that is similar to your project?

In what manner are these other projects the same as your project?

How are they different?

Are these similarities and differences strengths or weaknesses?

A creation

A project is an act of turning an unrelated set of resources into something that hadn't previously existed. I don't necessarily mean this in a theological or artistic way. It's creative in that something is coming into existence. That has two major implications.

First, the project will probably go through phases of development to become a product or service. Second, because a project usually involves a number of people and organizations, each with a stake in the project's outcome, communication about the project's status throughout its phases is critically important and often difficult. The project management term for this process is *progressive elaboration*.

Progressive elaboration is the communication of a project's status in a manner that facilitates progress through the phases of a project. This can be tricky. The project manager has to communicate to the principals of a project in a manner that complements the unique technology and professional language of each. You use specifications to talk to engineers. You use models and simulations when talking to customers. You use reports when talking to investors.

I heard someone define writing as the act of pushing the pen into the unknown. Using my book example, the members of this project team and I are pushing this project through its stages of completion. Each stage has its expected product and a method of progressive elaboration for clear communication of the project's status.

As you'll soon see, Microsoft Project is a wonderful tool for progressive elaboration.

Questions:

What aspect of your project involves the creation of something?

What kinds of technology do you need to be conversant about in your project?

A product

A project's goal and only reason for existence is a *product* or service. The simplicity of this statement masks its significance. Maybe saying it as an equation will make it more obvious:

Project goal = product

A project's sole reason for existence is its outcome. We measure all of a project's value in the manner and to the degree that it accomplishes its goal.

Questions:

How clear is your project's goal?

Is the goal attainable?

Does the goal need a reality check?

Defining Project Management

Consider a project's product or service as the project's target. A goal is an arrow. The more carefully you craft a goal, the more likely its potential for accuracy of flight (Figure 1-1).

Figure 1-1:
William
Tell(s) of
project
management.

Two things are missing in this analogy: the bow and the archer. Consider the project team as the bow. The project team provides the leverage needed to propel the arrow. Using the word *project* as a verb for a moment: The project team projects the goal toward its target.

The William (or Wilhelmina) Tell of this analogy is the project manager. The project manager keeps the goal (arrow) on course. If the goal was well-crafted and the project team has the resources to project the goal throughout its course, the project manager then becomes the key to hitting the target.

Project management is the application of knowledge, skills, and tools to enable a project goal to hit its target.

As you'll see, Microsoft Project is a highly valuable management tool for you and your team. It helps you make sure that you have a good arrow, the right-sized bow, and a good target at which to aim. William Tell would be apple green with envy.

Projects Have Phases

I have to leave the archery analogy to describe another important aspect of projects and project management. Projects have phases (Figure 1-2). Each phase has its own beginning and end and desired outcome. All phases share the following traits:

- ✔ Each phase requires execution.
- ✔ Although the overall result of the project is a product, each phase has its own product too. (The project management term for a product is a *deliverable*.)
- ✔ Each phase has its own phase-end review process.

The model for phases is repetitious cycles.

William Tell(s) about changing hats

If you are a project manager, you wear a lot of hats. Depending on the organization, in varying degrees you are responsible for the *development of the project plan*. This may include:

- Defining tasks, their sequence, and their duration
- Scheduling
- Resource planning (people, equipment, and materials)
- Organizational planning
- Cost estimating and budgeting
- Risk identification
- Quality planning
- Communication of planning

The project manager is also responsible for the *execution of the project plan,* which includes these tasks:

- Staffing
- Team building
- Contract administration
- Procurement
- Cost control
- Risk control
- Quality assurance
- Performance reporting
- Problem solving
- Change control

There can be no bows (as in bending from the waist) until the *completion of the project plan,* which usually includes:

- Contract closures
- Administrative closures

Figure 1-2:
Each
project
phase is a
cycle that
builds
on the
deliverable
(product)
of the
preceding
cycle.

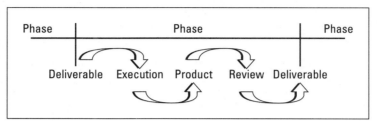

Most projects have five to seven phases, but some have a lot more. Simple projects usually have at least three phases as follows:

- ✔ Project planning phase
- ✔ Project execution phase
- ✔ Project closure phase

In this simple example, the deliverable of the project planning phase is a plan. (This deliverable will become the road map for the next phase.) Upon review, the plan is trimmed or expanded as well as improved overall until it's deemed acceptable. The phase ends with a technology transfer. Each phase ends with a deliverable that's the groundwork for the next phase to begin.

The deliverable of the execution phase is the product itself. (This deliverable will become the basis for approvals in the last phase.) For example, architects consider their product to be plans; engineers consider their product to be specifications. Upon review, the product is tightened up, clarified, and tweaked until it's considered an acceptable product. The phase ends with another technology transfer.

The deliverable of the project closure phase is the completion of the project. Upon review of all contracts and other administrative considerations, the bills are paid, the project team is disbanded, and the maintenance of the product is turned over to ongoing operations for the product's life. Although the product lives on, the project has terminated.

Microsoft Project is an excellent assistant during the project review and technology transfer of each phase. Figure 1-3 is a realistic example of project phases, illustrating a more complex series of phases that build a successful project.

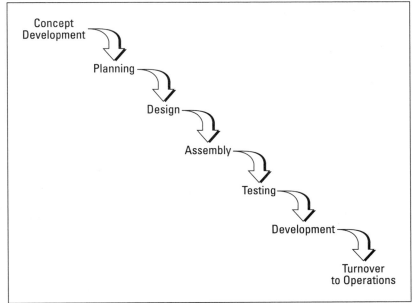

Figure 1-3:
A project
usually
consists of
several
phases,
each
contributing
to the
successful
overall
outcome.

Concept
Development

Planning

Design

Assembly

Testing

Development

Turnover
to Operations

Seven Steps of an Effective Project Plan

Successful project managers manage plans that are effective and based on achievable goals. Well-developed plans and goals are like a high-octane fuel: They have all that it takes to keep a project engine running smoothly and efficiently.

What follows are some steps to better ensure the quality of your project and to prepare you for using Microsoft Project. I suggest you get a paper and pencil or take this book over to your word processor and answer the following questions.

Scoping it out

A project's *scope* is a detailed description of what you are going to produce.

Questions:

What is your project's scope?

What is the importance or need of your project?

Who is your target customer, audience, or recipient?

Identifying stakeholders

Stakeholders are the organizations and individuals involved in or affected by a project.

Question:

Who are the stakeholders for your project?

Determining the quality

A business friend often says, "Anything worth doing is worth doing poorly." By this he means that if something is important enough to accomplish, it needs to be completed even if it falls short of perfection. Lowered standards may be acceptable in some situations but totally inappropriate in a lot of others. Everyone who has a stake in the project needs to agree on what yardstick of *quality* will be expected.

Questions of quality can be based on either explicit or implicit expectations. *Explicit expectations* involve standards overtly agreed upon by everyone involved. *Implicit expectations* are often the unwritten rules, opinions, and double standards that can turn a well-intended idea into a quagmire of inefficiency. Whenever possible, turn implicit expectations into explicit ones.

Questions:

What are the explicit expectations about quality in your project?

Are there explicit expectations based on industry or government standards and regulations?

Are there any explicit policies?

What implicit expectations could affect your project?

What can you do to turn implicit expectations into explicit expectations?

Listing constraints

Constraints are unavoidable time limitations imposed on your project. Typical constraints are deadlines or the availability of key resources or personnel.

Question:

What constraints can you identify for your project?

Assessing your muscle

No project exists in a vacuum (unless you're planning a space walk). A project is never more important than the organization that supports it. But quite often, pressures within an organization can make a project tougher than anticipated.

Some organizations are function-based; they have structures grouped by specialty, such as marketing, design, and accounting. Functional organizations are usually hierarchical. Each function has a boss, an assistant boss, and so on.

Other organizations are project-based. They exist to perform projects. Most organizations exist somewhere between these ends of the continuum.

Questions:

From where or whom does your authority come for this project?

Does your project team have autonomy, or must team members receive approvals within their own hierarchy?

Is there agreement in your organization about your project goals?

Are there persons unrelated to the project who believe that they are stakeholders? If so, what will you do about it?

Facing risks

Risks are circumstances outside your influence that may have a positive or negative effect on your project.

Questions:

Are there any significant risks to your project?

If so, what can you do to prepare for their eventuality?

Setting goals

Using the answers to all these questions, set goals for your project. Make your goals as detailed and clear as possible. Write them in such a way that they will answer any major questions by stakeholders.

Question:

What are your project goals?

Commonsense Project Management Concepts

The primary concern of management is producing expected results. Although this may sound rather cold-hearted, some people skills are also fundamentally important to just about any management responsibility. These are often called *transferable skills*. As a project manager, knowing your relative strengths or weaknesses in these transferable skills is important. Very few people are strong in all of them.

Smart project managers know that the word *staff* should be taken literally — managers are expected to lean on their staff. Sharing leadership responsibilities can elicit strong character strengths from your associates. It's common sense that the project goal is more important than the pride of the project manager. This section introduces some transferable skills worth considering for your project.

Leading

Leading and managing are not synonymous, but both are necessary. Leading involves:

- ✔ Knowing and believing the vision — having a vision of where you're going and knowing what has to be changed to get there.

- ✔ Sharing the vision — communicating your goals and objectives so that they can be understood and acted upon.

- ✔ Bringing the vision to life — helping the project team own and interpret the vision in a manner that energizes them to overcome obstacles.

Communicating

We measure communication by its effectiveness. Managing involves establishing and maintaining methods of effective communication. This often requires speaking and listening in the technical language of the stakeholder.

Negotiating

Negotiation is the grease that keeps projects moving smoothly. The ability to settle an argument and to successfully modify an agreement is critical to the success of most projects. Throughout a project, the project manager has to tweak plans to keep things on course.

Problem solving

Problem resolution involves accurately identifying what a problem is and knowing what you're going to do about it. For some people, the problem-solving skill comes naturally and is an enjoyable part of their job. Other people hate any kind of confrontation and will avoid it any cost. A project manager needs to expect problems — they're part of the job.

Looking in the mirror and around you

Using your trusty pointing device and matrix tablet (formerly known as pen and paper), do yourself a major favor by answering these questions.

Questions:

What management skills are your strengths?

Would your associates agree with this?

What mix of people and skills are necessary for the proper management of your project?

Do yourself a major favor by answering the questions in this chapter. It's a tough exercise, but it could save you many wasted arrows.

Chapter 2
Tasks, Schedules, and Resources

. . . .

In This Chapter

▶ Identifying major groups

▶ Determining tasks

▶ Setting duration

▶ Marking milestones

▶ Assigning resources

. . . .

*T*he success of a project is in the attention you give to details. Getting to the stage where you can identify details, however, can be laborious. And managing those details can be overwhelming. Perhaps more than anything else, Microsoft Project is a powerful tool for identifying details, managing their relationship with other details, and tracking their evolution throughout a project.

Even on small projects, it's not possible or appropriate for the project manager to know all the details. But what is possible and necessary is to make sure that each detail is being attended to by someone.

Project management is a discipline that oversees the attention to numerous, often unrelated, details in a way that ensures success. And success means that maybe you'll get that fire engine red Porsche for a Christmas bonus after all. Hey! Where does it say that project managers can't fantasize?

Starting with Categories and Phases

A good way to get to the details is by identifying categories or phases of a project. By *categories,* I mean things that naturally fit together. By *phases,* I mean a series of events that has to happen before another phase can begin. Table 2-1 lists some sample categories and phases.

Table 2-1	Sample Categories/Phases
Project Type	*Category/Phase*
Residential construction	Contract
	Design
	Lot preparation
	Footing and foundation
	Framing
	Electrical/mechanical rough-in
	Finishing
	Yard preparation
	Approvals
	Occupancy
	Contract completion
Video production	Contract
	Marketing
	Script development
	Graphics and animation development
	Preproduction
	Production
	Post-production
	Duplication
	Distribution
Event planning	Location preparation
	Award design
	Announcements
	Advance registration
	Catering contract
	Event management

On to Tasks

Categories and phases are helpful because they break the plan into major sections. Project management breaks categories and phases into *tasks*. A brief definition of a *task* is a job that has a beginning and an end.

A longer and more illustrative definition of a *task* is an element of work performed during the course of a project.

Tasks have a duration (a beginning and an end). Tasks usually have a cost. And tasks have resource requirements; that is, someone has to do the task with something someplace.

Table 2-2 lists some samples of tasks.

Table 2-2	Task Samples	
Project Type	*Category/Phase*	*Task*
Residential construction	Contract	Customer selections (house model, lot, carpeting, paint colors, kitchen cabinets, and so on)
		Write specifications
		Write contract
		Signatures
	Design	Plot plans
		Elevations
		Floor plans
		Mechanical plans
		Electrical plans
	Lot preparation	Surveying
		Well drilling
		Septic system
		Electrical service
		Natural gas service
		Excavation
		Landscaping

(continued)

Table 2-2 *(continued)*

Project Type	Category/Phase	Task
	Footing and foundation	Footing
		Foundation
		Basement walls
		Basement drainage and floor
		Inspection
	Framing	Wood framing
		Exterior sheathing
		Roofing
	Electrical/mechanical	Plumbing lines
		Furnace and A/C ducts
		Electrical wiring
		Inspection
	Finishing	Gypsum wallboard
		Stairway construction
		Painting
		Trim
	Yard preparation	Sidewalks and driveway
		Landscaping
		Seeding
	Approvals	Customer walkthrough
		Punch list corrections
	Occupancy	Final inspection
	Contract completion	Contract closure
		Administrative closure

Defining Duration

A brief definition of *duration* is the amount of time it takes to finish a task.

A long definition of *duration* is the number of work periods it takes to complete a task. This does not include nonworking periods, such as evenings, weekends, and holidays. You can express a work period in minutes, hours, days, and weeks.

Using a simple example, you could measure a work period for carpenters in days. This measurement is based on a limited time period per day, such as 7 a.m. to noon and 1 p.m. to 4 p.m. In contrast, you might measure the duration for contract writing in hours.

Start estimating the duration for tasks when you create your project management plan.

As you'll see, Microsoft Project helps you keep track of your task durations and judge their accuracy. Microsoft Project also helps edit your duration estimates.

Table 2-3 shows an example of estimating duration as part of project planning.

Table 2-3	Estimating Duration	
Category/Phase	**Task**	**Duration**
Contract	Customer selections	1 week
	Write specifications	1 day
	Write contract	3 hours
	Signatures	1 hour
Design	Plot plans	1 day
	Elevations	2 days
	Floor plans	2 days
	Mechanical plans	1/2 day
	Electrical plans	1/2 day
Lot preparation	Surveying	2 hours
	Well drilling	1 day
	Septic system	1 day
	Electrical service	1 day
	Natural gas service	1/2 day

(continued)

Table 2-3 *(continued)*		
Category/Phase	*Task*	*Duration*
	Excavation	1 day
	Landscaping	1 day
Footing and foundation	Footing	1 day
	Foundation	2 days
	Basement	1 week
	Basement floor	1 day
	Inspection	1 hour

Defining Milestones

Perhaps you think of a mile marker when you see the word *milestone*. Or you might picture some great event, such as the first time you said the word *aluminum* correctly. In project management, both of these pictures are true. A milestone marks places in your project and denotes important events.

A *milestone* is the beginning or the completion of a significant event or series of events in a project. Usually, a milestone marks a major stage of completion in a project, often the completion of a *deliverable*. (Sorry, I had to get technical on you.)

A *deliverable* is some outcome that must be produced as a stage of completion of a project. Examples of a deliverable might be a contract or an installed well or an approved inspection.

Table 2-4 lists some planned milestones for a project.

Table 2-4	Planned Milestones	
Category/Phase	*Task*	*Duration or Milestone*
Milestone	*Project begins*	*June 2*
Contract	Customer selections	1 week
	Write specifications	1 day
	Write contract	3 hours
	Signatures	1 hour
Milestone	*Contract begins*	*(anchored) July 1*
Design	Plot plans	1 day
	Elevations	2 days

Category/Phase	Task	Duration or Milestone
	Floor plans	2 days
	Mechanical plans	$1/2$ day
	Electrical plans	$1/2$ day
Milestone	*Plans completed*	*June 20*
Lot preparation	Surveying	2 hours
	Well drilling	1 day
	Septic system	1 day
	Electrical service	1 day
	Natural gas service	$1/2$ day
	Excavation	1 day
	Landscaping	1 day
Footing and foundation	Footing	1 day
	Foundation	2 days
	Basement	1 week
	Basement floor	1 day
	Inspection	1 hour
Milestone	*Inspection approved*	*(anchored) July 15*

There are some important things to notice in this example. For instance, the first milestone is the date when this project begins. Marketing dollars may have been invested, model homes built, and many hours spent by sales-people to turn a prospect into a customer. All of this may have happened before the first milestone. But, as far as the project is concerned, its date of birth is June 2.

One of the desired outcomes of laying out a plan is to expose its seeming inconsistencies. For instance, look at the second milestone; the date (July 1) is later than the date of the third milestone (June 20). The design phase has to be incorporated into the contract phase so it can finish in time to be one of the deliverables of the contract phase. As you soon see, Microsoft Project is a whiz at keeping track of these kinds of complexities.

Observe, too, that due to the nature of the contract, the inspection mile-stone is a fixed, or anchored, date. The event can't be later or the contractor will be penalized. You can manage this easily with the assistance of Microsoft Project. You can associate some tasks to be dependent on the completion of others. You can assign other tasks to run concurrently. In the example, the well drilling, the electrical service, and the natural gas service can all happen at the same time.

Identifying Resources

Resources can be people and things. Who will do it? What equipment or facilities will be necessary? The identification, assignment, and management of resources are the trickiest part of project management. It's also one of the best features of Microsoft Project.

Using the residential construction example, Table 2-5 lists some sample resources.

Table 2-5	Sample Resources	
Task	*Duration or Milestone*	*Resource*
Project begins	*Milestone: June 2*	
Customer selections	1 week	Sales, 4 half-days
Write specifications	1 day	Specifier, 1 day
Write contract	3 hours	Counsel, 3 hours
Signatures	1 hour	Sales, 1 hour, Conf. Rm.
Contract begins	*Milestone: July 1*	
Plot plans	1 day	Drafting, 1 day, CAD
Elevations	2 days	Drafting, 2 days, CAD
Floor plans	2 days	Drafting, 2 days, CAD
Mechanical plans	½ day	Contractor 1
Electrical plans	½ day	Contractor 2
Plans completed	*Milestone: June 20*	
Surveying	2 hours	Contractor 3, 2 hours
Well drilling	1 day	Contractor 4
Septic system	1 day	Contractor 4
Electrical service	1 day	Contractor 2
Natural gas service	½ day	Utility
Excavation	1 day	Contractor 5
Landscaping	1 day	Contractor 6
Footing	1 day	Contractor 5
Foundation	2 days	Contractor 5
Basement	1 week	Contractor 5
Basement floor	1 day	Contractor 5
Inspection	1 hour	City
Inspection approved	*Milestone: July 15*	

This is only one example of resource allocation, but it provides some insight into the type of project plan analysis you can make after you start plugging resources into tasks. For instance, look at the duration for customer selections. It's one week, but within that time only 4 half-days are set aside for staff input. A week is set aside to do tasks that are a few days in duration. This is a common situation.

Resources can be not only people, but also things. If something is necessary to perform a task, and if it's not automatically available, it can be included in the project plan. Using the preceding example, someone on the sales staff has to reserve the conference room for an hour on July 1. The room is used for many purposes by a variety of staff and customers. In such a situation, the conference room might be a managed resource.

Overallocation of resources is one of the most common problems in project management. As you allocate resources to tasks, you can double-check the availability of those resources and their commitment to other projects or operations. In the preceding example, drafting will devote 5 days within a 10-day period to this project. The builder might be wise to double-check the availability of these personnel to perform the tasks in the allotted time.

In addition to resource overcommitment to multiple projects, resources can also be overallocated in a single project. In our example, contractor 5 is responsible for 12 days of work in a 15-day period. You might need to ensure that the contractor has allotted enough labor and equipment to meet the milestone. To add to the concern, remember that foul weather is not reflected in the milestone.

Determining critical path

Two important scheduling terms of project management are critical task and critical path.

A *critical task* is one that must be completed on schedule for the project to finish on time. If a critical task is delayed, the project completion date is delayed also. A project's *critical path* is comprised of a series of critical tasks.

In Chapter 16, you use Microsoft Project to control critical tasks and critical paths.

Refine your project plan

By now, you've probably thought of some ways to develop your own project. Putting some thoughts together while they're fresh in your mind is a good idea. Here are some guidelines to help you:

1. **Identify the phases and categories of your project, using the previous examples.**

2. **Break your phases and categories into tasks.**

3. **Determine milestones and deliverables for your project.**

4. **Identify resources and their limitations.**

5. **Map out the critical path of your project.**

So, you have your phases. You've even broken them down (into tasks). Durations are doable, and milestones are reachable. You've determined the deliverables and identified the resources. You know the critical path and you've refined the project. Man! You are one serious project manager!

Chapter 3

What Microsoft Project 4.1 Does (And Doesn't Do)

In This Chapter

▶ Get going in Microsoft Project

▶ What you see

▶ Using your mouse

▶ Selecting your tools from toolbars

▶ Getting help

*M*icrosoft Project is an easy-to-use project management software program. It's a member of the Microsoft Office family and is now designed for the Windows 95 operating system. It works with common toolbars and commands, drag-and-drop editing, and long filenames.

Even though Microsoft Project is easy to use, it is a powerful planning, analysis, management, and reporting tool. It gives you, your project team, and your stakeholders the ability to see both the forest and the trees of the most complex plans. With it, you can split a project into manageable parts without sacrificing or confusing relationships. It helps you identify risks and solve problems before they occur.

Starting Microsoft Project

This book will help you use Microsoft Project 4.1 successfully. In writing the book, I made a few assumptions about you and your computer.

I assume that you've installed Microsoft Project 4.1 on your computer. If you haven't, don't cancel the rest of your year or anything. Installing the program is a snap.

I also assume that your computer is operating with Windows 95. If not, you're probably using an earlier version of Microsoft Project. This book is about the Windows 95 version.

With all the improvements to Windows and to Microsoft Project, upgrading is more than worth the investment.

To start Microsoft Project, click Start (see Figure 3-1) on the taskbar at the bottom of the screen, click Programs, and then click Microsoft Project.

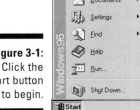

Figure 3-1:
Click the
Start button
to begin.

Screens

When you start Microsoft Project, the Welcome screen appears, as shown in Figure 3-2. From here, you have several choices. You can:

- Create a project for the first time
- Open the file you worked on last
- Take a guided tour
- Work on your own
- Select an option to not show the Welcome screen again

For now, select the Don't display this startup screen again check box.

The Create Your First Project option uses an online tutorial to take you through the process of building a project file. You can use your own information or sample data.

Select the Take a Short Guided Tour option. After you're finished, select the Work on Your Own option. The default screen, or view, appears, as shown in Figure 3-3.

Figure 3-2:
The
Welcome
screen is a
helpful first
view of
Microsoft
Project.

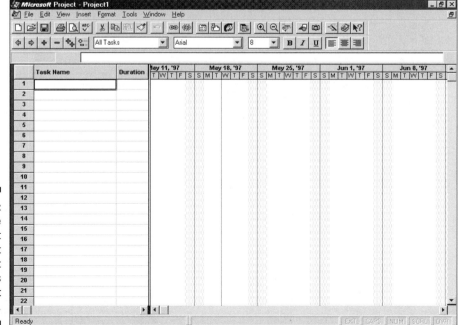

Figure 3-3:
The
Microsoft
Project
default
screen is
the Gantt
chart.

A *view* is usually a chart or graph combined with a table and a filter. Using views, you can enter, organize, and examine information in a variety of formats.

Microsoft Project has three types of views:

- ✔ Charts or graphs, such as a Gantt chart, a PERT chart, a resource graph, or a calendar
- ✔ Sheets, which provide information in rows and columns like a spreadsheet
- ✔ Forms, which provide or solicit information about a task or a resource in a format like a dialog box

Microsoft Project's default view is called a *Gantt chart* (named after Henry Gantt, the person who first developed it). The default view, like just about everything else in Microsoft Project, can be changed.

To change the screen default, choose Tools⇨Options. Click the View tab. In the Default View list, select a new default view. Then click OK.

A Cursory Look at Cursors

Microsoft Project has some unique cursors. They'll drive you bananas if you don't know what they mean. In other chapters, I discuss the significance of various cursor commands in some detail. For now, Table 3-1 lists the different cursors and their functions:

Table 3-1	Cursors and Their Functions
Cursor	**Function**
⬉	This is the default pointer. It appears all the time, except when one of the following cursors takes its place.
I	The I-beam appears whenever your cursor crosses or rests in a text box.
✛	This pointer appears whenever you are in the task detail area of a view.
⬉?	The help pointer appears when you select the help button. Then when you click somewhere on the screen, a description about that part of the screen appears. You can disable the help pointer by pressing Esc.
←‖→	This pointer appears when you rest the cursor on the divider between parts of a view or on the edge of a column heading. You can then drag the divider or the edge of a column heading horizontally.

Cursor	Function
↑ ⎓ ↓	This pointer appears when you rest the cursor on the bottom of a view. You can drag the bottom of the view to expose or hide parts of a split screen.
↑ ←→ ↓	This pointer appears in some views. It indicates that you can drag an object.

Double-clicking a portion of a view displays a dialog box relevant to the area you double-clicked. For example, double-click the task list area (the area where the plus cursor appears). The task information dialog box appears. Click Cancel.

Selection Bars

Microsoft Project selection bars are similar in layout to other Microsoft programs, but they offer shortcuts to numerous features unique to project management. Maybe the best news is that you don't need a photographic memory or a degree in buttonology to use them.

How Project 4.1 differs from earlier versions

Microsoft Project for Windows 95 includes the following new features and improvements:

AutoCorrect: Misspelled words can be corrected automatically. You can also create your own list of abbreviations that AutoCorrect will automatically change to the full word as you type.

Improved speed: 32-bit Microsoft Project for Windows 95 is faster than 16-bit Microsoft Project version 4.0 (for Windows 3.1).

Long filenames: Microsoft Project for Windows 95 uses the Microsoft Windows 95 file system that allows filenames of up to 255 characters. This enables you to name your projects with descriptive names and phrases.

Finding and opening files: The File Open dialog box helps you locate and open your files quickly. You can use shortcuts stored on your local machine to open files stored somewhere else. Refer to the Windows 95 help files for information on creating shortcuts.

ScreenTips: ScreenTips provide additional information about buttons and dialog box items. To see a ScreenTip for a button, click the Help button on the Standard toolbar, and then click the button. You can see ScreenTips for each item in a dialog box by clicking the Question Mark button in the title bar and then clicking the item.

The title bar

The top horizontal bar (Figure 3-4) is called the *title bar*. To the far left are the program's name and a program icon for opening or closing the program. Next is the name of the current file. To the far right are the minimize button, the program window button, and the close button.

The menu bar

The second horizontal bar (Figure 3-5) is called the *menu bar*. The far left project icon controls the current window. By selecting it, you can:

- ✔ Close the current window
- ✔ Switch to another window
- ✔ Create a combination window

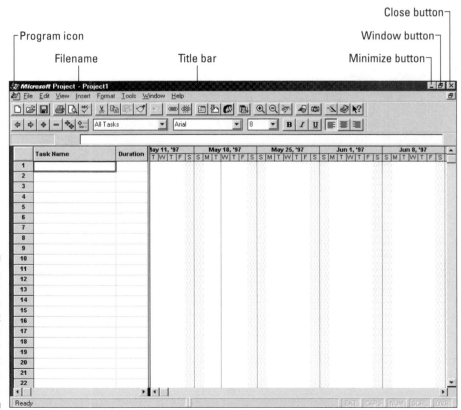

Figure 3-4:
The title bar contains the project filename and window controls for the program.

Project icon

Resize window

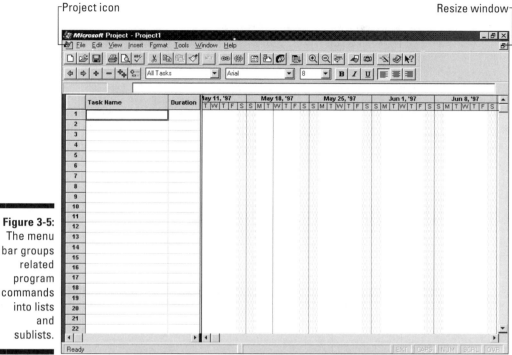

Figure 3-5:
The menu
bar groups
related
program
commands
into lists
and
sublists.

You can have up to 20 windows loaded. Much like a word processor and multiple documents, this enables you to work with or refer to numerous projects and subprojects at the same time.

The far right button controls the size of the current window.

The menu bar has a number of selections. When you choose a menu item, a list box appears. For example, choose the Edit menu. The list box shows the possible selections. Note that some items are unavailable. These items become available when some additional criteria exists in your file. The rest of the menu bar consists of a number of menu items.

Now choose View⇨Calendar. The Gantt chart is replaced by a Calendar view. Choose View again. This time, the Calendar item has a bullet in front of it; this means that you are currently in the Calendar view.

Choose Gantt Chart again. The view changes back to its original view.

The Standard toolbar

The third horizontal row (Figure 3-6) is the *Standard toolbar*. The toolbar contains most of the buttons necessary for performing basic functions in Microsoft Project.

Microsoft Project offers additional toolbars, which are described in other chapters. These additional toolbars don't replace the Standard toolbar. To add a toolbar, right-click anywhere on the toolbar and make your selection. To remove the additional toolbar, right-click anywhere on the toolbar and select the toolbar that you want to remove.

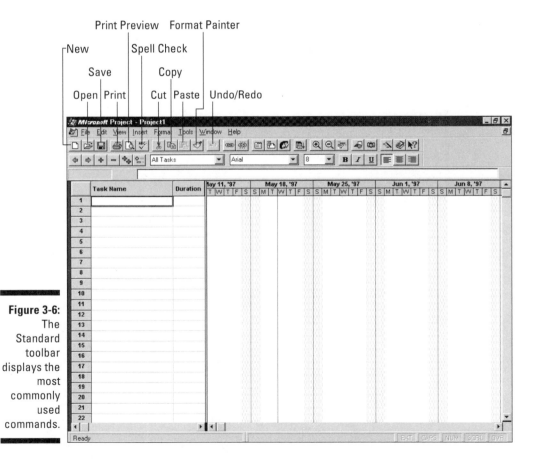

Figure 3-6: The Standard toolbar displays the most commonly used commands.

The first eleven buttons on the Standard toolbar are common to Microsoft Office applications:

New: Opens a new project window

Open: Opens the default or current folder

Save: Saves the active project

Print: Prints a copy of the active project with current print settings

Print Preview: Shows how the printed document will look

Spell Checker: Provides a spell check of your active project

Cut: Cuts a selection and puts it onto the Clipboard

Copy: Copies a selection

Paste: Pastes from the Clipboard, replacing the selection

Format Painter: Copies and applies text format

Undo/Redo: Undoes or redoes the last command

The other buttons of the Standard toolbar are unique to Microsoft Project.

When you select a toolbar button to perform a basic operation, you don't have a choice of settings. For instance, if you click the Print button, the print commands will be either default ones or your latest changes. You don't have the opportunity to modify the print properties. In contrast, if you choose File⇨Print from the menu bar, you have a choice of print properties.

The Formatting toolbar

The fourth horizontal bar (Figure 3-7) is the *Formatting toolbar*. The six buttons and two list boxes on the right are typical word processing selections. The seven buttons and the list box on the left are unique to Microsoft Project functions. The Microsoft Project functions are described in later chapters.

What You Won't Remember

Microsoft Project has a bunch of buttons that provide great shortcuts to performing project management functions. The trick is knowing and remembering what these buttons are.

All the buttons are cleverly iconographic. But even after you've been using the program for a long time, it's sometimes hard to remember, for example,

Formatting toolbar

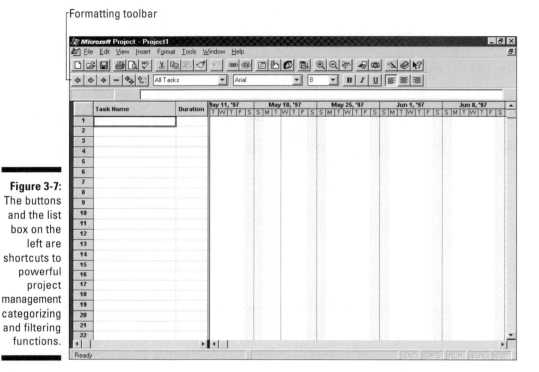

Figure 3-7:
The buttons
and the list
box on the
left are
shortcuts to
powerful
project
management
categorizing
and filtering
functions.

what the two faces and the finger pointing at the box are for. Not a problem!
You can easily find out what the buttons are and what they do through two
online help functions in Microsoft Project.

Tool tips

Tool tips are simple but immensely helpful little functions that identify each
button on the toolbar. Place your mouse over one of the toolbar buttons
(but don't click). In about a second, a descriptive phrase or word appears.

If the tool tip doesn't appear, it's probably turned off. To turn it on, choose
View➪Toolbars. Select the Show tool tips check box. Click Close.

Help button

The Help button is one of the winner innovations of Microsoft Office products. Click it and then click a button on the Standard toolbar. A text box
appears giving a nutshell description of the purpose of the button.

Keeping Project from turning into a project

One of the strengths of any good software program is its ease of use. If it's designed well, you'll be able to concentrate on your work instead of how to make the application function. The term designers use for the attention and vigilance you use to perform a task is *primary work*. The term for the attention and vigilance you use to make the software program function properly is *secondary work*. As you can imagine, the greater effort expended to perform secondary work, the less vigilance and attention you'll have left to accomplish your actual job.

You're probably not paid to use Microsoft Project — you're paid to perform a project management responsibility. You've chosen Microsoft Project to lessen your load in doing the task of project management. The less you have to remember to efficiently use Microsoft Project, the more you will be able to give to succeeding in your project management.

The techno-gurus who designed the program had their act together in limiting the number of things you need to know to effectively use the program. Some things have to be studied and understood. But you can gain a lot of knowledge about the program intuitively or through built-in helps.

Knowing where you are

Escape! In Microsoft Project, one of the most important keyboard keys you can know is the Esc key. If you're hung up in a complex dialog box or you think you're getting into trouble with a complicated activity, the Esc key is a quick and easy way to return to a screen view. It cancels whatever you are working on.

Knowing what you're doing

Microsoft Project offers a number of online aids to answer your questions or show you how to perform project management functions.

 Click the Help Topics button or press F1 on the keyboard. The Help dialog box appears. Following are instructions for each option in the dialog box. Feel free to explore any of them.

To find answers to your problems:

1. Click the Answer Wizard tab to get to its page.

2. In the text box, type change view.

3. Click Search.

The Answer Wizard searches the help database and provides the list of help topics.

To find what kind of help is available:

1. Click Help Contents.

2. Double-click The Project Planning Process.

The dialog box displays a number of topics to assist you in the use of Microsoft Project.

3. Double-click Creating a Schedule, double-click How Do I, and then double-click Enter a recurring task.

A multiple-step tutorial leads you through the steps of entering a recurring task.

4. To return to the Help Topics dialog box, click the Help Topics button.

To check out Microsoft Project's Index option:

1. Click Index.

2. In the text box, type baseline.

3. Double-click the word *purpose*.

A text box appears explaining the purpose of a baseline. If you want, click the green word or phrase; it usually provides a definition.

4. To return to the Help Topics dialog box, click the Help Topics button.

To search for specific words and phrases in the help files:

1. Click Find.

To use this function, Microsoft Project has to first create a search database. (The search database needs to be created only once.) Microsoft Project asks you whether you would like to have the database created.

2. If you want to have the search database created, click OK.

3. In the text box, type tracking toolbar.

Microsoft Project lists all the 46 topics it found relating to the Tracking toolbar.

To return to the Gantt screen, click Cancel.

Knowing when and how to communicate with others

When all else fails, you can get live, free technical support. At the time of this publication, Microsoft provides two free technical support calls. (You pay for the call.) After that, support costs a chunk of change per call, so save this option as a last resort.

You'll need the product ID number if you ever have to call technical support. Be smart and write down and file the number now, before you need help. That way, if you ever have trouble getting into the software program, you'll at least have the product number. To find it, choose Help⇨About Microsoft Project.

Technical support options

A number of technical support options are available short of the live telephone call.

1. **Click the Help Topics button or press F1.**

2. **Click the Contents tab.**

3. **Double-click Product Support.**

4. **If you are in the United States or Canada, double-click Product Support Within the United States and Canada.**

5. **Double-click Information Services.**

   A text box appears listing free support services.

6. **Scroll to the bottom of the box.**

   You see hot words that can connect you to other types of support, such as Information Services or Text Telephone.

7. **Select a support service or press Cancel to return to the Gantt screen.**

The services listed in the Help topics aren't your only line of support. You can get help with your project in lots of ways. In Chapter 22, I list ten of them.

Wizards Are Everywhere!

Wizards are one of the great innovations of Microsoft Office products. Take full advantage of their assistance while you are learning to use Microsoft Project effectively. Doing so can greatly reduce your secondary work. Remember, secondary work is the drain on your attention that keeps you from completing your task. In other chapters, I discuss alerts from the Planning Wizard as they relate to specific tasks. (By *alert,* I mean that Microsoft Project will interrupt your work with a question from the Wizard if the program detects that you are on the verge of making a mistake.)

To use the Planning Wizard feature, choose Tools⇨Options. Click the General tab. Select all Planning Wizard check boxes if they are not already selected. Click OK after you're finished.

 To see how a Planning Wizard might work, click the Gantt Chart Wizard button on the Standard toolbar.

Part II
Putting Your Project Together

The 5th Wave — By Rich Tennant

"IT'S AMAZING HOW MUCH MORE SOME PEOPLE CAN GET OUT OF A PC THAN OTHERS."

In this part . . .

After you define your project's scope and set the goals, you can create a schedule and start defining the relationships of the various project parts. In this part, using sample information, you develop tasks, set durations, add resources, outline your project, clarify relationships, and set times.

Be careful, you might find yourself craving the company of other project managers so that you can talk Gantt charts and resource pools.

Chapter 4

Creating a Schedule

● ●

In This Chapter

▶ Using Windows to manage files

▶ Putting your schedule in Project

▶ Changing your tasks

▶ Setting milestones

▶ Relating tasks

● ●

*I*n this chapter, I introduce you to the procedure for creating a schedule in Microsoft Project. As you'll see, it's a friendly, straightforward procedure. If you occasionally do a "big shop" at a grocery store, you're ready to tackle this type of work. Before you shop, you probably create a list of what you need. If you're familiar with the store, you probably order the list to match the layout of goods in the store's aisles. You order your project in Microsoft Project in much the same way. Instead of putting eggs and peanut butter in your cart, though, you enter a list of tasks into a file. And instead of planning your shopping by aisles, you make sense of your tasks' order by assigning time and associating responsibilities.

The first order of business is to mess around with some Windows stuff, such as creating a folder and saving a file. After that, it will be time to do some scheduling. While you're there, will you pick up a quart of milk?

Start Microsoft Project, if necessary. If the Welcome dialog box appears, select the check box titled: Don't display this startup screen again. Then click Work on Your Own.

The Tip of the Day dialog box may appear, offering a helpful hint about using Microsoft Project. If you want, you can clear the Show Tips at Startup check box. The next time you start the program, there won't be a tip. Click OK to close the dialog box.

The screen displays a blank, default Gantt chart. You can either begin a new project or open an existing one. In this chapter, you create a new project.

Description of the Practice Project

Suppose that you are a new project manager for Dream Homes, a small company dedicated to the custom design and construction of medium- to high-priced homes. Your project is the new home construction described in Chapter 2. You are building a home for Ferdinand and Isabella Smith. For the sake of the example, the current date is May 21, 1997. The start date of the project is June 2. The home must be completed and ready for occupancy on October 1. Others in your company scoff and say it can't be accomplished. Not you. With your knowledge of the industry and your newly acquired project management skills, it's a shoe-in (or a Smith-in).

To begin your project and set the dates, choose File⇨Project Info. The Project Info dialog box appears, as shown in Figure 4-1.

Figure 4-1:
Use the
Project
Information
dialog box
to set the
start and
end date of
a project.

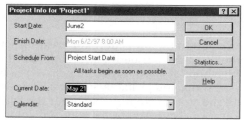

1. **In the Start Date text box, type** June 2.

2. **In the Current Date text box, type** May 21.

3. **Click OK.**

You don't need to type in the time or the year. 8:00 a.m. is the default start time for all work days, and the current year is the default year. You also don't need to worry about the finish date because it is adjusted based on your scheduling. After you set the start date, your schedule's length will automatically set the finish date.

Managing Files

File management in Microsoft Project conforms to the new features in Windows 95. If you're accustomed to working with Windows 3.1 or Windows for Workgroups, you'll find the new management tools easy to figure out and safer to use. They're especially helpful in Microsoft Project. For instance, you can use spaces and uppercase and lowercase letters for names. Now you can create realistic names such as `My first project` instead of that crazy old eight-character alphabet soup `my1stprj`. You even get to bring deleted files back from the grave!

Creating a new folder

Forgive me if this sounds obvious, but in Windows 95, you keep files organized in folders. (If you were a Windows 3.1 user, you probably remember that folders used to be called directories.) Nothing is more embarrassing than reaching into a drawer to give a customer a pen and then discovering that you've just handed over your toothbrush. (I hate it when that happens.) The same idea is true of computer files. You keep groups of related information in individual drawers (folders).

So what's in a name? Not much, I suppose. But in addition to the new name, Windows 95 enables you to manage folders with more freedom than before. That's significant.

One of the ways life is easier is that you can create a folder on-the-fly and without losing your train of thought. (In this section, you create a Practice Files folder. If you have already installed the disk files that come with this book, this folder is already on your hard drive.) For instance, you can make a folder while in the Save mode. To do so:

1. **Click the Save button on the Standard toolbar.**

   The File Save dialog box appears, as shown in Figure 4-2.

   Folders within the current folder (displayed in the Save in text box) are shown in the window.

Create New Folder

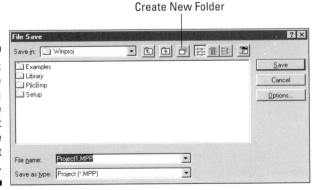

Figure 4-2:
The File
Save dialog
box lists the
current
folder in the
Save in text
box.

2. Click the Create New Folder button.

The New Folder dialog box appears, as shown in Figure 4-3.

3. In the Name text box, type Practice Files.

4. Click OK.

Windows 95 accepts file folders names with uppercase letters, spaces, and up to 255 characters.

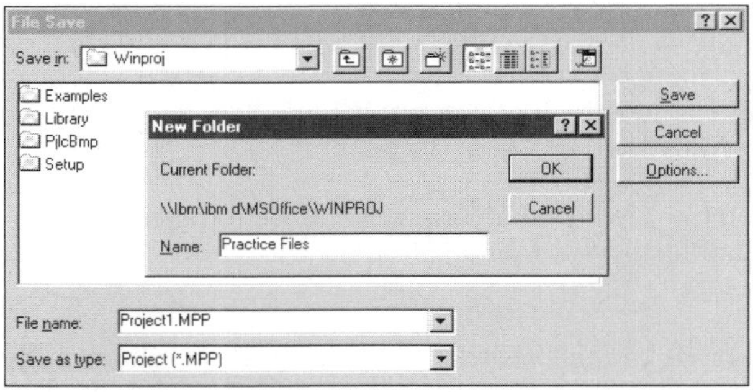

Figure 4-3:
The New
Folder
dialog box
shows the
current
folder,
where your
new folder
will reside.

Saving a file

You've set a project start date. In so doing, you've begun a project plan. Kind of a heavy thought, huh? It isn't absolutely necessary to save your file at this time, but it's a good idea. That way, everything from this point forward isn't floating around in random memory. Your project will have a home.

I assume you're still in the File Save dialog box. If you're not, click the Save button on the Standard toolbar. To save a file in your new folder:

1. In the File Save dialog box, double-click the Practice Files folder.

2. In the File name text box, type Smith Home.

3. Click the Save button.

The Microsoft Project title bar should now display the Smith Home project name, as shown in Figure 4-4.

Microsoft Project uses three file extensions: .MPP (project), .MPT (template), and .MPX (Microsoft Project exchange). The first, .MPP, is the default project file extension. The next, .MPT, is the template extension. You can save a file with the template extension as the basis for other projects. For instance, you can make a generic project containing all the tasks that are usually necessary to complete a project and then save it as a template. The

Figure 4-4:
The
Microsoft
Project
title bar
displays the
project's
name.

next time you begin a similar project, you can open your template instead of starting from scratch. The last, .MPX, is an ASCII, record-based text format used to transfer a file between applications that support the .MPX file format.

Opening a project file

Although you're in the beginning stages of creating your own project file, it may be nice to sneak a peek at a finished one — just to see an example of how all this stuff might appear when it's finished. Don't worry, you don't need to close your project. Microsoft Project will keep it loaded even if you open another project, kind of like walking and chewing gum at the same time or, in this case, planning a party for when the house is finished.

To open a project file:

1. Click the Open button on the Standard toolbar.

The File Open dialog box appears, as shown in Figure 4-5. Your Practice Files folder should still be open. If it isn't, that's okay. Just double-click it.

UpOneLevel

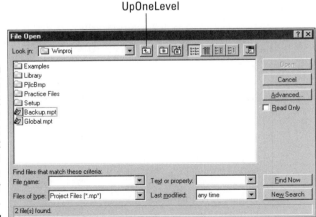

Figure 4-5:
Notice that
the File
Open dialog
box doesn't
offer the
Create a
New Folder
option.

2. Click the UpOneLevel button.

The Look in text box should now say Winproj.

3. Double-click the Library folder.

4. Double-click the Eventpln.MPT file.

An event-planning template file is now the active screen. See Figure 4-6.

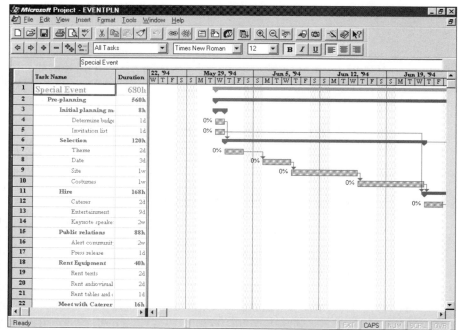

Figure 4-6:
A new
project
called
EVENTPLN
appears.

The event-planning template is one of eleven template files that come with Microsoft Project. After you load a template file, you can use it like any other project. It's called a template because it lets you reuse existing information that's already created for you. In this event-planning file, a number of tasks and sample durations have already been created for you.

We're not going to work on this event-planning project. I asked you to load it so that you could practice getting around a little bit in project folders and so that you could see a sample of a project plan that's partially completed.

The loading of the event-planning template didn't replace your Smith Home project. Microsoft Project lets you have up to 20 projects open at one time. This is for people who like walking into walls. Well, there _is_ a good reason for all those projects being open at one time. In really big projects, instead of having one huge project file, you can break it into a bunch of bite-sized pieces called _subprojects_. When you do this, loading a lot of files at once is sometimes necessary.

Choose Window. You can see that the Smith Home project is still loaded.

Before closing the event-planning file, you might enjoy navigating it to see an example of what your project will soon be like. Be sure to check out the Calendar and PERT Chart views by selecting View on the menu bar.

To close the Eventpln.MPT file, choose File⇨Close (or press Ctrl+F4). If a dialog box appears asking whether you want to save changes, click the No button. Smith Home should now be the active project window.

Making a Schedule

The first step in creating a schedule is to enter the project tasks.

I'm going to be using some common project management terms, terms such as task, duration, resource, constraint, and milestone. If you're not familiar with these project management terms and principles used by Microsoft Project, read Chapter 2 and check out the glossary. I'll also be asking you to use your mouse to get around in Microsoft Project. If you need some more confidence in this, check out Chapter 3.

Customizing columns

Your screen should show the Smith Home project in Gantt Chart view. A Gantt Chart view is actually a Gantt chart on the right and a Gantt table on the left.

Everything's set for you to begin building the schedule. But because you're not a vanilla kind of project manager, you might want to focus a little on your project. As you see in upcoming chapters, you can customize your project in oodles of ways. One way is by changing the names of columns in the Gantt table. To do this:

1. **Double-click the Task Name column heading.**

    The Column Definition dialog box appears, as shown in Figure 4-7.

Figure 4-7:
The Column
Definition
dialog box
provides a
group of
options for
defining the
properties
of your
column.

2. **In the Title text box, type** Dream Home Tasks.

3. **Click OK.**

Creating a task

Microsoft Project offers more than one way to enter tasks. The simplest way to enter task information is cell by cell. A *cell* is the same as a field in a spreadsheet—the intersection of a column and a row.

To enter a task:

1. **In the Dream Home Tasks column, move your cursor to the first cell and click.**

   The cell is highlighted.

2. **In the cell, type** Customer selections.

3. **Press Enter.**

   When you press Enter, the task resides in the cell. You've created the first task (Figure 4-8).

Two other things happen. One, the next cell is highlighted. Two, a duration of one day (1d) appears next to the first task. The one-day duration is the default duration for all tasks. You can change that in a little while.

Now that you have the hang of this, how about entering a whole list of tasks? It's easy. Simply:

1. **Select the next empty task cell if it isn't already highlighted.**

2. **Type the task name.**

3. **Press Enter.**

Entry bar

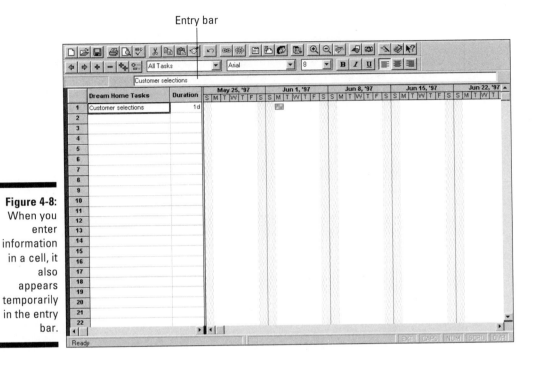

4. Repeat for each task.

Type the following tasks into successive task cells:

Write specifications	Furnace and A/C
Write contract	Electrical wiring
Signatures	Inspection
Plans	Wallboard
Water service	Stairway
Electrical service	Painting
Excavation	Trim
Landscaping	Landscaping
Footing/foundation	Customer walkthrough
Inspection	Punch list corrections
Wood framing	Final inspection
Roofing	Contract closure
Plumbing lines	Administrative closure

If you make a mistake, the easiest way to correct it is to choose the errant cell and then retype the information in the text box below the Formatting toolbar. This text box displays the contents of any active cell. To make a change, highlight the word you want to correct and type the correct word. When everything is the way you want, click the green ✔ button. If you don't want to make the change, click the red x button.

The number to the left of each task is its ID. This number has two functions. It indicates the order of a task and is the unique identifier of the task. Because each task has its own ID, you can have multiple tasks with the same name.

Way to go! You've created an entire list of tasks. This isn't the only way to do it, but it's the simplest. Entering a list means that you did your homework — you know what the tasks are before you start building the project. After you've entered all the tasks in the list, press the Page Up key. This takes you to the top of the task list. So far, your project should look like Figure 4-9. The task column is filled with the Smith Home tasks.

Figure 4-9:
Notice that you have more than one inspection task, but each task has its own ID.

	Dream Home Tasks	Duration
1	Customer selections	1d
2	Write specifications	1d
3	Write contract	1d
4	Signatures	1d
5	Plans	1d
6	Water service	1d
7	Electrical service	1d
8	Excavation	1d
9	Landscaping	1d
10	Footing/foundation	1d
11	Inspection	1d
12	Wood framing	1d
13	Roofing	1d
14	Plumbing lines	1d
15	Furncace and A/C	1d
16	Electrical wiring	1d
17	Inspection	1d
18	Wallboard	1d
19	Stairway	1d
20	Painting	1d
21	Trim	1d
22	Landscaping	1d

Entering durations

Duration is the amount of time it takes to finish a task. You can't have a schedule without estimating each task's duration. In this section, you do just that. Later, you discover some secrets to improve the accuracy of your estimates.

Microsoft Project lets you use the following durations:

✔ m (minutes)

✔ h (hours)

✔ d (days)

✔ w (weeks)

✔ 0 (milestones)

If that last one is confusing, don't worry. You find out more about it later in the chapter.

Microsoft Project assigns five days to a work week, and eight hours to a workday.

You enter durations in the same way that you enter task names. Simply select the cell, if necessary, and type. Press Enter, and the next cell is highlighted automatically. Type the following durations next to their respective tasks:

Task	*Duration*
Customer selections	**1w**
Write specifications	**1d**
Write contract	**3h**
Signatures	**1h**
Plans	**6d**
Water service	**1d**
Electrical service	**1d**
Excavation	**1d**
Landscaping	**1d**

Task	Duration
Footing/Foundation	8d
Inspection	1h
Wood framing	3w
Roofing	4d
Plumbing lines	3d
Furnace and A/C	3d
Electrical wiring	3d
Inspection	1h
Wallboard	1w
Stairway	4d
Painting	2w
Trim	1w
Landscaping	2d
Customer walkthrough	3h
Punch list corrections	4d
Final inspection	1h
Contract closure	1d
Administrative closure	2d

Whew. You've entered all the durations. Press the Page Up key. Your project should now look like Figure 4-10.

Saving an active file

 It's wise to frequently save your work as you add new information to your project. So be wise and click the Save button on the Standard toolbar now.

The Planning Wizard appears, as shown in Figure 4-11, and asks whether you'd like to save a baseline for your project.

A *baseline* is a snapshot of your project plan. You use it as the basis of comparison between what you've planned and what actually happens after the project begins.

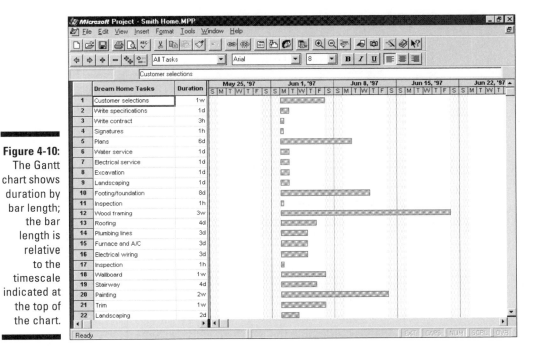

Figure 4-10:
The Gantt chart shows duration by bar length; the bar length is relative to the timescale indicated at the top of the chart.

You haven't finished creating your project plan, so for now:

1. Select the Save 'Smith Home.MPP' without a baseline option.

2. Click OK.

You've resaved the file.

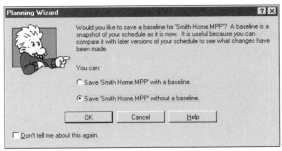

Figure 4-11:
The Planning Wizard asks you whether you want to save a baseline.

Editing Tasks

One of the nicest features of Microsoft Project is how easy it is to make changes. Adding, deleting, and moving tasks is a piece of cake. Even late into the project, the program can keep up with your changes and alert you to their effects on other aspects of the project.

You're only at the beginning of your project, but it's already time to make a few changes. Suppose that you've reviewed your tasks and you notice the following:

- The design of the home takes place after the contract signatures. Normally, design plans are part of the project. You'll need to move the task.

- Water service and electrical service can be put in only after the foundation has been erected or poured. You need to move this small group of tasks.

- The landscaping task is listed twice. Sometimes there might be a good reason to list a task twice, but not this time. All landscaping work would be ruined in the early stages of construction. You need to delete one landscaping task and change the other's duration.

- You need to add some tasks, specifically, milestones.

Moving a task

Moving a task and its duration is simple. To move Plans so that it precedes Signatures:

1. **Select task number 5.**

2. **Drag the cursor up until it rests on the line between tasks 3 and 4.**

   A gray line appears.

3. **Release the mouse button.**

   Task 5 has just become task 4 and vice versa.

Notice that the durations have automatically realigned with the new task positions.

Moving a group of tasks

You can move a group of tasks in much the same way that you move an individual task. *Your* next task, Mr. Phelps, if you accept it, is to move the Water service and Electrical service tasks so that they follow the Footing/foundation task. To do so:

1. **Select the ID number of task 6.**

2. **Press and hold down the Shift key.**

3. **Select the ID number of Task 7.**

   This highlights the block of tasks and their ID numbers.

4. **Release the mouse button and Shift key.**

5. **Click in the highlighted number area and then drag the cursor down until it rests on the line between tasks 10 and 11.**

   A gray line appears.

6. **Release the mouse button.**

   Tasks 6 and 7 are now tasks 9 and 10.

Good grief! That must be something like what the astronauts feel when they're trying to dock into a Russian spaceship. With a little practice, it gets less stressful.

Oops. Undoing changes

 If you make a mistake or change your mind, you can undo your most recent action by clicking the Undo button on the Standard toolbar.

Deleting a task

The final corrections (at this point anyway) are to delete one of the Landscaping tasks and change the other's duration. The Landscaping task at task 7 needs to go because, as mentioned, it occurs too soon.

To delete task 7 and its duration:

1. **Select anywhere on the task 7 row in the Gantt table.**

   When I say Gantt table, I mean the information on the left side of the vertical bar. The Gantt chart is on the right of the vertical bar.

2. **Press the Delete key.**

   That Landscaping task is gone. The tasks that followed now ripple into their new position.

3. **Change the duration of Task 21, Landscaping, to 4 days.**

Press the Page Up key. Your project should now look like Figure 4-12.

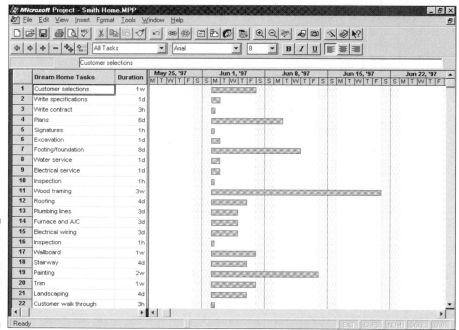

Figure 4-12: The edited Gantt chart shows all current changes.

The new information is only temporary until you save it, so save your project again:

1. **Click the Save button on the Standard toolbar.**

2. **Select the Save 'Smith Home.MPP' without a baseline option.**

3. **Click OK.**

Inserting tasks

Inserting a task or tasks is as simple as moving and deleting them. Just click on an existing task and press the Insert key. Space is inserted for your new task at that point, and the former occupant of the cell moves to the next cell down. In the next section, I show you how to insert space for additional tasks — in this instance, project milestones.

Inserting milestones

A *milestone* is the beginning or completion of a significant event or series of events in a project. Milestones are places where you stop to assess your progress. Often, milestones occur when contractors should be finished with their responsibilities so that others can begin. Sometimes milestones are a place for changing some project team members.

On the Smith Home project, some milestones are linked to stage-of-completion commitments in the contract. Another contract stipulation is that occupancy must occur on or before October 1 of the same year.

In Microsoft Project, you designate a milestone by entering a duration of 0. To insert a milestone, you click in the cell where you want to insert the milestone. The task that currently holds that place will trickle down one task line (as will all subsequent tasks).

To add your first milestone to the Smith Home project:

1. **Select task 1, Customer selections.**

2. **Press the Insert key.**

3. **Type** Project begins **as the milestone, and** 0d **as the duration.**

   Notice that after you leave the duration field, the Gantt chart creates a black diamond with the date 6/2, your start date in Project Info. Your screen should look like Figure 4-13.

4. **Insert these other milestones into your project, all with a duration of 0d:**

   a. Before Excavation, insert a milestone called Contract begins.

   b. Before Wood Framing, insert Foundation stage complete.

   c. Before Wallboard, insert Framing stage complete.

   d. Before Contract closure, insert Finishing stage complete.

   e. After Administrative closure, enter Project complete.

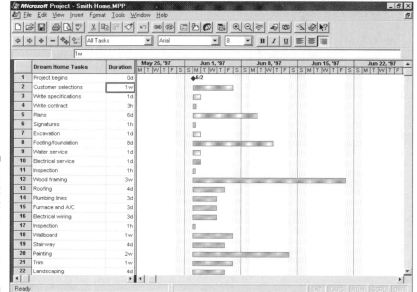

Figure 4-13:
The default
Gantt chart
designation
of a mile-
stone is a
black
diamond.

You can scroll the Gantt table by clicking the scroll bar on the right of the
Gantt chart.

Press the Page Up key. Your project should now look like Figure 4-14.

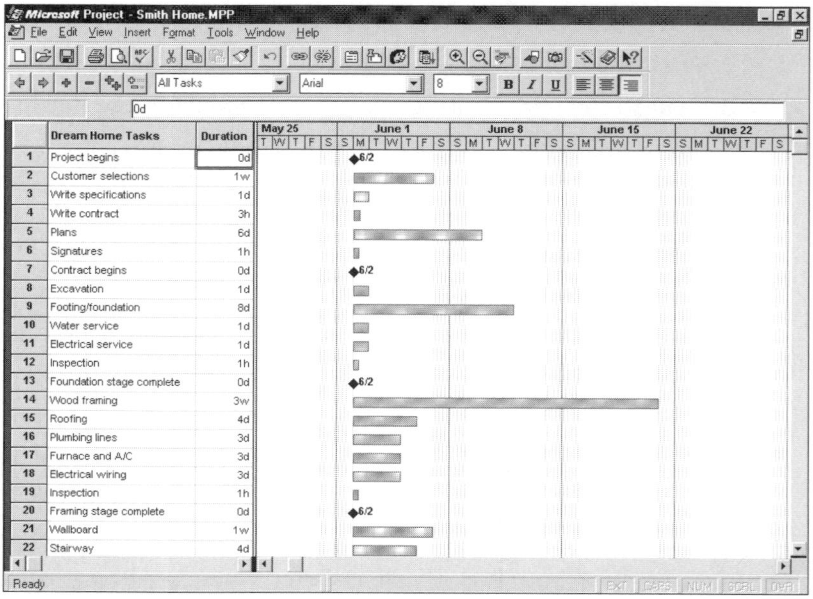

Figure 4-14:
The mile-
stones have
been
added, but
their actual
dates have
not been
set.

Don't be bothered by the fact that all the milestones have the same date as the project start date. You'll change those dates shortly.

Your project's value increases with each entry of information. Make sure that you save your file frequently, or your Van Gogh might lose an ear.

1. **Click the Save button on the Standard toolbar.**
2. **Select the Save 'Smith Home.MPP' without a baseline option.**
3. **Click OK.**

Linking Tasks

As you scan the project, you'll notice that all the project's tasks are set to start on the same date. The painters are going to have trouble getting to the second floor of a house that hasn't been designed yet. Hmm. Something is missing. Although the task durations are all relatively accurate, the overall project has no layout in time.

To add the element of time to a project, you link tasks. The default link is that a task will not begin until previous ones have finished. It's called a *finish-to-start* link. You can link two or all your tasks.

This chapter works only with the default finish-to-start link. To find out about other types of links, check out Chapter 6.

To link all the tasks on the Gantt chart:

1. **Select task 1, keeping the mouse button held down.**
2. **Drag the cursor through all the tasks.**

   All the tasks are selected.

3. **Click the Link Tasks button on the Standard toolbar.**

Now the Gantt chart comes alive. Tasks are linked in the finish-to-start relationship and stretch out beyond the screen's width (unless you have a monitor shaped like a 2 x 4). In Microsoft Project, what you see is called a *view*.

To view your links on the Gantt chart:

1. **Press the Page Up key to return to the first task.**

   The Gantt chart looks much different now.

2. **Press the Page Down key to move to the last task.**

   There seem to be no bars to the right of these tasks.

3. **Select the final task cell, Project Complete.**

4. **Click the Goto Selected Task button on the Standard toolbar.**

The Gantt chart should like something like Figure 4-15. We have troubles. The project, in its current state, will finish on October 1, exactly the contractual finish date. That's unrealistically optimistic. What about that thing called rain? Unless you know some weather magic, you need to do some project management magic to shorten the project's length. But like all other forms of magic, project management is a craft. You need to know about a number of things to make the Smith Home project realistically shorter. That's what the upcoming chapters are about — optimizing work through quality time management.

While you're looking at the chart, notice the lines with arrowheads. A line indicates a link. An arrowhead indicates relationship.

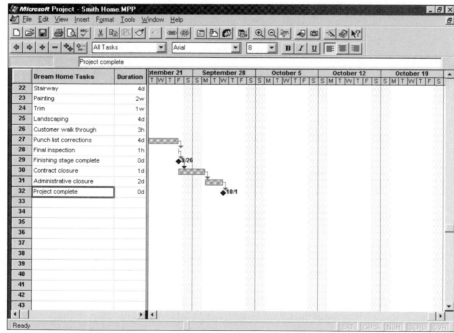

Figure 4-15:
The Gantt chart shows the timescale projection of linked tasks.

Unlinking tasks

One of the magic feats you need to know is how to unlink tasks. Sometimes you'll need to unlink tasks so that you can reorganize task relationships. Use the tasks in the Smith Home project to see how this works:

1. **Click the first task.**

2. **Click the Goto Selected Task button on the Standard toolbar.**

3. **Select the first task, keeping the mouse button held down.**

4. **Drag the cursor down through all the remaining tasks.**

   All the tasks are selected.

 5. **Click the Unlink Tasks button on the Standard toolbar.**

   The project returns to its previous unlinked condition.

Undoing an action

Although project managers are pros at making things appear and disappear, they sometimes reach their hand in the hat and pull out something they weren't expecting. Or sometimes, if you're up close, you might hear them mutter a slight "Oops" when they saw a project in two. But you'll see no sweat on their brow. They know that the Undo button is only a click away.

 In the case of the Smith House project, you can undo your most recent action. To restore the project to its linked condition, click the Undo button on the Standard toolbar.

Phew. Your project should be linked again. All that linking and unlinking and relinking makes one thirsty. Time for a break. But before you get up from your chair, resave the Smith Home project:

1. **Click the Save button on the Standard toolbar.**

2. **Select the Save 'Smith Home.MPP' without a baseline option.**

3. **Click OK.**

So you've created your schedule. Kind of makes your heart flutter to think of all those nicely arranged tasks and durations and milestones and links. You've accomplished the tasks in a very short time, er, duration.

Chapter 5

Outlining Your Project

● ●

In This Chapter

▶ Creating summary tasks

▶ Promoting and demoting tasks

▶ Modifying the Gantt chart timescale

▶ Using outlining features

● ●

*M*icrosoft Project provides a dynamic way to order, view, and control related groups of tasks. It does this through outlining. In project management, an *outline* is an ordered structure for a project showing how some tasks fit into broader groupings, called *summary tasks*. Tasks grouped within a summary task are called *subtasks*. Figure 5-1 is an example of a summary task and subtasks.

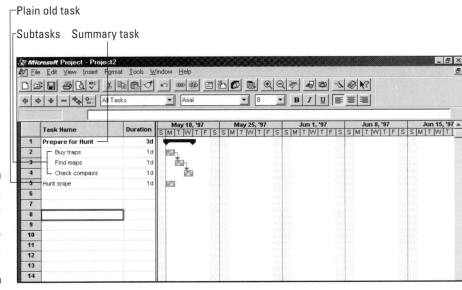

Figure 5-1: An example of a summary task and subtasks.

Why Project 4.1 (And You) Works Better with Outlines

Outlining your project into summary tasks and subtasks has strong benefits. One important advantage is that you can report on the project's progress using varying levels of detail. For instance, the bank may want to know only the current stage of construction and therefore needs only a summary task report. Or your procurement department may want a detailed report of only the upcoming phase of a project so that the materials can be delivered on time without unnecessary stockpiling of inventory.

With outlining, you're more likely to manage a project successfully because you associate tasks with their related activities and deadlines. For instance, a public utility will want a two-week lead time before installing the electric service. In addition, they will install the service only after you have completed the footing and foundation work. Your management of these two tasks will be easier if you associate them as subtasks of the same summary task.

A summary task is just what its name implies: a summary of the duration, cost, and resources of all the subtasks related to the summary task. You can assess the overall status of a group of subtasks by looking at summary task information.

Kinds of Outlines

You can prepare two basic types of outlines: top-down outlines and bottom-up outlines. A *top-down* outline identifies a project by all its phases or major categories. Typically, these become your summary tasks. After you list these major categories, you break the project down into a series or group of tasks within each category. These become your subtasks.

A *bottom-up* outline is the reverse. You list everything that needs to be accomplished in the project. Then you cluster, or order, the tasks into major phases or groups. The result is the same as for top-down outlining; you just get there from the opposite direction.

The project you develop in Chapter 4 is an example of a bottom-up outline. You develop the tasks, but do not identify the summary tasks and subtasks.

This chapter — and the rest of Part II — uses an example project file (Smith Home project) that you create in Chapter 4. If you haven't already created the file, check out Chapter 4.

Adding Summary Tasks

Your project, the Smith Home, is a bottom-up outline. You created the tasks, and now it's time to put them into summary tasks — kind of like putting sliced loaves of bread into wrappers. The wrapper doesn't add anything to the slices, but it contains them and tells all about them. Got any pumpernickel projects?

In the bottom-up approach, you add summary tasks by inserting them (in the same way that you insert any other task). Here goes:

1. **Click the Open button on the Standard toolbar.**

2. **Double-click the Practice Files folder.**

3. **Double-click the Smith Home.MPP project file.**

4. **Select the Customer selections task, and press Insert.**

5. **Type** Contract/Design.

This newly inserted task isn't a summary task yet. It becomes a summary task after you identify (demote) its subtasks.

Demoting Tasks

Demotion is not a popular word these days, but it's a rad term in project management. If you want to create a subtask, you *demote* it; that is, you place it under the hierarchy of a summary task. You don't need to furrow your brow, buy antacids, or close the office door to do it either.

Demoting tasks in Microsoft Project is simple. All you have to do is select the cell or cells that you want to demote and click the right arrow on the Standard toolbar. So roll up you sleeves and get ready to do some demoting.

To demote subtasks in your project:

1. **Move the cursor to the beginning of the Customer selections task.**

2. **Click and drag down to the end of the "Contract begins" milestone.**

   Tasks 3 through 8 are selected.

3. **Click the Indent button on the Formatting toolbar.**

Your project should now look like Figure 5-2.

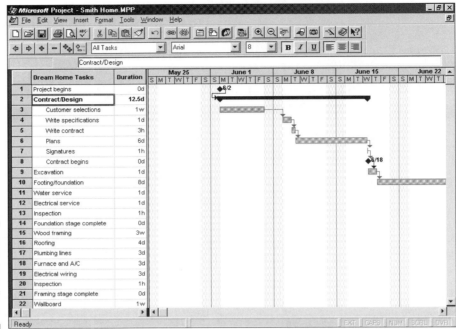

Figure 5-2:
Tasks 3
through 8
are now
subtasks of
task 2.

The following changes have taken place:

- ✔ The selected tasks have been indented to the right.
- ✔ The summary task, Contract/Design, has been changed to bold.
- ✔ The summary task duration is now the sum of the six subtasks.
- ✔ A summary bar is now in the Gantt chart. It begins with the start of the first subtask and ends with the finish of the last subtask and the date of the milestone.

You can have up to nine levels of demotion.

Now insert another summary task into your project:

1. Select Excavation task, and press Insert.

2. In the entry box, type Foundation Stage.

3. Press Enter.

Don't worry if Microsoft Project interprets that the new task is another subtask of Contract/Design. After you insert the task, you can modify its place in the hierarchy of the outline.

After all that tough demotion stuff, it's time to do some promotion.

Promoting Tasks

To free the Foundation Stage task from the subtask category, you promote it. Task promotion is as simple as demotion. To promote the task:

1. Select the Foundation Stage task.

 2. Click the Outdent button on the Formatting toolbar.

Foundation Stage moves to the left, indicating that it is no longer a subtask of Contract/Design.

Now that you have the hang of the outlining procedure, insert the following additional summary tasks:

1. Select Wood framing, press Insert, and type Framing Stage.

2. Select Wallboard, press Insert, and type Finishing Stage.

3. Select Contract closure, press Insert, and add Close-Out Stage.

Demote the tasks that follow each new summary task as follows:

1. Click and drag over the tasks that follow a new summary task.

2. After the group of tasks is selected, click the Indent button on the toolbar.

3. Repeat for each group of subtasks.

When you have completed this process, press the Page Up key.

Changing the Gantt Chart Timescale

To improve your analysis of the project, you can zoom in and out on your Gantt chart by pressing the zoom buttons on the Standard toolbar.

 For example, click the Zoom In button on the Standard toolbar. Notice that the timescale on the Gantt chart has changed to six-hour blocks.

Now click the Zoom Out button on the Standard toolbar. The chart is back where it started, with weeks as a major scale and days as a minor scale. Click the Zoom Out button two more times. The major scale is now months, and the minor scale is now weeks as shown in Figure 5-3. This view makes seeing the entire project by scrolling up and down possible. Such a compacted view is somewhat limited in value, but it's helpful from time to time to step back and see (or print) the full picture.

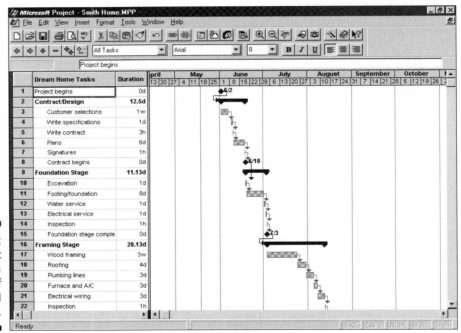

Figure 5-3:
The Gantt chart with a timescale of months and weeks.

 If needed, you can zoom all the way in to quarter-hour intervals, and you can zoom all the way out to quarter-year intervals.

Click the Zoom In or Zoom Out button on the Standard toolbar to return the Gantt chart timescale to the default days and weeks scale.

1. Click the Save button on the Standard toolbar.

 2. Select the Save 'Smith Home.MPP' without a baseline option.

3. Click OK.

Editing Summary Tasks

I have good news and bad news about editing summary tasks. The good news is that you can move them, add them, and delete them like any other task. The bad news is that, if you're not careful, you might affect subtasks in a way you weren't intending. For instance, if you delete a summary task, you delete its subtasks, too.

But even the bad news isn't all bad. Microsoft Project warns you if you might be making a mistake.

Chapter 4 has more information on editing tasks.

Deleting summary tasks

Got a summary task that doesn't look as brilliant as it first appeared? Have circumstances changed and you need to cluster a few groups of subtasks under a single summary task? You can delete a summary task — carefully!

Because the Smith Home project is for practice, it's a good place to make your first attempt at deleting a summary task:

1. **Select the Foundation Stage summary task.**

2. **Press the Delete key.**

   The Planning Wizard appears (Figure 5-4). It warns you that Foundation Stage is a summary task and that deleting it will also delete its subtasks. Pretty sharp, huh?

3. **Click Cancel.**

   You retreat from this point of no return. (Well, you could click Undo as a last resort.)

Figure 5-4: Choose the Cancel button or the Cancel check box to avoid deleting the summary task.

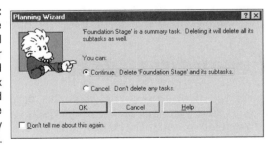

If the Planning Wizard didn't appear:

1. **Click the Undo button on the Standard toolbar.**

   This retrieves your deletion.

2. **Choose Tools⇨Options.**

3. **Click the General tab.**

4. **Select the Advice from Planning Wizard box and all three of its check boxes.**

5. **Click OK.**

   From now on, Planning Wizard will appear as described in the book. Leaving all the wizards on until you're proficient with the program is good.

To delete a summary task without affecting the subtasks, you need to first promote the subtasks to tasks. You do this by selecting the tasks, and then clicking the Outdent button on the Formatting toolbar. You can then delete the summary task.

Moving summary tasks

If you move a summary task, you move its subtasks as well. Subtasks stick to their summary task like glue.

If you move a summary task into an existing summary group, the summary task and its children will become a subtask and sub-subtasks, respectively, of that group.

When you move a summary task, the move affects the relationships of subtasks to other tasks. The subtasks are groupies of the summary task. Where the summary task goes, its subtasks follow — even if this doesn't make sense to your schedule. You probably need to modify task relationships if you have already linked tasks. For information about changing task relationships, see Chapter 6.

Collapsing and Expanding Tasks

One of the great features of Microsoft Project is its flexibility in presentation of information. For instance, after you have outlined a project, you can simply point and click to expand or collapse the project.

To collapse a summary task:

1. Select the Foundation Stage task.

2. Click the Hide Subtasks button on the Formatting toolbar.

The subtasks of the summary task Foundation Stage are collapsed (Figure 5-5).

Collapsed summary task

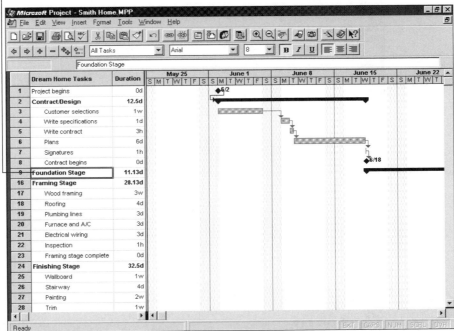

Figure 5-5:
Click the
Hide
Subtasks
button to
collapse a
summary
task.

3. Repeat Steps 1 and 2 to collapse the other subtasks.

Fortunately, the instructions for expanding tasks don't need to be expansive. To expand a summary task:

1. Select the Foundation Stage task.

2. Click the Show Subtasks button on the Formatting toolbar.

The subtasks of the summary task Foundation Stage are expanded (Figure 5-6).

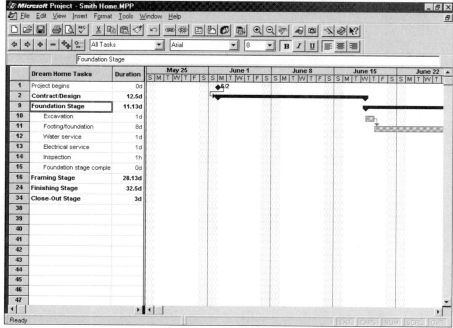

Figure 5-6:
Click the
Show
Subtasks
button to
expand a
task.

 To expand all subtasks, click the Show All Tasks button on the Formatting toolbar.

Adding Symbols or Numbers to an Outline

You can add a plus symbol to all summary tasks and a minus symbol to all subtasks. Why would you want to do this? Well, if you collapse a group of subtasks, the plus sign of their summary task will indicate the existence of the subtasks.

 Click the Outline Symbols button on the Formatting toolbar. A plus appears next to each summary task, and a minus sign appears next to each subtask.

Microsoft Project also offers outline numbering. This outlining feature works much like legal or regulatory outlining. You know the type — 1.1.1.1.1. instead of I.A.1.a.i.

The outline option aligns with a project management system called *Work Breakdown Structure*. In this system, tasks are organized for detailed reporting of schedules and for tracking costs. Each additional indent of a subtask is an increasingly detailed definition of a project's component.

To activate the outline option:

1. Choose Tools⇨Options.

2. Click the View tab.

3. Click to clear the Show Outline Symbol check box.

4. Select the Show Outline Number check box.

5. Click OK.

The tasks and subtasks now have outline numbers associated with them (Figure 5-7).

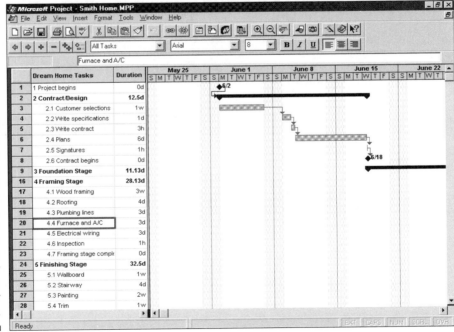

Figure 5-7: When you set the outline numbers to be visible, they remain so until you clear the Show Outline Number check box.

The outline numbers reflect the number of a summary task, the numbers of related subtasks, and the level of hierarchy within the summary task. This differs from a task ID. For instance, task ID 6 might be 2.4 in the outline numbering. This means it is the fourth subtask of summary task 2.

Adjusting the width of the task column

All of a task's name doesn't have to fit in the task name cell. The full name still exists even if you can't see all of it. But for outlining and reporting, the schedule looks better if everything fits.

To make the task names fit, you can either shorten the names or enlarge the task column to fit the longest task name.

For example, look at task 23 in Figure 5-7, Framing stage complete. It just doesn't fit.

To make it and all the tasks fit, you can do one of three things:

- Drag the column edge to the right.

- Double-click the Dream Home Tasks heading. The Column Definition dialog box appears. For Width, enter a number larger than the current 24 (up to 255 characters).

- Double-click the Dream Home Tasks heading. In the Column Definition dialog box, choose Best Fit. The column is automatically sized based on the length of the task name.

Now that you've gone to all this trouble to create your project, it would be simply *outlinedish* to risk someone tripping on your power cord or dropping a box of nails on your keyboard. Hey kids! Do you know what time it is? Right. It's time to save the file again:

1. **Click the Save button on the Standard toolbar.**

2. **Select the Save 'Smith Home.MPP' without a baseline option.**

3. **Click OK.**

After I've outlined a project, I'm always glad I did, even though the process is a pain in the subtask. In other chapters, you reap the reward of those who toil. May all your tasks be promoted!

Chapter 6
Task Relationships

Microsoft Project is all about relationships — it's a master of whodunits (or who'sgoingtodoits). As the project manager, you are the great storyteller. You get to choose the twists and turns and control the outcomes. The players of the story, the tasks, are *dependent* on other tasks to begin or finish. The tasks are also the cause of other tasks beginning — the predecessors. *The Predecessors!* What a title! You'll sell a million. Can I come to your file signing?

The success of your project is largely the result of the care you put into your task relationships. Sometimes the players are constrained by circumstances beyond their control. In this chapter, you have an opportunity to establish various task relationships and constraints in your project.

The example in this chapter is based on the Smith Home project file you create in Chapter 4 and further develop in Chapter 5. You use this example throughout Part II. If you haven't already created the file, you might want to follow the instructions in Chapter 4 and Chapter 5.

If it isn't already open, open Smith Home.MPP in the Practice Files folder.

Using Constraint and Feeling Good about It

Some tasks have to begin or end on certain dates. This might be due to the availability of a key consultant or limited access to an important piece of equipment. Other tasks can start just as soon as their predecessors finish. In either case, priorities govern the beginning and end of every task. In project management, these priorities are called constraints.

A *constraint* is a time limitation placed on a task. All linked tasks have constraints. Looking at your home building project, you can see that Microsoft Project linked each task to follow directly on the heels of its predecessor. Microsoft Project used its default constraint, called *As Soon As Possible*. Fortunately, you aren't limited to this constraint because reality isn't limited to it. In fact, Microsoft Project uses eight kinds of constraints:

Constraint	*Description*
As Late As Possible (ALAP)	The task must start as late as possible without impeding the start date of subsequent tasks. This constraint has no actual constraint date.
As Soon As Possible (ASAP)	The task must start as early as possible. This constraint has no actual constraint date. This is the Microsoft Project default constraint for tasks.
Finish No Earlier Than (FNET)	The task must end no sooner than a certain constraint date.
Finish No Later Than (FNLT)	The task must finish no later than a certain constraint date.
Must Finish On (MFO)	The task must finish on a certain date. The date is anchored in the schedule.
Must Start On (MSO)	The task must start on a certain date. The date is anchored in the schedule.
Start No Earlier Than (SNET)	The task must start on or after your constraint date.
Start No Later Than (SNLT)	The task must start on or before your constraint date.

Microsoft Project used its ASAP constraint when it linked all the tasks in your home building project. Some remodeling is in order — not of the house, but of some task constraints:

- ✔ The ASAP default set the signing of the contract on June 18. It actually is scheduled for 11:00 a.m. on July 1.

- ✔ The contract begins at the signing of the contract, but the actual scheduled beginning of the work is July 7 at 8 a.m.

Microsoft Project usually provides multiple ways to enter information. One way is to enter information directly into the Gantt table. You'll use this method to change the contract signing constraint.

Using the Gantt Table

The Gantt table presents your project plans in a table format. As you see in Part III, the table provides more information than you can shake a Gantt bar at. Who knows what lurks behind the Gantt chart? The project manager knows. That's you, or at least it will be you soon. Let's take a look:

1. **Select the vertical separator bar between the Gantt table and the Gantt chart.**

2. **Drag the bar to the right until it reveals all the columns, including Resource Names.**

    Two columns, the Start column and the Finish column, might be full of hatch marks.

3. **Double-click the Start column heading.**

    The Column Definition dialog box appears.

4. **Click Best Fit.**

5. **Widen the Finish column in the same manner.**

 The subtasks of the Foundation Stage may still be collapsed, so click the Show All Tasks button on the Formatting toolbar. Your screen should now look like Figure 6-1.

Figure 6-1:
The Gantt
table
displays
all its
columns.

The Gantt chart figure shows the Microsoft Project - Smith Home.MPP window with menu items File, Edit, View, Insert, Format, Tools, Window, Help. The table displays the following:

	Dream Home Tasks	Duration	Start	Finish	Predecessors	Resource
1	1 Project begins	0d	Mon 6/2/97 8:00 AM	Mon 6/2/97 8:00 AM		
2	2 Contract/Design	12.5d	Mon 6/2/97 8:00 AM	Wed 6/18/97 12:00 PM	1	
3	2.1 Customer selections	1w	Mon 6/2/97 8:00 AM	Fri 6/6/97 5:00 PM		
4	2.2 Write specifications	1d	Mon 6/9/97 8:00 AM	Mon 6/9/97 5:00 PM	3	
5	2.3 Write contract	3h	Tue 6/10/97 8:00 AM	Tue 6/10/97 11:00 AM	4	
6	2.4 Plans	6d	Tue 6/10/97 11:00 AM	Wed 6/18/97 11:00 AM	5	
7	2.5 Signatures	1h	Wed 6/18/97 11:00 AM	Wed 6/18/97 12:00 PM	6	
8	2.6 Contract begins	0d	Wed 6/18/97 12:00 PM	Wed 6/18/97 12:00 PM	7	
9	3 Foundation Stage	11.13d	Wed 6/18/97 1:00 PM	Thu 7/3/97 2:00 PM	8	
10	3.1 Excavation	1d	Wed 6/18/97 1:00 PM	Thu 6/19/97 12:00 PM	8	
11	3.2 Footing/foundation	8d	Thu 6/19/97 1:00 PM	Tue 7/1/97 12:00 PM	10	
12	3.3 Water service	1d	Tue 7/1/97 1:00 PM	Wed 7/2/97 12:00 PM	11	
13	3.4 Electrical service	1d	Wed 7/2/97 1:00 PM	Thu 7/3/97 12:00 PM	12	
14	3.5 Inspection	1h	Thu 7/3/97 1:00 PM	Thu 7/3/97 2:00 PM	13	
15	3.6 Foundation stage complete	0d	Thu 7/3/97 2:00 PM	Thu 7/3/97 2:00 PM	14	
16	4 Framing Stage	28.13d	Thu 7/3/97 2:00 PM	Tue 8/12/97 3:00 PM	15	
17	4.1 Wood framing	3w	Thu 7/3/97 2:00 PM	Thu 7/24/97 2:00 PM		
18	4.2 Roofing	4d	Thu 7/24/97 2:00 PM	Wed 7/30/97 2:00 PM	17	
19	4.3 Plumbing lines	3d	Wed 7/30/97 2:00 PM	Mon 8/4/97 2:00 PM	18	
20	4.4 Furnace and A/C	3d	Mon 8/4/97 2:00 PM	Thu 8/7/97 2:00 PM	19	
21	4.5 Electrical wiring	3d	Thu 8/7/97 2:00 PM	Tue 8/12/97 2:00 PM	20	
22	4.6 Inspection	1h	Tue 8/12/97 2:00 PM	Tue 8/12/97 3:00 PM	21	

The Start date and time for the contract signatures is Wednesday, June 18, 1997, at 11:00 a.m. You need to change it to Tuesday, July 1, 1997, at 11:00 a.m. Simply do the following:

1. **Double-click the Start cell for the Signatures task.**

   The Task Information box appears. This is a handy tool for making changes to a task.

2. **Select the entire Start Date text box.**

3. **Type** 7/1 11:00 AM **in the text box.**

   Don't use periods with the *AM* designation.

4. **Click OK.**

   A Planning Wizard dialog box appears, as shown in Figure 6-2. The Planning Wizard is alerting you that you are about to modify the relationship of the Signature task and its predecessor, the Plans task.

   If the Planning Wizard doesn't appear, click the Undo button on the Standard toolbar. Then choose Tools⇔Options. Select the General tab, and then select the Advice from Planning Wizard check box. Make sure that all the advice check boxes are checked. Click the OK button, and repeat Steps 1 to 4.

Figure 6-2:
The
Planning
Wizard
asks
whether
you want
to maintain
a link even
though
you have
changed a
constraint.

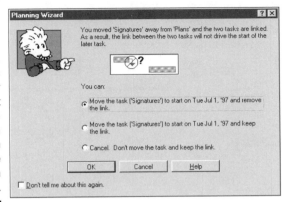

5. **Select the second option, the one that moves the task and keeps the link.**

6. **Click OK.**

   You have changed a constraint from ASAP to SNET (Start No Earlier Than).

Using the Task Information Box

One of the more efficient ways to assess and make changes to tasks is by using the Task form. As you are about to see, it puts all kinds of information at your fingertips simultaneously. You can access the Task form by selecting a task and then clicking the Information button on the Standard toolbar.

But perhaps a better way to see the Task form is through a combination view. A *combination view* contains two views about information. The lower pane shows detailed information about the highlighted task or resource in the upper pane.

Before changing to a combination view, you need to expose more of the Gantt chart and less of the Gantt table:

1. **Select the vertical bar separating the Gantt table and the Gantt chart.**

2. **Drag it to the left until it exposes only the task and duration columns.**

3. **Choose <u>W</u>indow⇨Split to change to a combination view.**

   Your screen should now look like Figure 6-3.

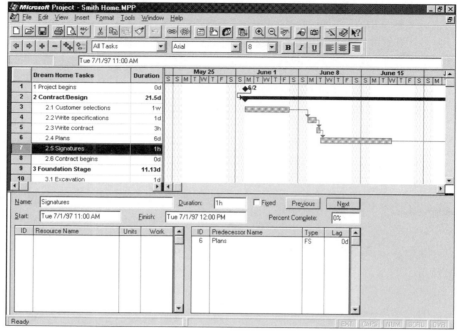

Figure 6-3:
The screen is split, revealing the Gantt chart and the Task Information box.

Welcome to a combination view! In this crazy little world, you can see a portion of the Gantt table, the Gantt chart, and the Task form. This isn't exactly a view from Pike's Peak, but it's about the best that Microsoft Project has to offer.

You can manipulate each of the three windows. For example:

1. **Select the Signatures task.**

 2. **Click the Goto Selected Task button on the Standard toolbar.**

3. **Click the Zoom In button on the Standard toolbar a few times to see the hourly timescale.**

4. **If necessary, click the Goto Selected Task button again to line up the view with the Signatures task.**

5. **After you're finished, click the Zoom Out button until you return to the weeks/days timescale.**

Use the Task form in a combination view to change a duration and a task relationship. Click the Next button until the Excavation task is highlighted and *Excavation* appears in the Name box of the Task form.

The Start Date for the Excavation task is wrong. Excavation is the first task after the contract has been signed. As the schedule is currently written, the excavation is slated to begin right after lunch on the same day as the contract signing. Realistically, the excavation contractor will need a four-day lead time.

To do this, you need to change the constraints on the Excavation task. The standard Task form doesn't offer a constraint option, so first you need to change to the Task Details Form:

1. **Choose View⇨More Views to change to the Task Details Form.**

   A list box appears.

2. **Scroll through the list box until you find Task Details Form.**

3. **Double-click Task Details Form.**

   The Task Details Form, shown in Figure 6-4, replaces the standard Task form.

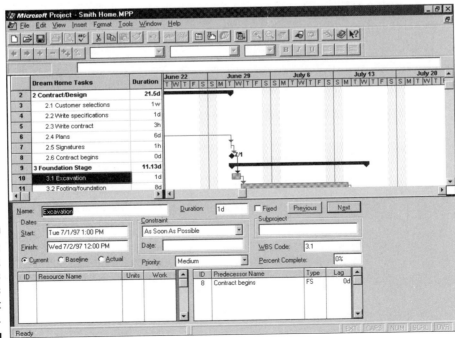

Figure 6-4:
The Task Details Form has constraint options.

4. **Under Constraint, click the down arrow.**

   A list box appears.

5. **Select Start No Earlier Than.**

6. **In the Date box under Constraint, type** 7/7.

7. **Click OK.**

   Notice that the start and finish dates for the task have changed in the Task Details Form. Also notice that the Gantt chart has moved the Excavation date to Monday, July 7 (Figure 6-5).

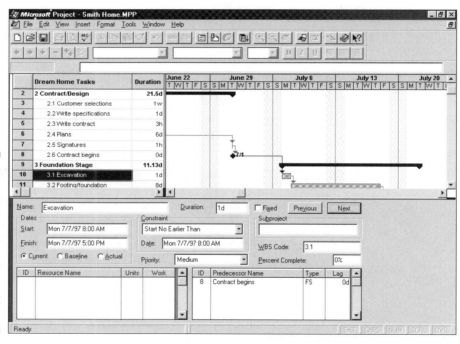

Figure 6-5:
The changes to the start and finish dates are reflected in the Gantt chart.

While you're in the Task Details Form, click Previous until you reach the Signatures task. Notice that the constraint change you made to Signatures is recorded in the list box under Constraints. Click Next until you're back to the Excavation task.

You won't be making any other constraint changes for now, so change the form view back to the standard Task form:

1. **Choose View⇨More Views.**

2. **In the list box, double-click Task form.**

   You're back to the standard Task form.

While you're in the split view, you might want to see how you're doing with the projected completion date as shown. Click anywhere in the Gantt chart. Notice the thin vertical bar on the far left of the window? This indicates that the Gantt window is the active view.

Press Page Down as many times as necessary until the final task appears, Project complete. Select the Project complete task. The Task form probably says that the project finish date is Friday, October 17, 1997. This is unacceptable. The customer contract has a firm move-in date of no later than Wednesday, October 1. You have some project management to do to meet this deadline. One of the ways you can do some time managing is by changing task relationships.

Press Page Up until the Excavation task appears again. Then click anywhere in the Task form to make it active.

Changing Task Relationships

You need to find ways to manage time. It's time to change some task relationships in your home building project. You can schedule tasks to happen concurrently. Water and electric service meet this bill (sorry, no pun intended). So those are the first relationships to change:

1. **Click Previous or Next until you reach the Water service task.**

   The Task form shows that the predecessor of Water service is Footing/ foundation, ID 11. This is okay.

2. **Click Next.**

   You should be at Electrical service. Its predecessor is Water service, ID 12. To make Electric service occur concurrently with Water service, the Electric service and the Water service must share the same predecessor.

3. **Change the Electric service predecessor by selecting the ID column in the Task form and typing** 11.

4. **Click OK.**

   Notice that the predecessor name has changed to Footing/Foundation.

5. **Click anywhere in the Gantt chart to activate the Gantt window to view the result.**

6. **With Electrical service highlighted, click the Goto Selected Task button on the Standard toolbar.**

   Your screen should look similar to Figure 6-6.

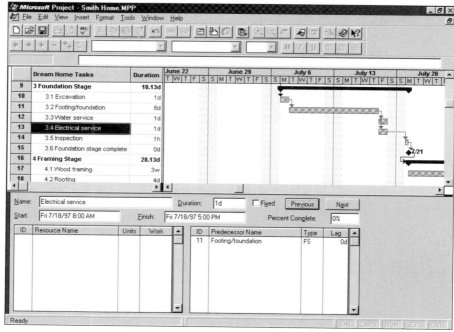

Figure 6-6:
The
Electric
service
and Water
service
tasks now
share the
same
predecessor.

Notice that the Gantt chart now assigns the same predecessor to Water service and Electric service. They both start on the same day. Because both tasks have the same duration, they also end on the same day. As you see a little later, this isn't always the case.

Lagging

Sometimes you need to make room in a project to allow for some flexibility of time. (And maybe in your life, too. I know I do.) The allowance of time between dependent tasks is called *lagging*.

In the Task form, you can see that the Finish date and time for the Electrical service task is Friday, July 18, at 5:00 p.m. Click the Next button to arrive at the Inspection task. Its Start date is Monday, July 21, at 8:00 a.m. This is the next work day and the next work hour. You need to add some lag time to this task relationship.

Lag time can be in minutes, hours, days, or weeks. In the following, you add a one-day lag:

1. **Select the Lag column and type** 1d.

2. **Click OK.**

Notice that the Lag column now says 1d and that the start date has changed to Tuesday (Figure 6-7). Also notice that the Gantt chart has changed to reflect the lag. In addition, because the Inspection task is a subtask of the Foundation Stage summary task, the summary bar has elongated. Way to go, you ole project manager!

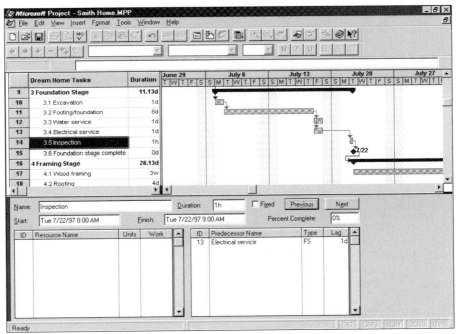

Figure 6-7:
The Gantt chart shows a one-day lag.

Sharing predecessors

Using what you know so far, you need to make some task relationship changes in the Framing Stage. The Roofing, Plumbing lines, Furnace and A/C, and Electrical wiring tasks could share the same predecessor and, therefore, happen at the same time. For all these tasks, make Wood framing, ID 17, their predecessor:

1. **Click Previous or Next until you reach the task (such as Roofing).**

2. **Change the task's predecessor by selecting the ID column and typing 17 in the column.**

3. **Click OK.**

4. **Follow Steps 1 through 3 for the remaining tasks.**

After you're finished:

1. **Click anywhere in the Gantt chart.**

2. **Select the Electrical wiring task.**

3. **Click the Goto Selected Task button on the Standard toolbar.**

4. **Scroll the Gantt chart until your screen appears similar to Figure 6-8.**

   The tasks should be stacked as you specified when you gave them all the same predecessor.

Fixing time glitches in the task form

You've fixed one problem only to create another. Task ID 22, Inspection, has Electrical wiring as its predecessor. The problem is that this task's duration is shorter than the Roofing task. Inspection can't occur until all Framing Stage construction subtasks are complete. Sheesh. Does it feel like you're trying to rub out an ink spot? It's really not that bad. As you edit your project, changes sometimes require other changes. In this case, you have to do only two things. You need to change the Inspection task predecessor, and you need to provide a one-day lag as you did before the Foundation Stage inspection.

To edit the milestone:

1. **Click the Next button in the Task form until you come to ID 22, the Inspection task.**

2. **Change the predecessor ID to 18.**

   This ID is the Roofing task, the longest of the four preceding stacked tasks.

3. **Select the Lag column and type 1d in the column.**

4. **Click OK.**

Your project should now look like Figure 6-9. You've made big progress.

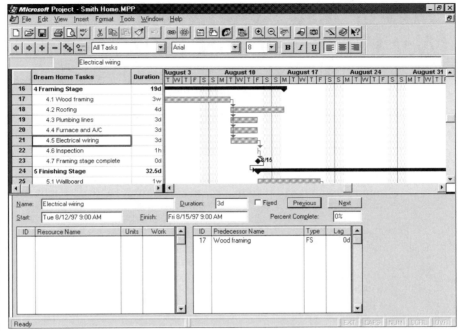

Figure 6-8:
Four
tasks
share
the same
predecessor.

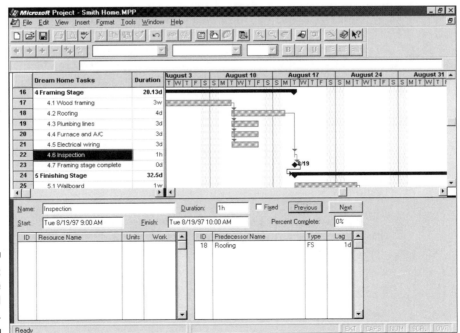

Figure 6-9:
The
corrected
milestone.

Kinds of Task Relationships (Not Your Friends at Work)

Microsoft Project has four kinds of task relationships: finish-to-start, start-to-start, finish-to-finish, and start-to-finish.

The finish-to-start (FS) relationship is the default Microsoft Project task relationship. It means that task A must finish before task B can begin. When you create a link, the default relationship is finish-to-start.

The start-to-start (SS) relationship means that task A and task B begin simultaneously. An example of this is heating a store-bought pizza. Task A is preheat the oven. Task B is prepare the pizza on a pan.

The finish-to-finish (FF) relationship means that task A and task B finish at the same time. An example of this is a long bomb in a football game. Task A is the quarterback dropping back into his pocket and unleashing a 50-yarder to a place no one is yet occupying. Task B is a split end racing down the sideline on an exact route that will place him at a precise place at a precise time (without looking back to give the defender any clues). I love football!

The start-to-finish (SF) relationship means that task B can't finish until task A starts. An example of this is a temporary electrical generator that can't stop until power is turned on to a permanent electrical system.

As you've probably guessed by now, some task relationships in the home aren't the default finish-to-start. Specifically, you need to change some relationship types in the Finishing Stage of the project.

The Wallboard task (ID 25) and the Stairway task (ID 26) should both start at the same time. They should have a start-to-start (SS) relationship.

The Painting task (ID 27) should also have a start-to-start (SS) relationship with the Wallboard task (ID 25), but it should lag by four days. That way, the wallboard crew can finish a portion of the house so that the painter can begin priming and applying the first coat.

The carpenter can begin doing the finish woodwork as soon as the paint dries. When one third of the Painting task (ID 27) is completed, the Trim task (ID 28) should begin. This is also a start-to-start (SS) relationship.

The Landscaping task should coincide with the completion of the Painting task. This is a finish-to-finish (FF) relationship.

The Customer walk-through task (ID 30) should follow the completion of the Painting task (ID 27) and should have a 2-day lag. This is a finish-to-start (FS) and a lag.

This may seem like a lot, but it's not. Each of these conditions is normal to a project plan and is easy to perform (and understand) in Microsoft Project. Scout's honor.

To begin changing task relationships, start with the Wallboard and Stairway relationship:

1. **Click the Next button until the Task form reaches ID 26, the Stairway task.**

   The predecessor is already ID 25, Wallboard. But you need to change the Type.

2. **Select the Type column and type** ss.

   The letters *ss* stand for start-to-start.

3. **Click OK.**

   As the Gantt chart shows, the Stairway task has a start-to-start relationship with the Wallboard task.

Next, you change the Painting and Wallboard relationship. As mentioned, you need to set a start-to-start relationship of this task to its new predecessor, the Wallboard task (ID 25). And you need to set a four-day lag.

1. **Click the Next button until the Task form reaches ID 27, the Painting task.**

2. **Select the Predecessor ID column, and type** 25.

3. **Select the Type column, and type** ss.

4. **Select the Lag column, and type** 4d.

5. **Click OK.**

   As the Gantt chart shows, the Painting task has a start-to-start relationship with the Wallboard task and has a lag of four days.

The grayed areas of a Gantt chart are nonworking periods. In Chapter 7, you modify the default working schedules.

Next, you need to set a start-to-start relationship with the Trim task's existing predecessor, the Painting task (ID 27). In this case, you need some lead time.

Lead time is the opposite of lag time. With lead time, you give the predecessor a certain head start before the dependent can begin. Lead time is expressed as a percentage or in minus minutes, hours, days, or weeks.

In this example, the Painting task should have a 33 percent lead before the Trim task starts. To change the Painting and Trim relationship:

1. **Click the Next button until the Task form reaches ID 28, the Trim task.**

2. **Select the Type column, and type** ss.

3. **Select the Lag column and type** 33%.

4. **Click OK.**

   In the Gantt Chart, the Trim task now has a start-to-start relationship with the Painting task and gives the Painting task a 33 percent lead.

The Landscaping task should coincide with the completion of the Painting task (ID 27). This is a finish-to-finish (FF) relationship:

1. **Click the Next button until the Task form reaches ID 29, the Landscaping task.**

2. **Select the Predecessor ID column, and type** 27.

3. **Select the Type column, and type** ff.

   The letters *ff* stand for finish-to-finish.

4. **Click OK.**

   In the Gantt Chart, the Landscaping task now has a finish-to-finish relationship with the Painting task. They both end at the same time.

You can change a task relationship also by double-clicking a link in the Gantt chart.

Next, the Customer walk-through task should follow the completion of the Painting task (ID 27) and have a 2-day lag. To change the Customer walk-through and Painting relationship:

1. **Click the Next button until the Task form reaches ID 30, the Customer walk-through task.**

2. **Select the Predecessor ID column, and type** 27.

3. **Select the Lag column, and type** 2d.

4. **Click OK.**

You have completed your changes to the Finishing Stage.

Removing split (or making your eyes horizontal again)

Had enough of this magnificent combination view? Are your eyeballs working independently? Well, you have just about beat the living tar out of the Task form. Why not let it cool down for awhile and return to a single view?

To remove a split, choose <u>W</u>indow⇨Remove Split. The screen returns to a full Gantt chart. Scroll the Gantt chart so that the Finishing Stage summary task begins near the top left corner of the chart. Your Gantt chart should now look similar to Figure 6-10.

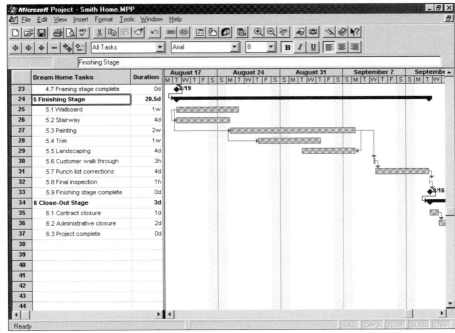

Figure 6-10: The Gantt chart shows the new task relationships in the Finishing Stage task.

After all that work, it's time to resave the project file:

1. **Click the Save button on the Standard toolbar.**
2. **Select the Save 'Smith Home.MPP' without a baseline option.**
3. **Click OK.**

A task is to a project what dirt is to a garden. It isn't much to look at, but try growing a begonia without it. Tasks are the groundwork of a project — nothing happens without them.

But begonias need more than dirt; they need people and tools for planting, watering, and weeding. And so it is with a project. Tasks, left to themselves, usually don't bear worthwhile fruit. In project management lingo, the planters, waterers, and weeders are called resources. Properly managed resources can make a bouquet from a briar patch. To find out about resources, check out Chapter 7.

Chapter 7

Resources

. . . .

In This Chapter

▶ Identifying people and things as resources

▶ Making the most of what you have

▶ Relating resources to responsibilities

▶ Putting the details into resources

▶ Controlling time with multiple calendars

▶ Shortcut ways to assign resources

. . . .

So, you're responsible for a project. Its success is important to you and your organization. If you get it right, the world will be put on notice that one serious strategist is in its midst. If you don't get it right . . . well, that's not an option.

The project needs to run like a well-oiled machine. Deadlines must be kept and goals must be met. Of course, things won't always run like clockwork. People overbook, materials arrive late, equipment breaks down. But those situations don't change the fact that the project has to meet its goals on time and on budget.

This isn't as bleak as it appears. It just means that getting your name into next year's Who's Who of project management may require managing your project resources.

What You and Your Chair Have in Common

Resources are equipment and the people who perform work on your project. In project management, resources aren't *every* piece of equipment and *every* person who performs work on your project.

For instance, ensuring that every member of the project team has a desk and a chair may be out of the scope of your project management responsibilities. That may be part of the operational givens of the organization that initiates the project. In contrast, if you and your project team need to meet in a conference room every Monday morning at 8:30, that conference room may be one of the resources of your project. Its availability may need to be managed.

The same is true of people. It may be an operational given that the shipping department provides the people power to handle all incoming and outgoing mail and parcels. If you have a mass mailing that must go out on a certain date, however, the shipping department personnel have just become a project resource. The proper scheduling of and communication about that mailing is a project management responsibility.

The art of resource planning is a beauty to behold when performed well. But it can be ugly to the bone when performed poorly.

Resources and Cost Estimating

You can't separate resources from their cost. Resources and cost are so interrelated that any decision about one usually affects the other. As you'll see here (and in Chapter 15), Microsoft Project makes it possible for you to work on both simultaneously. You can

- Determine whether the resource cost accrues up front, throughout the work, or at the end
- Set hourly and overtime rates
- Indicate flat per-visit charges
- Establish that a resource is working on a contractual fixed cost

Determining and managing the right quality, quantity, and availability of resources separates project managers from wanna-be's. But this isn't as scary as it might seem. A project manager isn't necessarily a walking encyclopedia of technical and managerial knowledge. More often, an effective project manager makes expert judgment by knowing how to get and use good information. Here are some tips.

Tie resources to tasks

Ensuring a successful marriage of resources to the project is much easier if you specifically assign resources to individual tasks or groups of tasks. As you'll soon see, Microsoft Project recognizes only resources that are tied to tasks.

Find out how the same thing was accomplished before

A man visiting Ernest Hemingway for the first time, so the story goes, was shocked by what he found. Everywhere, in every room, in every available space, he saw stacks and stacks of books. When the visitor queried Hemingway why so many books, the novelist simply said that a writer has to read. The significance of this story to you, the project manager, is that the easiest and safest step to success is to find out how similar projects have been accomplished by experts (who happen to be people just like you).

Remember your goal

A new project manager may be tempted to spend hours developing a dynamite set of goals and objectives and then file them somewhere as though they were unrelated to the reality of the moment. Nothing could be farther from the truth. As you assign resources, they should directly relate to your goals, objectives, and project scope. If they don't, be warned! The horse is getting out of the barn. Back up, take a deep breath, meet with your project team, and solve the discrepancy immediately.

Create a resource pool

You'll find out the details about the resource pool in a little bit, but consider this for now: A *resource pool* is the sum of people and equipment you have available for your project. Some resources are unlimited in their availability; others are specific as to when and to what degree they can be utilized. Some carry no direct cost to your project, some are a fixed cost, and others are available a la carte. Prepare the list accordingly.

Know your limitations

Knowing your limitations means that you should be well versed in company policy about rentals, consulting fees, and equipment purchases. Near misses count only in horseshoes and hand grenades. Be sure that you know what is and isn't expected.

A real-life blunder illustrates my point. A friend of mine once managed a multimillion-dollar video production project that involved stakeholders in Los Angeles, Indianapolis, and Washington, D.C. The project deadlines were killers, and approval for all production phases required signatures from all three stakeholders. Therefore, overnight delivery of materials was almost a daily occurrence. At the conclusion of the highly successful project, my friend received a negative performance appraisal because he had violated his company's policy regarding overnight deliveries.

Get help

Expert judgment is more often than not a team achievement. See whether other parts of your organization can give you expert counsel. Find out whether any professional or trade associations have light to shed. Search the Internet.

If you're not a regular cruiser on the Net, you can find out how to perform powerful searches in *The Internet For Dummies*, 4th Edition (written by John Levine, Carol Baroudi, and Margaret Levine Young and published by IDG Books Worldwide, Inc.).

Resource-Driven and Fixed-Duration Tasks

Microsoft Project assumes that you are working with resource-driven tasks unless you tell it otherwise. If you increase the amount of resources assigned to a *resource-driven* task, the task will be shorter in duration. For example, if it takes two people six hours to unload boxes of oranges from a truck, four people could do it in three hours. In contrast, a *fixed-duration* task is unaffected by resources. For example, the procedure of signing a mortgage takes an hour. If fifteen people were in the room, it would still take an hour.

You use the Task form to designate a task as fixed duration. From the Gantt Chart view, choose Window⇨Split. Select the appropriate task and then select the Fixed option on the Task form. Now the task duration will remain the same no matter what changes you make to the task's resources.

Hitching Resources to Tasks

Before you go through all the trouble of assigning resources to tasks, you might ask yourself if you really need to do so. Some projects don't need that kind of specificity. If you don't associate resources to tasks, Microsoft Project does its schedule calculations using the project's task duration and task relationship information.

In most cases, you'll find a real value in assigning resources to tasks. Microsoft Project is a trooper, keeping track of and automatically updating even the most complex resource and cost relationships. By assigning resources to tasks, you'll be able to

- ✔ Keep your hands on costs
- ✔ Determine when too many or too few resources are allocated to a task
- ✔ Find out when resources are scheduled to be in two places at one time
- ✔ Track the stages of completion of a task by various resources
- ✔ Understand and report with accuracy

The example in this chapter is based on an example project file (Smith Home Project) that you create in Chapter 4 and further develop in Chapters 5 and 6. You use this example throughout Part II. If you haven't already created the file, you might want to follow the instructions in Chapters 4, 5, and 6.

Using the Resource Assignment dialog box

In Microsoft Project, resources can be hitched to tasks in a number of ways. The simplest way is by using the Resource Assignment dialog box. This dialog box directly associates a resource list to a specific task.

The dialog box has two columns: Name and Units. *Name* is the title you assign to a resource. *Units* is a quantity of resource units dedicated to the selected task. Microsoft Project's default unit assignment is 1. This means that 1 unit (person or equipment) is assigned 100 percent of its time per day throughout a task's duration.

Let's use the Smith Home project to look at the Resource Assignment dialog box and to practice assigning resources:

1. **If it isn't already open, open Smith Home.MPP in the Practice Files folder.**

2. **Select task 3, Customer selections.**

3. **Click the Resource Assignment button on the Standard toolbar.**

4. **Type** Sales **in the Name box and press Enter.**

So far, you've created a resource but you haven't assigned it to the task. Before you do, determine the unit assignment of the resource. The Customer selections task has a duration of 1 week. Although the selection process might take a week, the resource allocation is quite different. Of the entire sales force of 10 full-time employees, you're assigning one person one-fourth of her or his time to this customer. The unit designation for this is 0.25. Type **0.25** in the Units box and press Enter (Figure 7-1).

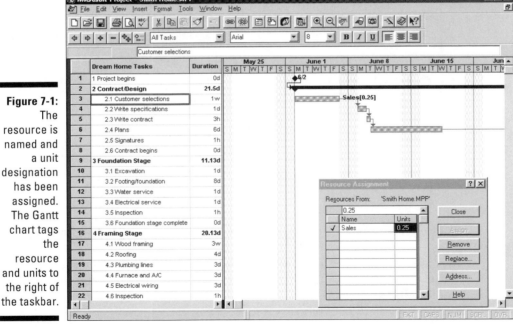

Figure 7-1: The resource is named and a unit designation has been assigned. The Gantt chart tags the resource and units to the right of the taskbar.

Three things have just happened:

- ✔ A check mark appears next to the resource name in the Resource Assignment dialog box. The check indicates the resource assignment.
- ✔ The resource name appears next to the taskbar on the Gantt chart.
- ✔ The unit allocation appears next to the resource name on the Gantt chart.

The first time you assign resources and their units to a task, Microsoft Project assumes that the resource assignment equals the duration you first estimated. After you assign a resource and unit designation, the task becomes a resource-driven task by default. Therefore, if you change the units, the task duration changes automatically. If this is not what you want, you can make the duration unchangeable (regardless of the resources or units) by converting the task to a fixed-duration task.

The resource pool

A fast and easy way to prepare your project for resource assignments is by creating a resource pool. A *resource pool* is a set of resources that has been assembled for assignment to project tasks.

To create a resource pool for the Smith Home project:

1. **Highlight the Customer selections task, if it isn't already selected.**
2. **Click the Resource Assignment button on the Standard toolbar.**
3. **In the Resource Assignment dialog box, type** Specifications.
4. **Select the next line, and type** Counsel.
5. **Repeat step 4 for the following:**

    Drafting

    Excavation Contractor

    Water Utility

    Electric Utility

    Building Inspector

    Framing Crew

    Plumbing Contractor

    Mechanical Contractor

    Electrical Contractor

Wallboard Crew

Paint Crew

Finish Carpenters

Project Manager

6. After you're finished, scroll back to the top of the list.

The Resource Assignment dialog box should look like Figure 7-2.

A smart way to enter resources is by title rather than by a person's name and by specialty rather than by a company name. This gives you some leeway for changes in personnel and contracts.

Creating a resource pool is a major step in resource allocation. This is a good time to resave the project file:

1. Click the Save button on the Standard toolbar.

2. Select the Save 'Smith Home.MPP' without a baseline option.

3. Click OK.

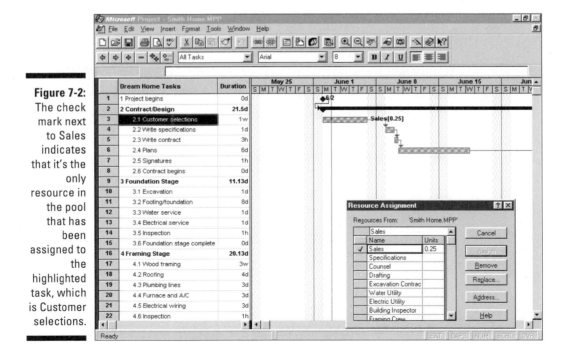

Figure 7-2:
The check
mark next
to Sales
indicates
that it's the
only
resource in
the pool
that has
been
assigned to
the
highlighted
task, which
is Customer
selections.

Resource details

Microsoft Project lets you get as detailed about your resources as your project requires. Some resources may be assigned staff whose salaries are not directly attributed to the project budget. Other resources may be hourly workers who directly affect the budget. And still other resources may be contractors who are working against a fixed amount. Whatever the case, the details are manageable.

If you have closed the Resource Assignment dialog box, open it again by highlighting a task and selecting the Resource Assignment button on the Standard toolbar. Double-click Framing Crew, and the Resource Information dialog box appears, as shown in Figure 7-3.

In the Resource Information dialog box, you can enter a number of details specific to this resource. These details are true of this resource no matter which task you assign it to:

- **Name:** All resources are identified by their name or their initials.

- **Initials:** A substitute for the Name field. This can save you some keystrokes when you're assigning resources.

- **Max Units:** The total number of units available for the project. The number can range from 0 to 100. Microsoft Project uses this number when calculating whether you have enough resources for a task or multiple simultaneous tasks.

- **Std Rate:** The cost for regular work. Microsoft Project's default multiplier in this box is hours. If you type 15, for example, it interprets that to mean $15/hour. Possible time units are minutes (m), hours (h), days (d), and weeks (w).

- **Ovt Rate:** The cost for overtime work. Use this if the resource expects an overtime rate for overtime work. Like Std Rate, enter an amount followed by a time unit abbreviation.

- **Per Use:** The cost per use fee. An example of this is the building inspector's fee of, say, $65 per visit.

- **Accrue at:** When the cost for the resource actually occurs. The three choices are Start (incur total actual cost as the tasks using this resource start), Prorated (incur actual costs as the tasks using this resource progress), and End (incur total actual cost as the tasks using this resource end). Microsoft Project defaults to an Accrue at Prorated cost unless you specify otherwise.

✓ **Base Cal:** The base calendar. Microsoft Project offers three flavors of base calendars: Standard, Night Shift, and 24 Hours. These three calendars are based on default settings. For instance, the Standard work calendar is Monday through Friday, from 8 a.m. to 5 p.m. with one hour for lunch and no holidays.

✓ **Group:** The name of a resource group. Any resource using this group name will be part of the group. (For instance, you might put water and electric service in a group called Utilities.) Then you can sort by the group name.

✓ **Code:** An alphanumeric code for the resource. This is a helpful tool for accounting.

Using the Resource Information dialog box, assign the following details to the Framing Crew resource:

Option	Value
Initials	FC
Max Units	16
Standard Rate	10
Overtime Rate	15
Group	Carpenters

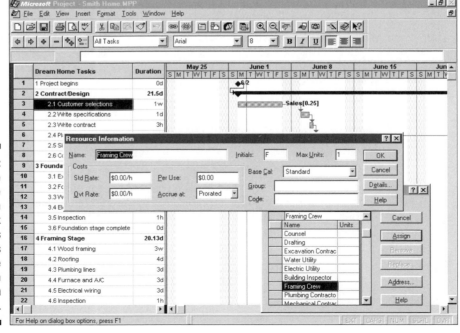

Figure 7-3:
Use the
Resource
Information
dialog box
to enter as
much or as
little
information
as you
choose.

The Resource Information dialog box should now look like Figure 7-4. Click OK. The Resource Information dialog box automatically interprets rates as a per hour amount unless you use m for minute, d for day, or w for week.

Dragging a resource

An easy way to assign resources from the resource pool is by dragging them. Using the home building project as an example:

1. **Scroll the Gantt chart to the top.**

2. **Select Specifications from the resource pool.**

3. **Move the mouse cursor to the left-most column of the Resource Assignment dialog box.**

   The cursor changes into a two-faced Resource Assignment button.

4. **Click and drag the cursor over the Write specifications task.**

5. **Release the mouse.**

The screen should now look like Figure 7-5. The Specifications resource is now checked. Note that a unit of 1 is associated with the resource for that task. In addition, the Gantt chart lists the resource name.

The drag feature automatically assigns a unit of 1 to the resource. This changes the task into a resource-driven task. After you've assigned the resource, change the task units to modify the task duration. So, if you're planning an initial unit assignment of something other than 1.0, don't use the drag feature. Instead, enter a unit value in the units column of the Resource Assignment dialog box and click the Assign button.

Assigning a resource to multiple tasks

Using the resource pool, you can assign a resource to several tasks at the same time. If the tasks are grouped sequentially, select the first task, hold down the Shift key, and select the last task in the sequence. Release the Shift key. All the tasks in the sequence should be highlighted.

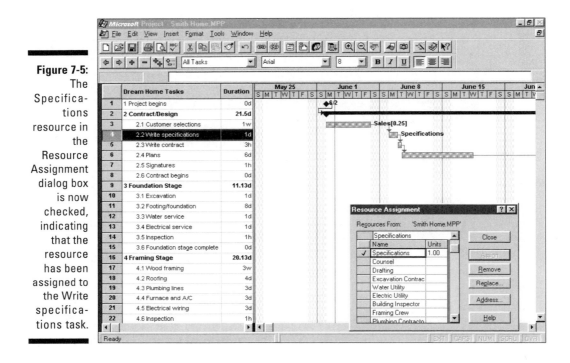

Figure 7-5:
The Specifications resource in the Resource Assignment dialog box is now checked, indicating that the resource has been assigned to the Write specifications task.

If the tasks are not grouped sequentially, select the first task, hold down the Ctrl key, and select the tasks you want. When you have selected the final task, release the Ctrl key. All the nonsequential tasks you selected should be highlighted.

After you select the tasks, select the resource from the resource pool. If you want, you can add a unit assignment. When you are satisfied with your selections, click the Assign key.

You can use the same method to assign multiple resources to a single task. You can also assign multiple resources to multiple tasks.

Using the home building example, you assign two resources to three tasks. It just so happens that the project manager and the building inspector must both perform the inspection task. To make this easy and visual, you make some preliminary changes to the Gantt Chart view and then assign the resources to the tasks:

1. **Scroll the Gantt chart until the first Inspection task, task 14, is the top-most visible task.**

2. **Select task 14.**

3. **Click the Goto Selected Task button on the Standard toolbar.**

4. **Click the Zoom Out button twice.**

   The timescale is now months and weeks.

5. **Drag the Resource Assignment dialog box to the upper-right corner of the screen.**

   This gives you a fuller view of the Gantt chart.

6. **Select the first Inspection task, task 14 (if it isn't still selected).**

7. **Hold down the Ctrl key.**

8. **Select the other two Inspection tasks, tasks 22 and 32.**

9. **Release the Ctrl key.**

10. **In the Resource Assignment dialog box, select Building Inspector.**

11. **Hold down the Ctrl key.**

12. **Scroll to the bottom of the resource pool.**

13. **Select Project Manager.**

14. **Release the Ctrl key.**

15. **Click the Assign button in the Resource Assignment dialog box.**

    The Gantt chart and the Resource Assignment box should look like Figure 7-6.

    Assigning multiple resources to a task doesn't affect the task's duration. But a change of units in a multiple resource assignment, just like in a single resource assignment, changes the task's duration unless the task is a fixed-duration task.

16. **Restore the Gantt chart to its normal timescale by clicking the Standard toolbar's Zoom In button twice.**

17. **Click the Close button in the Resource Assignment dialog box.**

Removing and adding resources

Changing resource assignments can be simple or tricky depending on when in the project you do it. Early on, changing resource assignments is a piece of hot fudge ice cream cake. Select the task in the Gantt table, click the Resource Assignment button on the Standard toolbar, select the resource in the resource pool, and click the Remove button.

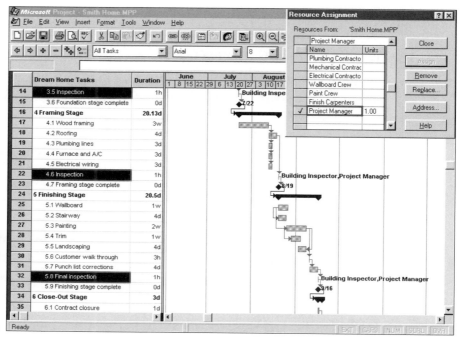

Figure 7-6:
Assigning
multiple
resources
to a task.

You need to change a few things in the home building example. First, an important person is missing from the resource pool, namely the project foreman. Second, the project foreman rather than the project manager should perform the inspection tasks with the building inspector. To make these changes:

1. **Select the three Inspection tasks (if they aren't still selected):**

   Select the first Inspection task, task 14. Hold down the Ctrl key and select the other two Inspection tasks, tasks 22 and 32. Then release the Ctrl key.

 2. **Click the Resource Assignment button on the Standard toolbar.**

3. **In the first empty Name box, type** Project Foreman.

4. **Select Project Manager.**

5. **Click the Replace button.**

   The Replace With dialog box appears.

6. **Select Project Foreman.**

7. **Click OK.**

8. **Close the Resource Assignment dialog box.**

The three inspection tasks change to show the removal of the project manager and the addition of the project foreman to each task.

Deleting a resource

Deleting a resource from the resource pool requires that you work in the Resource Sheet view. This view is especially helpful in summarizing details about all resources. You can also use it to make changes to resources.

To change to the Resource Sheet view, choose View⇨Resource Sheet. The screen now looks like Figure 7-7.

In the home building example, the Plumbing task and the Furnace task will now be performed by a single contractor. Therefore, you must delete a resource and modify a resource name:

1. **Select Resource 10, Plumbing Contractor.**

2. **Press the Delete key.**

   The Plumbing Contractor resource is deleted.

3. **Select the new Resource 10, Mechanical Contractor.**

4. **In the Resource Name box, type** Mech./Plumb. Contractor.

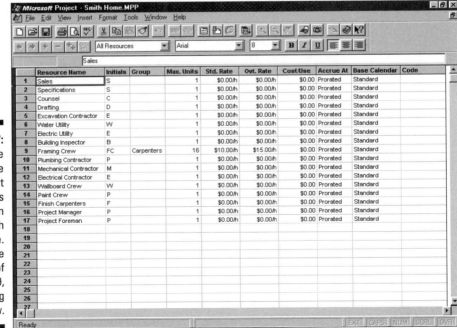

Figure 7-7: The resource sheet displays information about each resource. Notice the details of resource 9, Framing Crew.

A new combined resource replaces two previously distinct resources. After you've had a chance to look over the resource sheet, change back to the Gantt Chart view by choosing View⇨Gantt Chart.

You did some heavy-duty project plan development. You made major resource assignments, added some resource details, and did some editing. This is a good time to save the project file:

1. **Click the Save button on the Standard toolbar.**
2. **Select the Save 'Smith Home.MPP' without a baseline option.**
3. **Click OK.**

More Than One Calendar

It's not unusual for various resources to have different expectations about working hours and working days. Microsoft Project is an excellent tool for managing time with more than one clock.

Microsoft Project works with two kinds of calendars — project calendars and resource calendars. A *project calendar* is also called a standard calendar. It's the default calendar that applies to all tasks and resources. This calendar measures duration by assigning Monday through Friday as working days and by assigning 8 a.m. to 5 p.m. as working hours, with one hour off for lunch at noon. By default, the project calendar does not include any holidays. What a grump!

You can change any part of a project calendar or all of it. You can make it so that any day of the week with a *y* in the name is a day off. Or you can schedule a siesta from noon to 3 p.m. It's up to you and your understanding, totally cool boss.

A *resource calendar* can march to the beat of a different drummer. You can customize the resource calendar to match the availability and work times of a specific resource. For instance, using the home building example, you can create a resource calendar for painters and wallboarders so that the two groups work at separate times. Why? Painters hate dust. And you can assign a special holiday just for the wallboard crew so that they can observe the invention of the screw gun.

It's time to make some changes to the home building example. You need to include some holidays that everyone knows and loves. In addition, you need to accommodate some groups who want to work different hours. Finally, you need to make some specific changes to a particular resource calendar. In the next sections, you

- ✔ Modify the project calendar
- ✔ Create a second base calendar
- ✔ Create a resource calendar

Modifying the project calendar

First, you add some holidays to the project calendar. The house is being built in the United States, so add July 4 and September 1 as holidays:

1. Choose Tools➪Change Working Time.

The Change Working Time dialog box appears (Figure 7-8).

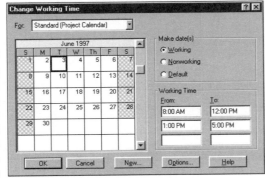

Figure 7-8: Shaded days represent default nonworking days.

2. Manipulate the scroll bar until you come to July 1997.

3. Select July 4.

4. Under Make date(s), select the Nonworking option.

5. Repeat this process for Labor Day, September 1.

6. Click OK.

7. Select task 10, the Excavation task, to see the effect of your change.

 8. Click the Goto Selected Task button on the Standard toolbar.

The Gantt chart indicates that Friday, July 4, is a nonworking day. The day is gray on the chart (Figure 7-9). So the changes to the project calendar could have adjusted all tasks after July 4 to be one day later. That didn't happen here because task 10 is already scheduled to begin on Monday, July 7.

Gray is a rotten color for a nonworking day! In Chapter 9, you can customize the look of your Gantt chart. May all your nonworking days be sunny and sky blue!

Save the project file again:

1. **Click the Save button on the Standard toolbar.**

2. **Select the Save 'Smith Home.MPP' without a baseline option**.

3. **Click OK.**

Creating a new calendar

Having another calendar to compliment the project calendar is often necessary. Stop! Don't throw this book at the computer. Multiple calendars are simple to understand and use in Microsoft Project. Sometimes you have groups of resources with things in common. For instance, in the home building example, all the construction folks want to arrive at the job at 7 a.m., have half an hour for lunch, and leave in mid-afternoon. In contrast, the office folk want to arrive at work at 8 a.m., have an hour for lunch starting at noon, and leave at 5 p.m. — the standard calendar working hours.

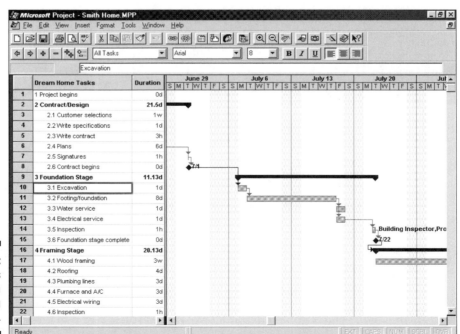

Figure 7-9:
July 4 is now a nonworking day.

To resolve this, you need to create a second calendar, called a base calendar. You create it by first duplicating the project calendar. This way, any changes to the project calendar, such as holidays, will be carried over to the new calendar. Simple, right? An example should remove any mud or muddle:

1. **Choose Tools⇨Change Working Time.**

   The Change Working Time dialog box appears.

2. **Click the New button.**

   The Create New Base Calendar dialog box appears.

3. **In the Name box, type** Construction Hours Calendar**.**

4. **Make sure that the second option (Make copy of) is selected, and that it reads Make copy of Standard calendar, as shown in Figure 7-10.**

   Anything you did to the standard calendar is carried over to the Construction Hours calendar. In this case, the July 4 and September 1 holidays are included.

5. **Click OK.**

The creation of a new calendar doesn't replace the standard calendar. All resources base their working hours and days on the standard calendar, until selected otherwise.

Figure 7-10:
The Create
New Base
Calendar
dialog box.

Now change the working hours for the Construction Hours calendar:

1. **Select the columns for working days by clicking on M (Monday) and dragging horizontally to F (Friday).**

2. **In the Working Time area, type** 7:00 AM **in the From box and** 11:00 AM **in the To box.**

3. **On the next line in the Working Time area, type** 11:30 AM **in the From box and** 3:30 PM **in the To box.**

   Your screen should look like Figure 7-11.

4. **Click OK.**

Figure 7-11:
Use the
Change
Working
Time dialog
box to
create a
custom
work
schedule
that
includes
changes
made in the
standard
calendar.

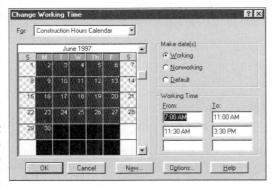

The last step is to apply this calendar to all appropriate resources. An easy way to do this is in the Resource Sheet view:

1. **Choose View➪Resource Sheet.**

2. **In the Base Calendar column, select the cell for resource 5, Excavation Contractor.**

   A down arrow appears next to the entry box.

3. **Click the down arrow.**

   Four choices appear, as shown in Figure 7-12.

4. **Select Construction Hours Calendar.**

   Construction Hours Calendar replaces *Standard* in the Base Calendar cell for resource 5, Excavation Contractor.

5. **Double-click the column title cell, Base Calendar, and then choose Best Fit.**

   The default column size was too small to fit the full name of the calendar. Best Fit corrects that.

6. **Follow steps 2 through 4 for resources 6, 7, 9 to 14, and 16.**

   The results should look like Figure 7-13.

After you review your changes, return to the Gantt Chart view.

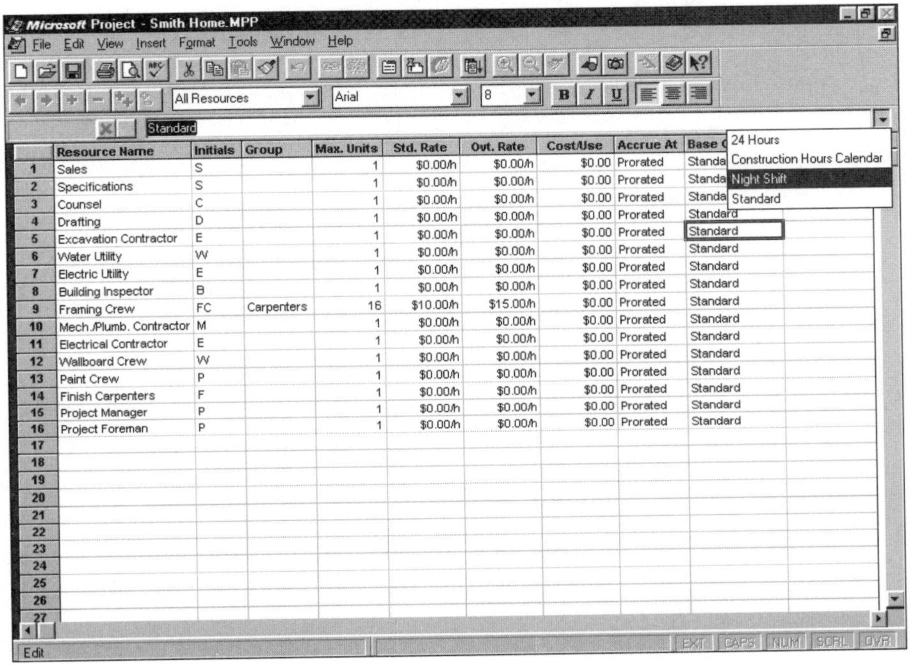

	Resource Name	Initials	Group	Max. Units	Std. Rate	Ovt. Rate	Cost/Use	Accrue At	Base C
1	Sales	S		1	$0.00/h	$0.00/h	$0.00	Prorated	Standa
2	Specifications	S		1	$0.00/h	$0.00/h	$0.00	Prorated	Standa
3	Counsel	C		1	$0.00/h	$0.00/h	$0.00	Prorated	Standa
4	Drafting	D		1	$0.00/h	$0.00/h	$0.00	Prorated	Standard
5	Excavation Contractor	E		1	$0.00/h	$0.00/h	$0.00	Prorated	Standard
6	Water Utility	W		1	$0.00/h	$0.00/h	$0.00	Prorated	Standard
7	Electric Utility	E		1	$0.00/h	$0.00/h	$0.00	Prorated	Standard
8	Building Inspector	B		1	$0.00/h	$0.00/h	$0.00	Prorated	Standard
9	Framing Crew	FC	Carpenters	16	$10.00/h	$15.00/h	$0.00	Prorated	Standard
10	Mech./Plumb. Contractor	M		1	$0.00/h	$0.00/h	$0.00	Prorated	Standard
11	Electrical Contractor	E		1	$0.00/h	$0.00/h	$0.00	Prorated	Standard
12	Wallboard Crew	W		1	$0.00/h	$0.00/h	$0.00	Prorated	Standard
13	Paint Crew	P		1	$0.00/h	$0.00/h	$0.00	Prorated	Standard
14	Finish Carpenters	F		1	$0.00/h	$0.00/h	$0.00	Prorated	Standard
15	Project Manager	P		1	$0.00/h	$0.00/h	$0.00	Prorated	Standard
16	Project Foreman	P		1	$0.00/h	$0.00/h	$0.00	Prorated	Standard

Figure 7-12: The entry box lists the base calendars for the project. Three calendars are defaults. Construction Hours Calendar is the one you created.

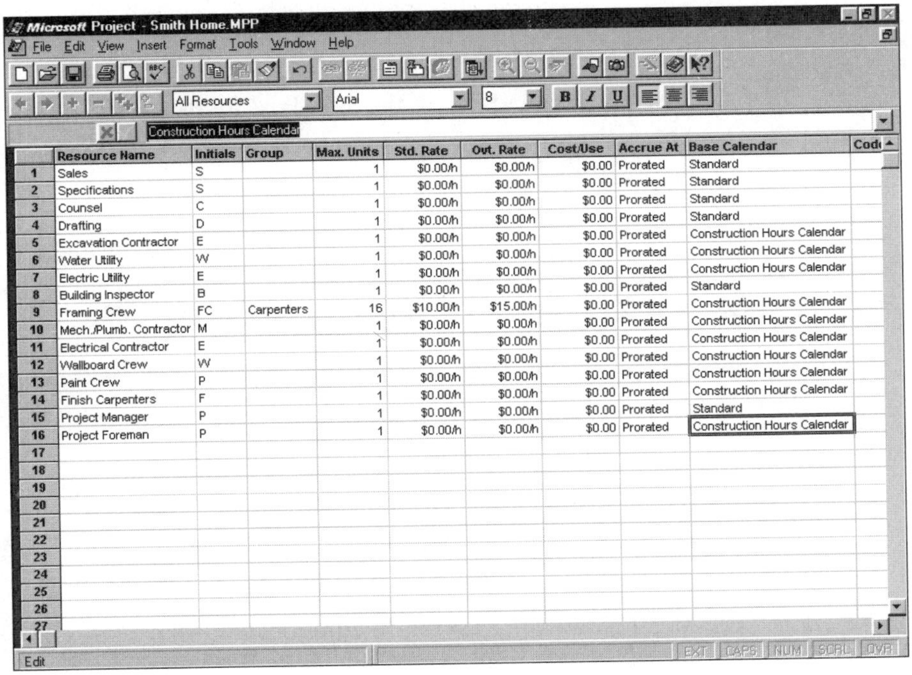

	Resource Name	Initials	Group	Max. Units	Std. Rate	Ovt. Rate	Cost/Use	Accrue At	Base Calendar	Cod
1	Sales	S		1	$0.00/h	$0.00/h	$0.00	Prorated	Standard	
2	Specifications	S		1	$0.00/h	$0.00/h	$0.00	Prorated	Standard	
3	Counsel	C		1	$0.00/h	$0.00/h	$0.00	Prorated	Standard	
4	Drafting	D		1	$0.00/h	$0.00/h	$0.00	Prorated	Standard	
5	Excavation Contractor	E		1	$0.00/h	$0.00/h	$0.00	Prorated	Construction Hours Calendar	
6	Water Utility	W		1	$0.00/h	$0.00/h	$0.00	Prorated	Construction Hours Calendar	
7	Electric Utility	E		1	$0.00/h	$0.00/h	$0.00	Prorated	Construction Hours Calendar	
8	Building Inspector	B		1	$0.00/h	$0.00/h	$0.00	Prorated	Standard	
9	Framing Crew	FC	Carpenters	16	$10.00/h	$15.00/h	$0.00	Prorated	Construction Hours Calendar	
10	Mech./Plumb. Contractor	M		1	$0.00/h	$0.00/h	$0.00	Prorated	Construction Hours Calendar	
11	Electrical Contractor	E		1	$0.00/h	$0.00/h	$0.00	Prorated	Construction Hours Calendar	
12	Wallboard Crew	W		1	$0.00/h	$0.00/h	$0.00	Prorated	Construction Hours Calendar	
13	Paint Crew	P		1	$0.00/h	$0.00/h	$0.00	Prorated	Construction Hours Calendar	
14	Finish Carpenters	F		1	$0.00/h	$0.00/h	$0.00	Prorated	Construction Hours Calendar	
15	Project Manager	P		1	$0.00/h	$0.00/h	$0.00	Prorated	Standard	
16	Project Foreman	P		1	$0.00/h	$0.00/h	$0.00	Prorated	Construction Hours Calendar	

Figure 7-13: The Resource Sheet shows the changes made. Microsoft Project automatically records these changes to any view that displays work times.

Creating a resource calendar

Now that you've modified the standard calendar and created an additional base calendar, creating a resource calendar will be easy. National Screw Gun Awareness Week, here we come! Using the home building example:

1. **Choose Tools⇨Change Working Time.**

2. **In the For box, select the Wallboard Crew resource.**

   Notice that the working days for a resource calendar are a light shade of gray.

3. **Scroll to July 1997.**

   The week beginning July 6 is the beginning of the wallboard workers' national holiday.

4. **Drag across the whole week to highlight it.**

5. **Under Make date(s), select the Nonworking option.**

   The wallboarders are now free to attend the National Screw Gun Olympics. Fortunately, your schedule didn't need them that week anyway.

6. **Click OK.**

   You've just modified a resource calendar!

Save the project file:

1. **Click the Save button on the Standard toolbar.**

2. **Select the Save 'Smith Home.MPP' without a baseline option.**

3. **Click OK.**

Another Way to Assign Resources

Another easy and effective way to assign resources to tasks is by using the Task form. To do so:

1. **Choose Window⇨Split.**

   The Task form appears in the lower half of the screen.

2. **Click Previous or Next until you come to task 5, Write contract.**

3. **Select the space below the Resource Name column title.**

   A highlighted box appears. In addition, a down arrow appears to the right of the entry bar (at the top of the screen).

4. Click the down arrow to the right of the entry bar.

A list of the resources in the resource pool appears, as shown in Figure 7-14.

5. Click Counsel.

The resource now appears below Resource Name.

You can enter as many resources as you want in the Resource Name column. They all become assigned to that particular task. When you're back in the single view, you can still see the resource assignments by highlighting the task and clicking the Goto Selected Task button on the Standard toolbar.

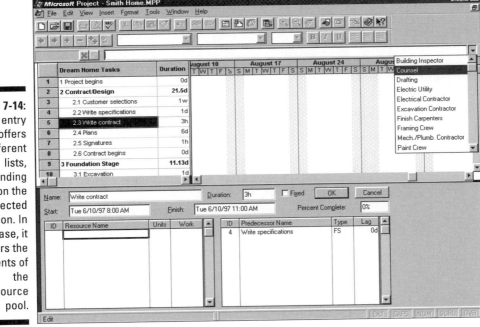

Figure 7-14:
The entry bar offers different lists, depending on the selected option. In this case, it offers the contents of the resource pool.

Part III
Viewing Your Project

The 5th Wave   By Rich Tennant

"I TOLD HIM WE WERE LOOKING FOR SOFTWARE THAT WOULD GIVE US GREATER PRODUCTIVITY, SO HE SOLD ME A DATABASE THAT CAME WITH THESE SIGNS."

In this part . . .

How many project managers does it take to change a lightbulb? Sorry, that's operations. Okay. How many lightbulbs does it take to change a project manager? Now, that's a good question. A project manager often needs all kinds of light shed on a subject before there's enough clarity to make a change. In project management, you add light to a subject by changing views.

In this part, you learn how to view charts, tables, and graphs. You use and customize the Gantt Chart view, the PERT Chart view, the Calendar view, and Resource view. You find out about filters. And you work with multiple projects.

Chapter 8
Kinds of Views

In This Chapter

▶ Making sense of views

▶ Getting around in views

▶ Using views

*I*n the predawn foggy stages of a project, the project manager, like a pilot, wants ready access to a map and an intelligent navigator. Microsoft Project has a powerful way to keep you on the right path — through views.

Views are to project management what flying by instrument is to a pilot. One perspective can't give you all the information you need. One reading might indicate that you're right on schedule with a full retinue of resources. But another reading might show that the resources are headed into a maze of conflicting tasks.

A *view* is the way you display project information. Microsoft Project has two major classifications of views — task views and resource views. This chapter is about task views. To find out about resource views, check out Chapter 9.

Triangulation and Project Management

One of the biggest breakthroughs in modern mapmaking was the adoption of the triangulation technique. *Triangulation* is based on the idea that you can pinpoint an object's location to a fraction of an inch by observing it from three vantage points. Although the concept of triangulation is simple and has been around for hundreds of years, it needed a technology to make it possible. Through the use of orbiting satellites, triangulation has greatly reduced the margin of error in determining the precise location of points on the earth's surface.

This concept of triangulation is a helpful way to relate project management and its dependence on technology. You want to know how a project is progressing and you use your computer to do the job. The technology of Microsoft Project and its multiple vantage points (views) allow you to more precisely analyze the moving target of an ongoing project.

The three major categories of views are charts, tables, and forms. The next section contains helpful descriptions and illustrations of these views.

Loading the Sample Files

If you haven't already extracted and copied the files from the accompanying disk, you might want to do so before proceeding with this chapter. The sample files have various conditions built into them that will assist you in your understanding of Microsoft Project. To do this:

1. **Insert the book's disk into your floppy disk drive.**

2. **Click the Start button, and then choose Run.**

3. **Type** A:\PROJECTS.EXE **(substitute your floppy disk drive letter if it's different than A).**

   The self-extractor window appears. The files will be copied to C:\MSOffice\Winproj\Practice Files by default. If you want to copy the files to a different location, type the new folder path in the Unzip To Folder box.

4. **In the self-extractor window, click the Unzip button.**

You're ready to go.

Open the sample project file called Smith Home 8.MPP from the Practice Files folder. To do so, start Microsoft Project (if necessary) and then

1. **Click the Open button on the Standard toolbar.**

2. **Open the Practice Files folder.**

3. **Double-click Smith Home 8.MPP.**

   The file opens.

A Friendly Guide to Charts, Tables, and Forms

Microsoft Project bases its views on two kinds of information: task views and resource views. A *task view* presents information about tasks. Among the task views are Gantt Chart, PERT Chart, Calendar, and various task tables and task forms.

A *resource view* presents information about resources. Among resource views are Resource Graph, Resource Sheet, Resource Usage, and resource forms. This chapter deals with task views.

Task views

The Gantt Chart view is a task view and also the default view of Microsoft Project. The default Gantt chart is actually a table and a bar chart. The bar chart shows tasks and their durations.

In this Smith Home 8 example, a baseline has been added to the Gantt chart. Chapter 17 describes the reason and procedure for adding a baseline. For the present discussion, think of a *baseline* as a snapshot (a point of reference) of how the project manager predicts the project will occur. After you set the baseline, any updating of information reflects actual events compared against the baseline.

For details on using and customizing the Gantt chart, see Chapter 9.

Using the Smith Home example, check out the Task view. To do so:

1. **Select task 18, Roofing.**

2. **Click the Goto Selected Task button on the Standard toolbar**.

The Gantt chart has black bars inside the blue bars. The blue bars indicate the time you allotted for each task; the black bars indicate the actual progress of the task. Looking at Figure 8-1, you can see that

- The Wood framing is completed.
- The Roofing task is partially completed.
- The Plumbing lines task hasn't started.
- The Furnace and A/C task has only begun.
- The Electrical wiring task is almost finished.

Task tables

Microsoft Project provides task tables and resource tables. Task tables can be seen in either the Gantt Chart view or in the Task Sheet view (the table minus the Gantt chart). Among these task tables are Entry, Cost, Schedule, and Summary.

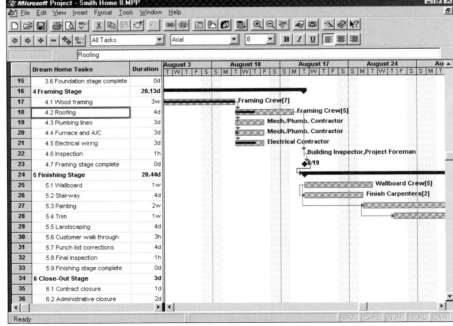

Figure 8-1:
The task duration is the lighter (blue) bar. Progress is reported with the darker (black) bar.

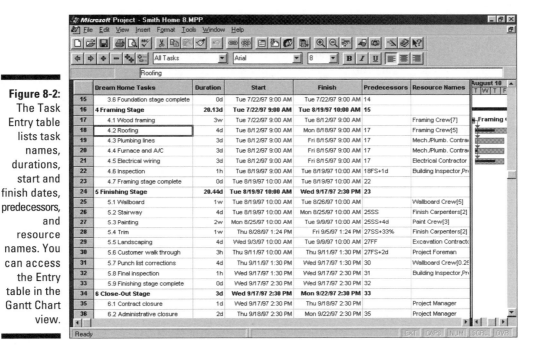

Figure 8-2:
The Task
Entry table
lists task
names,
durations,
start and
finish dates,
predecessors,
and
resource
names. You
can access
the Entry
table in the
Gantt Chart
view.

Entry table

The Gantt chart's default task table is the Task Entry table. To see it in all its glory, place your mouse over the vertical bar separating the table and the bar chart. The mouse cursor changes to two vertical bars and two arrows. Click and drag the vertical bar to the right until the entire table is visible (Figure 8-2).

If a table column has hatch marks instead of information, move the cursor to where the column titles join and then double-click when the cursor turns into a two-faced arrow.

The Task Entry table reflects the information that appears in bar chart form in the Gantt chart.

To change a default view, choose Tools⊅Options. Click the View tab. In the Default View list box, select a new default view. Click OK. The next time Microsoft Project starts, it will open to the new default view.

Cost table

Another task table available in the Gantt Chart view is the Task Cost table. To access it, choose View⇨Table Entry. The Task Table list appears (Figure 8-3).

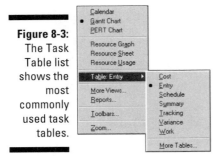

Figure 8-3:
The Task Table list shows the most commonly used task tables.

Select Cost. The Task Cost table, shown in Figure 8-4, provides information on the cost of the project's tasks.

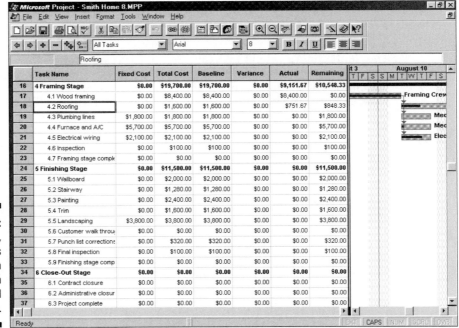

Figure 8-4:
Fixed costs, such as task 21, can be based on contractual agreement.

Notice task 18, the Roofing task. Based on the predicted duration and the per-hour fee for each unit of the Framing Crew resource, the predicted total labor cost of the Roofing task is $1,600. The actual cost so far is $751.67, and $848.33 remains.

Schedule table

The Schedule table shows task information about scheduled start and finish dates. It also shows the latest dates that tasks can start and finish without messing up the schedule. The difference between the planned start and finish and the latest start and finish is shown in the slack column. (See Figure 8-5.) *Free slack* is how much slack Microsoft Project allows a task before it conflicts with the successor task. *Total slack* is how much slack the task has until it delays the completion of the project.

Summary table

The Summary table summarizes how the project is doing task by task. In Figure 8-6, notice how Microsoft Project summarizes that the Framing Stage category is 71 percent complete, while its subtasks show stages of completion ranging from 0 percent to 100 percent complete.

	Task Name	Start	Finish	Late Start	Late Finish	Free Slack	Total Slack
16	**4 Framing Stage**	**Tue 7/22/97 9:00 AM**	**Tue 8/19/97 10:00 AM**	**Tue 7/22/97 9:00 AM**	**Tue 8/19/97 10:00 AM**	**0d**	**0d**
17	4.1 Wood framir	Tue 7/22/97 9:00 AM	Tue 8/12/97 9:00 AM	Tue 7/22/97 9:00 AM	Tue 8/12/97 9:00 AM	0d	0d
18	4.2 Roofing	Tue 8/12/97 9:00 AM	Mon 8/18/97 9:00 AM	Tue 8/12/97 9:00 AM	Mon 8/18/97 9:00 AM	0d	0d
19	4.3 Plumbing line	Tue 8/12/97 8:00 AM	Fri 8/15/97 5:00 PM	Wed 8/13/97 8:00 AM	Fri 8/15/97 5:00 PM	0.88d	0.88d
20	4.4 Furnace anc	Tue 8/12/97 9:00 AM	Fri 8/15/97 9:00 AM	Tue 8/12/97 9:00 AM	Fri 8/15/97 5:00 PM	0.88d	0.88d
21	4.5 Electrical wii	Tue 8/12/97 9:00 AM	Fri 8/15/97 9:00 AM	Tue 8/12/97 9:00 AM	Fri 8/15/97 5:00 PM	0.88d	0.88d
22	4.6 Inspection	Tue 8/19/97 9:00 AM	Tue 8/19/97 10:00 AM	Tue 8/19/97 9:00 AM	Tue 8/19/97 10:00 AM	0d	0d
23	4.7 Framing stag	Tue 8/19/97 10:00 AM	Tue 8/19/97 10:00 AM	Tue 8/19/97 10:00 AM	Tue 8/19/97 10:00 AM	0d	0d
24	**5 Finishing Stage**	**Tue 8/19/97 10:00 AM**	**Wed 9/17/97 2:30 PM**	**Tue 8/19/97 10:00 AM**	**Mon 9/22/97 2:30 PM**	**0d**	**0d**
25	5.1 Wallboard	Tue 8/19/97 10:00 AM	Tue 8/26/97 10:00 AM	Tue 8/19/97 10:00 AM	Mon 9/22/97 2:30 PM	0d	0d
26	5.2 Stairway	Tue 8/19/97 10:00 AM	Mon 8/25/97 10:00 AM	Tue 9/16/97 2:30 PM	Mon 9/22/97 2:30 PM	19.44d	19.44d
27	5.3 Painting	Mon 8/25/97 10:00 AM	Tue 9/9/97 10:00 AM	Mon 8/25/97 10:00 AM	Tue 9/9/97 10:00 AM	0d	0d
28	5.4 Trim	Wed 9/3/97 7:00 AM	Tue 9/9/97 5:00 PM	Mon 9/15/97 2:30 PM	Mon 9/22/97 2:30 PM	8.69d	8.69d
29	5.5 Landscapinc	Wed 9/3/97 10:00 AM	Tue 9/9/97 10:00 AM	Tue 9/16/97 2:30 PM	Mon 9/22/97 2:30 PM	9.44d	9.44d
30	5.6 Customer w	Thu 9/11/97 10:00 AM	Thu 9/11/97 1:30 PM	Thu 9/11/97 10:00 AM	Thu 9/11/97 1:30 PM	0d	0d
31	5.7 Punch list cc	Thu 9/11/97 1:30 PM	Wed 9/17/97 1:30 PM	Thu 9/11/97 1:30 PM	Wed 9/17/97 1:30 PM	0d	0d
32	5.8 Final inspect	Wed 9/17/97 1:30 PM	Wed 9/17/97 2:30 PM	Wed 9/17/97 1:30 PM	Wed 9/17/97 2:30 PM	0d	0d
33	5.9 Finishing sta	Wed 9/17/97 2:30 PM	Wed 9/17/97 2:30 PM	Wed 9/17/97 2:30 PM	Wed 9/17/97 2:30 PM	0d	0d
34	**6 Close-Out Stage**	**Wed 9/17/97 2:30 PM**	**Mon 9/22/97 2:30 PM**	**Wed 9/17/97 2:30 PM**	**Mon 9/22/97 2:30 PM**	**0d**	**0d**
35	6.1 Contract clo:	Wed 9/17/97 2:30 PM	Thu 9/18/97 2:30 PM	Wed 9/17/97 2:30 PM	Thu 9/18/97 2:30 PM	0d	0d
36	6.2 Administratix	Thu 9/18/97 2:30 PM	Mon 9/22/97 2:30 PM	Thu 9/18/97 2:30 PM	Mon 9/22/97 2:30 PM	0d	0d
37	6.3 Project comp	Mon 9/22/97 2:30 PM	Mon 9/22/97 2:30 PM	Mon 9/22/97 2:30 PM	Mon 9/22/97 2:30 PM	0d	0d

Figure 8-5: The Schedule Table.

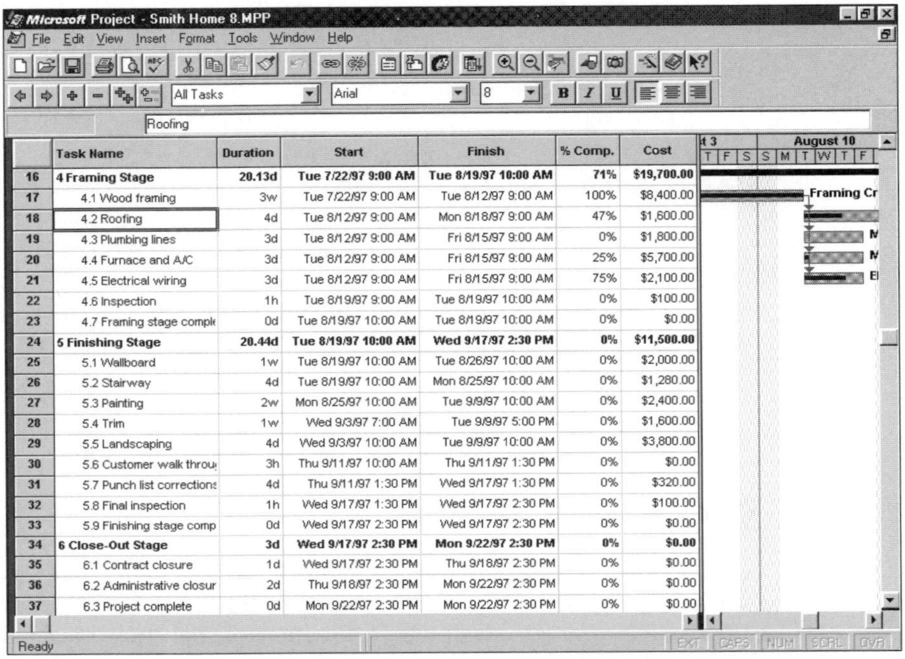

Figure 8-6:
The %
Comp.
column
displays the
sum of all
work to be
performed
by all
resources
for each
individual
category
and its
subtasks.

Using other task tables

Eight other task tables are available in the Gantt Chart view (see Table 8-1). If they aren't visible when you select View⇨Table, select View⇨Table⇨More Tables.

Table 8-1	Task Tables
Table	*What It Does*
Tracking table	Shows actual information about the progress of a project's tasks. You can keep your finger on the pulse of the schedule and the way money is being spent. Information includes the actual start and finish dates, the percentage of completion, the actual and remaining duration, the actual cost, and the actual amount of work that has been performed.
Variance table	Shows how the actual start and finish dates vary from the planned (baseline) start and finish dates in terms of task duration. The default measurement for this table is days.
Work table	Displays the variance between estimated work and actual work for individual tasks (similar to the Variance table). It also shows the percentage of completed work and remaining work. The default measurement for this table is hours.

Table	What It Does
Baseline table	Shows the baseline information for each task's duration, start and finish dates, hours of work, and cost.
Constraint Dates table	Shows the constraint type of each task. Unless you specify otherwise, Microsoft Project assigns a default As Soon As Possible constraint type to all tasks. The table also lists any specific constraint dates.
Delay table	Assists in leveling resources. Leveling, discussed in Chapter 16, is a way of stretching out task durations to lessen resource allocation at a given time.
Earned Value table	Compares work and cost amounts, including cost of budgeted work and scheduled work. Scheduled data is sometimes different than budgeted data because it can be based on updated information. The column abbreviations refer to the following: BCWS is Budgeted Cost of Work Scheduled; BCWP is Budgeted Cost of Work Performed; ACWP is Actual Cost of Work Performed; SV is Earned Value Schedule Variance; CV is Earned Value Cost Variance; BAC is Budgeted at Completion; FAC is Forecast at Completion. Excuse me for a few minutes, please. I have this irrational craving for alphabet soup.
Export	Transfers a Microsoft Project file to another application, such as a spreadsheet.

You can also create your own table in Microsoft Project. To find out more about this, see Chapter 13.

Using the Task Sheet

If you'd like to work on tasks without seeing the Gantt bar chart, select the Task Sheet view. The Task sheet presents information in a spreadsheet format. To change to the Task Sheet view:

1. **Choose View⇨More Views.**

   The More View list appears.

2. **Double-click Task Sheet.**

   The Entry table fills the Task sheet (Figure 8-7).

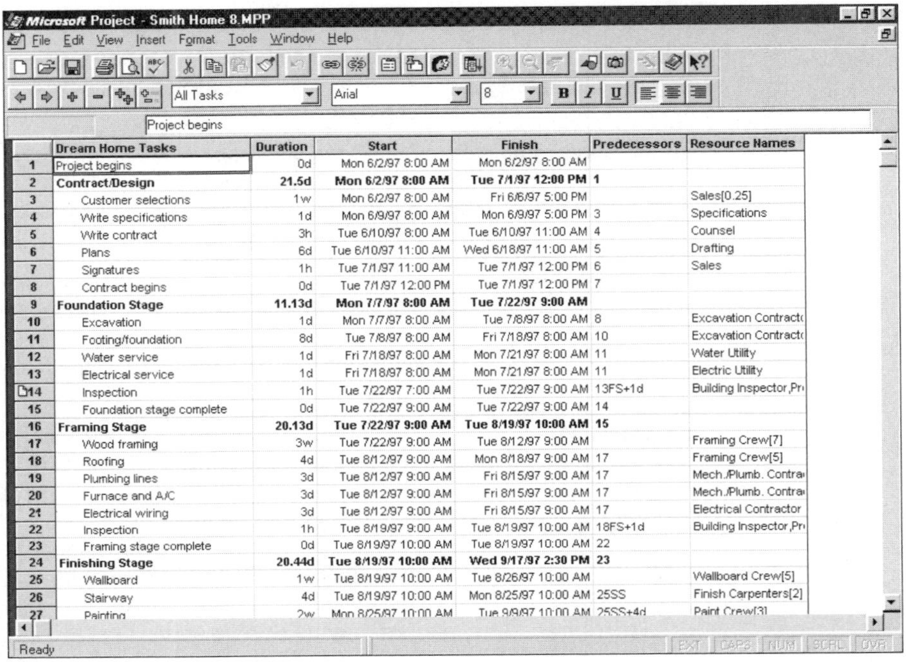

	Dream Home Tasks	Duration	Start	Finish	Predecessors	Resource Names
1	Project begins	0d	Mon 6/2/97 8:00 AM	Mon 6/2/97 8:00 AM		
2	**Contract/Design**	**21.5d**	**Mon 6/2/97 8:00 AM**	**Tue 7/1/97 12:00 PM**	**1**	
3	Customer selections	1w	Mon 6/2/97 8:00 AM	Fri 6/6/97 5:00 PM		Sales[0.25]
4	Write specifications	1d	Mon 6/9/97 8:00 AM	Mon 6/9/97 5:00 PM	3	Specifications
5	Write contract	3h	Tue 6/10/97 8:00 AM	Tue 6/10/97 11:00 AM	4	Counsel
6	Plans	6d	Tue 6/10/97 11:00 AM	Wed 6/18/97 11:00 AM	5	Drafting
7	Signatures	1h	Tue 7/1/97 11:00 AM	Tue 7/1/97 12:00 PM	6	Sales
8	Contract begins	0d	Tue 7/1/97 12:00 PM	Tue 7/1/97 12:00 PM	7	
9	**Foundation Stage**	**11.13d**	**Mon 7/7/97 8:00 AM**	**Tue 7/22/97 9:00 AM**		
10	Excavation	1d	Mon 7/7/97 8:00 AM	Tue 7/8/97 8:00 AM	8	Excavation Contract
11	Footing/foundation	8d	Tue 7/8/97 8:00 AM	Fri 7/18/97 8:00 AM	10	Excavation Contract
12	Water service	1d	Fri 7/18/97 8:00 AM	Mon 7/21/97 8:00 AM	11	Water Utility
13	Electrical service	1d	Fri 7/18/97 8:00 AM	Mon 7/21/97 8:00 AM	11	Electric Utility
14	Inspection	1h	Tue 7/22/97 7:00 AM	Tue 7/22/97 9:00 AM	13FS+1d	Building Inspector,Pr
15	Foundation stage complete	0d	Tue 7/22/97 9:00 AM	Tue 7/22/97 9:00 AM	14	
16	**Framing Stage**	**20.13d**	**Tue 7/22/97 9:00 AM**	**Tue 8/19/97 10:00 AM**	**15**	
17	Wood framing	3w	Tue 7/22/97 9:00 AM	Tue 8/12/97 9:00 AM		Framing Crew[7]
18	Roofing	4d	Tue 8/12/97 9:00 AM	Mon 8/18/97 9:00 AM	17	Framing Crew[5]
19	Plumbing lines	3d	Tue 8/12/97 9:00 AM	Fri 8/15/97 9:00 AM	17	Mech./Plumb. Contra
20	Furnace and A/C	3d	Tue 8/12/97 9:00 AM	Fri 8/15/97 9:00 AM	17	Mech./Plumb. Contra
21	Electrical wiring	3d	Tue 8/12/97 9:00 AM	Fri 8/15/97 9:00 AM	17	Electrical Contractor
22	Inspection	1h	Tue 8/19/97 9:00 AM	Tue 8/19/97 10:00 AM	18FS+1d	Building Inspector,Pr
23	Framing stage complete	0d	Tue 8/19/97 10:00 AM	Tue 8/19/97 10:00 AM	22	
24	**Finishing Stage**	**20.44d**	**Tue 8/19/97 10:00 AM**	**Wed 9/17/97 2:30 PM**	**23**	
25	Wallboard	1w	Tue 8/19/97 10:00 AM	Tue 8/26/97 10:00 AM		Wallboard Crew[5]
26	Stairway	4d	Tue 8/19/97 10:00 AM	Mon 8/25/97 10:00 AM	25SS	Finish Carpenters[2]
27	Painting	2w	Mon 8/25/97 10:00 AM	Tue 9/9/97 10:00 AM	25SS+4d	Paint Crew[3]

Figure 8-7: The same task tables that are available to the Gantt Chart view are available also to the Task Sheet view.

The Task sheet shows details about each task. It's your call whether you want to use this view or the Gantt Chart view. The methods for entering and editing information are identical in both views.

Calendar View

As mentioned, the Gantt chart is the default task view in Microsoft Project. Another task view is the Calendar view. The default Calendar view is a monthly calendar showing tasks in bar form, as shown in Figure 8-8. The length of the bar indicates the task's duration.

The Calendar view is a helpful communications tool when you need to print schedules. The Calendar view can also be used as a primary way to manage small projects. To access the Calendar view, choose View⇨Calendar.

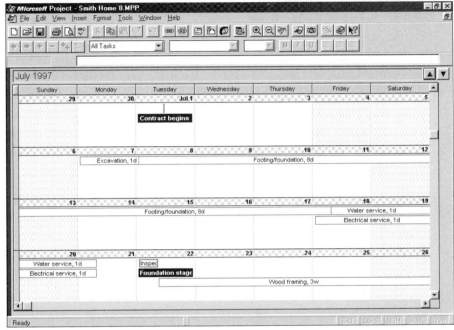

Figure 8-8:
Use the up and down arrows to change month views. The familiar method of presentation makes it easy for you to view and edit tasks and durations.

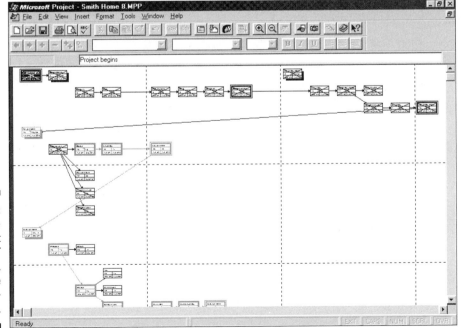

Figure 8-9:
To change the layout of the PERT Chart view, choose Format ⇨ Layout.

PERT Chart View

In addition to the Gantt Chart view and the Calendar view, Microsoft Project also provides the PERT Chart view. The PERT chart is a network diagram displaying all tasks and their relationships. To display the PERT Chart view, choose View⇨PERT Chart (Figure 8-9).

You can use this chart to create and edit your schedule, create and undo links, set durations, and assign resources to tasks. To uncover the details about PERT charts, read Chapter 10.

Chapter 9
The Gantt Chart

- -

In This Chapter

▶ Using the Gantt chart for fun and profit

▶ Fast ways to a good-looking chart

▶ Mousing around in the Gantt chart

▶ Making time fit the project

- -

*E*arly in the 19th century, Henry Gantt introduced a new way to show information in a bar chart and spreadsheet fashion. Voilà! The man was immortalized. Now, whenever project managers discuss their work, they indirectly pay homage to him. Just as Henry Gantt's creation was a winner, what you do with his chart in Microsoft Project may make you a winner, too.

In this chapter, you kick the tires and get behind the wheel of the Gantt chart. You find out the neat little options just waiting for you, and you modify the chart to emphasize and segregate various kinds of information. Ole Henry might have been the first to fiddle with this kind of chart, but you're going to make the Gantt chart sing.

If you haven't copied the files from the accompanying disk, you might want to do so before proceeding with this chapter. See Appendix C for instructions.

Start Microsoft Project, if necessary. Then, to open the sample project file called Award Program 9.MPP, do the following:

1. **Click the Open button on the Standard toolbar.**

2. **Open the Practice Files folder.**

3. **Double-click Award Program 9.MPP.**

Gantt Chart Text, Notes, and Graphics

Microsoft Project offers general text editing features and specialized formatting functions. Use these to polish your Gantt chart for on-screen readability, aesthetics, and reporting.

To practice, you'll correct a few errors in the example file. In addition, you'll improve the overall look and effectiveness of the information in several ways. The result will be a work of project management art.

Choosing words and speling corectly

One of the fastest ways you can make a negative impact on those you're most trying to impress is by misusing a word. Never use a word unless you're absolutely sure you know what it means. When you have a choice between a common word or an obscure word, use the common one. And make sure you spell the word correctly. Microsoft Project doesn't offer help in word selection, but it does provide a spell checker.

To use the spell checker, click the Spelling button on the Standard toolbar or press F7. The Spelling dialog box appears, as shown in Figure 9-1. The location of the word as a task or a resource is shown in the Found In box. Perform the corrections as needed.

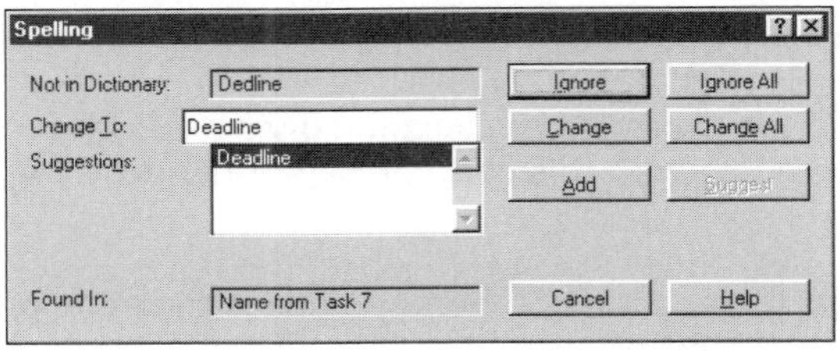

Figure 9-1:
The spell checker indicates the word that it determines was misspelled.

Just as in any word processing application, Microsoft Project's spell checker doesn't catch everything. Task 15 has the article *an* that should be the conjunction *and*. You'll have to correct that the old-fashioned way: Highlight the task and change the text in the entry bar.

Customizing text

What's black and white and read all over? The traditional answer is a newspaper. With Microsoft Project, it never has to be a Gantt chart. Colorful changes to text can result in easy-to-read, visually pleasing information. The Formatting toolbar is the ticket for making changes to fonts, font sizes, and colors.

Using the Award Program example, you'll change all category headings to 12-point Times New Roman. The headings are already boldface, and you'll leave them that way. To change the font style:

1. **In the Filter list box on the Formatting toolbar, select Summary Tasks (Figure 9-2).**

   The summary tasks are now the only tasks listed. (Chapter 13 discusses this filter and others in detail.)

2. **Highlight the summary tasks by clicking on task 1 and dragging the mouse through task 16.**

   The four tasks are highlighted.

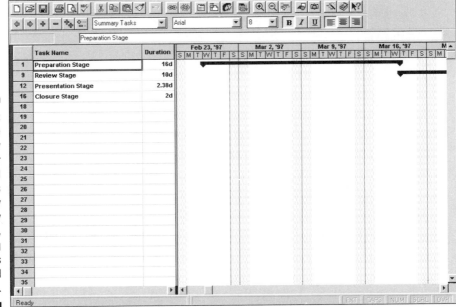

Figure 9-2:
The Summary Tasks filter isolates and displays only summary tasks, hiding subtasks and milestones.

3. **In the Font list box on the Formatting toolbar, select Times New Roman.**

The font of the four tasks changes to Times New Roman.

4. **In the Font Size list box on the Formatting toolbar, select 12.**

The font size of the four tasks changes to 12-point (Figure 9-3).

Filter list box ¬   Font list box   ⌐Font Size list box

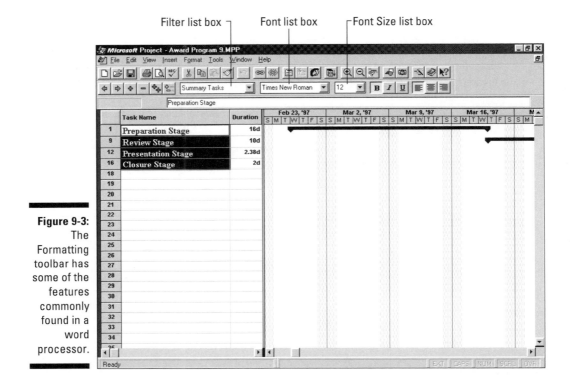

Figure 9-3:
The
Formatting
toolbar has
some of the
features
commonly
found in a
word
processor.

Not bad! But how about changing the Summary Task color, too? Not a problem, Ganttologist. To change the text color:

1. **Highlight all the summary tasks (if necessary) by clicking on task 1 and dragging the mouse through task 16.**

The four tasks are highlighted.

2. **Right-click in the highlighted area.**

3. **Select Font in the list box.**

The Font dialog box appears (Figure 9-4). The dialog box should already show that the selected tasks have changed from 8-point Arial to 12-point Times New Roman.

4. **Select Green in the Color list box, and then click OK.**

5. **In the Filter list box on the Formatting toolbar, select All Tasks.**

The task column now highlights the summary tasks in a new font, size, and color.

The number of available fonts may vary from one computer to the next. If you intend to share your project file, stick to commonly used fonts so that you can be sure how your project will look on another computer.

Figure 9-4:
You can change the font and its style, size, and color in the Font dialog box.

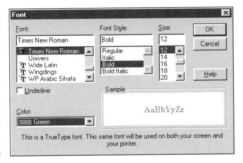

Adding notes

Sometimes you need to write yourself or others a note about a task, a resource, or the whole project. To write a note about a particular task in the Gantt Chart view, you use the Attach Note button on the Standard toolbar.

In the following, you use the Award Program example to attach a note to a task:

1. **Select any task.**

2. **Click the Attach Note button on the Standard toolbar.**

The Task Information dialog box appears, set to the Notes tab (Figure 9-5).

3. **In the Notes section, type your message.**

4. **Click OK.**

A note indicator appears next to the task number.

You can view the note at any time by selecting the task and then clicking the Attach Note button.

To delete a note, highlight the task and choose Edit⇨Clear. A Clear list box appears. Choose Notes to delete the task note.

Figure 9-5:
In the Task Information dialog box, you can enter task details, such as resources, pre-decessors, and start and finish dates.

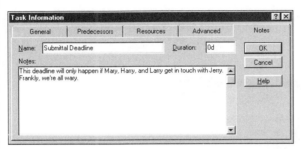

Adding graphics

You can draw on the Gantt chart with a limited set of drawing tools. To access the Drawing toolbar, right-click anywhere on the toolbar and choose Drawing from the list. Frankly, I think you'll be disappointed with what you can do, but go for it if you're interested. To remove the Drawing toolbar, right-click the toolbar and choose Drawing again. The toolbar disappears.

Adding graphics would be more effective. If you have a graphics program, you can use its clipboard to copy a graphics file. Then you simply use the Paste command in Microsoft Project to insert the graphic in the Gantt chart.

For example, you can put a graphic in the Award Program's Gantt chart. To do so, use the standard Paint program that comes with Windows 95. If you have a graphics program, feel free to use it instead.

To add the graphic into the Award Program's Gantt chart:

1. **On the Windows desktop, click Start and then Programs.**

2. **Choose Accessories⇨Paint.**

    The Paint application appears, as shown in Figure 9-6. Although it is a limited paint program, it is good for copying and pasting graphics.

Figure 9-6:
The Paint application recognizes only .BMP and .PCX extensions.

3. **Choose File⇨Open.**

4. **Change to the Practice Files folder.**

   The Practice Files folder should be in the MSOffice\Winproj directory.

5. **Double-click award.BMP.**

   An award graphic is now in the Paint application.

Now that you have this priceless work of art in the Paint application, you need to copy it to the clipboard for use in Microsoft Project. You can use the same procedure to insert a company logo, a relevant graph, or a photo that identifies the project.

To copy and paste the award graphic into the Microsoft Project file:

1. **Choose Edit⇨Select All on the Paint menu bar.**

2. **Choose Edit⇨Copy on the Paint menu bar.**

3. **Holding down the Alt key, press Tab to show the programs that are currently running.**

   If necessary, press Tab again until the Microsoft Project program icon is selected.

4. **Release the Alt key.**

   Microsoft Project should now be the active screen.

5. **Choose Edit⇨Paste Special.**

   The Paste Special dialog box appears.

6. **Double-click Bitmap Image in the selection box.**

   The Gantt chart should now look like Figure 9-7. If you want, you may close the Paint application.

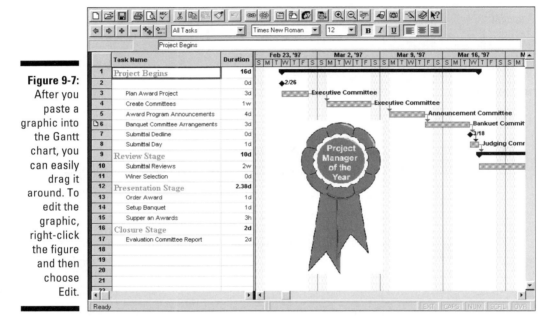

Figure 9-7:
After you paste a graphic into the Gantt chart, you can easily drag it around. To edit the graphic, right-click the figure and then choose Edit.

Customizing the Look of the Gantt Chart

You can change the way your Gantt chart looks without modifying the information you've entered. Doing so won't put you on the inside track for winning an art award, but it will make working with task information less of a task. You and your associates may be spending oodles of hours working on your project, so you may as well like the way it looks.

Changing gridlines

Gridlines are horizontal and vertical lines that appear in the Gantt Chart view and some other views. You can change the look and frequency of gridlines to aid in the reading of the Gantt chart. To do so:

1. **Right-click in one of the white areas of the Gantt chart (not the Gantt table).**

   A list box appears.

2. **Choose Gridlines.**

   The Gridlines dialog box appears.

3. **With Gantt Rows highlighted, click the down arrow of the Normal Type box. Select a line type.**

4. **In Normal Color, select any color you want for the Gantt row lines.**

   The gridlines appear with the selected color (Figure 9-8). Don't worry, if you don't like the color you can easily change it.

To clear the gridlines, choose Normal Type. Then select the blank box at the top of the list.

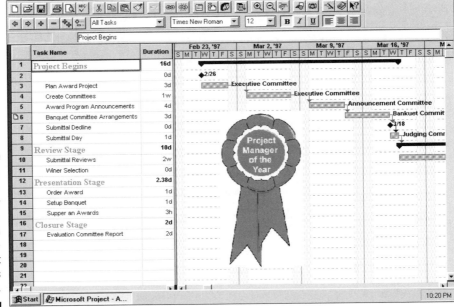

Figure 9-8: Here's one of the many ways you can customize the Gantt chart's gridlines.

Changing bar styles

Changing bar styles has nothing to do with the trend toward microbreweries. A bar style is the way in which you depict duration on the Gantt chart. Sometimes it's helpful to customize the information. If that's what you want to do, the Bar Styles dialog box is the place to be.

To modify bar styles:

1. **Right-click in one of the white areas of the Gantt chart (not the Gantt table).**

2. **In the list box, select Bar Styles.**

   The Bar Styles dialog box appears.

3. **Select the Summary option.**

   The Format Bar dialog box appears. With this, you can change all the summary bars in the Gantt chart.

   For now, don't make any changes to the summary bars. That way, you can follow along with the next example.

4. **Click Cancel.**

Individual bar style changes

I asked you to click Cancel because I wanted to show you something else. Sometimes it's neat to modify individual elements of the bar chart.

For example, you can choose a different color for each summary bar. To do this:

1. **Right-click the summary bar for task 1, Preparation Stage.**

2. **Choose Format Bar.**

   The Format Bar dialog box appears.

3. **Change the middle bar color to something other than black.**

   You can change anything else you want as well.

4. **Click OK.**

5. **Follow Steps 1 through 4 for the other three summary bars, using a different color or pattern for each.**

With each summary bar a different color, you may find it easier to identify the stages of the project.

Making other changes in looks

You can make other changes to the appearance of the Gantt chart. By right-clicking in the general chart area, you can change the color and look of nonworking time. Your days can finally be sky blue if you want! By double-clicking a particular area or element, you can change the look of that specific feature.

Changing links

One more double-click makes it possible for you to change more than a look. By double-clicking a link, you can modify the schedule.

For example, the Award Program has a scheduling blunder. The Announcement Committee is supposed to meet the day after it's formed, which is unrealistic. You need to create a one-week lag between tasks 4 and 5.

To do this:

1. **Double-click the link between tasks 4 and 5 on the Gantt chart.**

   The link is the graphic depiction of the relationship of tasks 4 and 5. The link's Task Dependency dialog box appears, as shown in Figure 9-9.

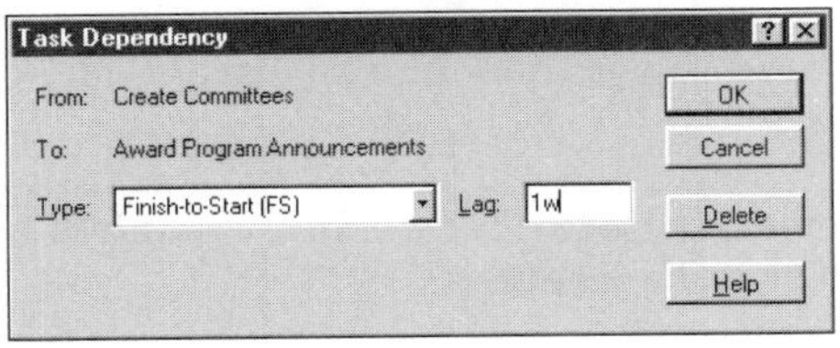

Figure 9-9:
You can change the task relationship as well as the lag time in the Task Dependency dialog box.

2. **In the Lag box, change the lag time from 0d to 1w.**

3. **Click OK.**

   All projects following task 4 move up one week.

Using the Mouse

You can use your mouse to solicit or change information from the Gantt chart. For instance, place your mouse cursor over the left edge of a task duration bar (one of the blue bars in the Gantt chart that represent task duration) until it becomes a percent sign, and then click and hold. An information box appears, giving the task's start and finish dates. By dragging left or right, you can register a percentage of task completion. Try it on one of the tasks. It's easy.

Click and hold in the middle of a task bar. Do the same for a summary task, and then a milestone. An information box reports the start time and duration of each task. These kinds of readouts are helpful when you're scanning the various stages of a project. By dragging the task duration bar right or left, you can move the entire task duration to new start and finish dates.

Getting Time on Your Side

In project management (and in life), the proper use of time is never easy. Microsoft Project can't solve all your time challenges, but at the very least, it can tell you whether time is helping or hurting your project. One of the time tools provided by Microsoft Project is the timescale.

The timescale is the indicator at the top of the Gantt chart (refer to Figure 9-8). Time is shown in major and minor increments. Major time increments are in the upper row of the timescale. For instance, the current setting shows a major timescale of one week. The date indicated is the first day of the week (Sunday). The second row is the minor timescale. The current setting shows individual days.

I'm not going to ask you to modify the timescale. But you might need to at some other time, so here's what it's all about:

1. **Double-click the timescale area of the Award Program's Gantt chart.**

   The Timescale dialog box appears, as shown in Figure 9-10.

2. **Click the Timescale tab, if it isn't already chosen.**

The default setting of the timescale is weeks in the major scale and days in the minor scale. Notice the default manner of depicting time in the major and minor scales. The major timescale time lists month, day, and year. The minor timescale time lists an abbreviation for days. For detailed instructions about the use of the Timescale dialog box, click Help.

The Count box under both Major Scale and Minor Scale affords you the opportunity to depict measurements of time sequentially or by skipping. Skipping is performed by changing the count from 1 to some other number. For instance, if the major setting is months (January, February, March), you can show every other month (January, March, May) by changing the count to 2. You can change any or all of the settings in the Timescale dialog box.

Figure 9-10:
The Timescale dialog box offers settings for working and nonworking time.

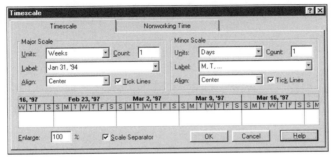

Chapter 10

The PERT Chart

I wish I could tell you that the PERT chart was designed by Henry Gantt's Aunt Pertha, but she probably wasn't responsible (unless she worked for the U.S. Navy in the late 1950s). The PERT in PERT chart stands for *Program Evaluation and Review Technique* —I'll stick with the acronym.

Microsoft Project offers the PERT chart as one of its views because you can use it to

✔ Review project tasks in a graphical format

✔ Study task relationships in a close-up view or a wide view

✔ Edit tasks

✔ Link tasks

✔ Create schedules

If you haven't copied the files from the accompanying disk, you might want to do so before proceeding with this chapter. See Appendix C for instructions.

In this chapter, you tinker with a sample PERT chart file. To begin, start Microsoft Project (if necessary). Then

1. **Click the Open button on the Standard toolbar.**

2. **Open the Practice Files folder.**

3. **Double-click PERT Sample 10.MPP.**

Basics of the PERT Chart

PERT charts are weak on duration and strong on relationship. As you're about to see, PERT charts are like flowcharts. They make it easy for you to concentrate on the implications of the links between tasks. On the flip side, PERT charts don't give you a lot of visual representation of the lengths of tasks or the timeline.

To see this mastery of the intricacies of relationship, choose View➪PERT Chart. The Gantt chart is replaced by the PERT chart. (See Figure 10-1.)

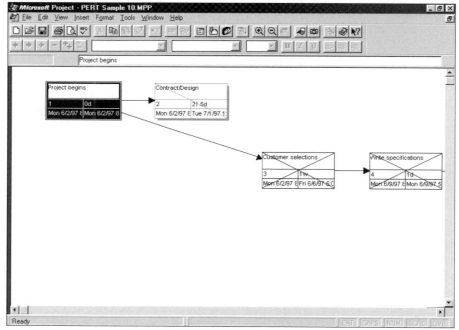

Figure 10-1:
The lines and arrows in the PERT chart indicate the tasks' relationships.

Zooming the view

One of the first things you need to know in a PERT Chart view is where to find the zoom controls so that you can see the whole picture as well as the details. You can use the Zoom In and Out buttons on the Standard toolbar to perform this function. But you might like the PERT zoom feature better. To use the PERT zoom feature

1. **Choose View➪Zoom.**

   The Zoom dialog box appears.

2. **Choose Entire Picture and then click OK.**

Most of the picture appears, as shown in Figure 10-2.

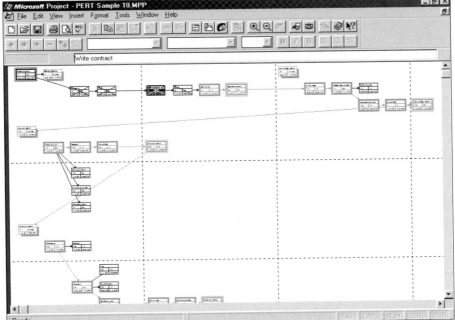

Figure 10-2:
You can
use the
Zoom
dialog box
or the Zoom
In and
Zoom Out
buttons on
the
Standard
toolbar.

Reading the view

The Entire Picture view shows a number of aspects about the PERT chart. Each box, or *node,* is an individual task. Predecessors are always to the left of and above successors. Summary tasks are always to the left of and above their subtasks.

Click the Zoom In button on the Standard toolbar once. At this level of magnification, you can see that some task boxes contain two diagonal lines, some contain a single diagonal line, and some have no diagonal line. Two diagonal lines mean that the task is completed. A single diagonal line indicates a task that is partially completed. No diagonal line means that the task hasn't begun yet.

A summary task has a single diagonal line if some but not all of its tasks have double diagonal lines.

An easy way to understand the various box frames and colors is by accessing the Box Styles dialog box. To do so:

1. **Double-click anywhere in the blank area of the PERT Chart view.**

   The Box Styles dialog box appears.

2. **Click the Borders tab.**

   The Box Styles dialog box looks like Figure 10-3.

Figure 10-3:
The shapes and colors of the nodes communicate information just as much as the text within them.

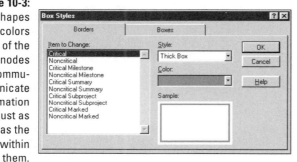

The Box Style dialog box is an editing tool. But it's also a good way to illustrate the meaning of node colors and shapes. By highlighting different Items to Change, you can see how they're graphically represented:

Item	*Default shape*
Critical task	Thick red border
Noncritical task	Narrow black border
Critical Milestone	Red frame
Noncritical Milestone	Black frame
Critical Summary task	Red shadow box
Noncritical Summary task	Black shadow box

You can use the Box Styles dialog box to change the styles or color of any of these items.

Viewing task information

In addition to illustrating and interpreting the meaning of node borders, the Box Styles dialog box also tells you about the information contained in the nodes.

To see what's in your nodes (no mirror is necessary), click the Boxes tab of the Box Styles dialog box. It's node mission control. Each PERT node box has five fields, as shown in Figure 10-4. Each field contains default information. Field 1 is usually used for the task name, as shown here. Fields 2 through 5 contain default information. But you can choose something else for each field if you want.

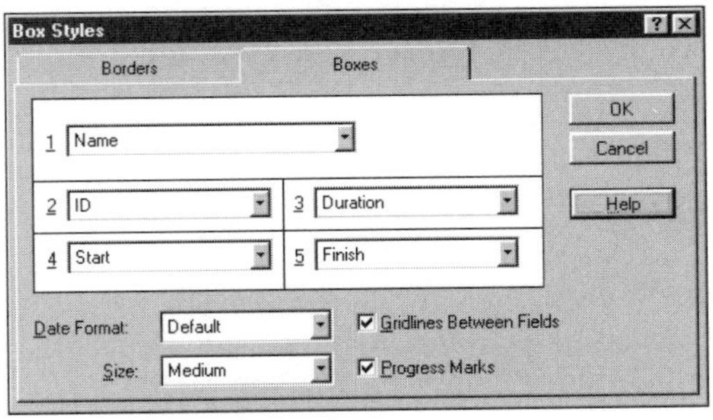

Figure 10-4:
In addition to changing box information, you can modify the box design: Select the Size box to change the size of PERT chart nodes.

To practice changing box information, you can modify field 2:

1. Select field 2.

2. Select Resource Group from the choices in the list box.

3. Click OK.

The Resource Group has replaced the task ID.

Some tasks don't have a resource group assignment. The PERT chart indicates this using nodes with an empty resource group field.

Viewing task relationships

Click the Zoom Out button on the Standard toolbar until the PERT chart is nearly a full view again. This view will assist in comparing task relationships. Task relationships appear as red and black lines. Red lines represent *critical path relationships* (tasks that must be completed on time to keep the project on schedule). Black lines represent *noncritical path relationships* (tasks that can completed late but won't keep the project from being completed on schedule). Critical path is described in detail in Chapter 16.

Editing Tasks and Relationships

Adding a task or changing a link on the PERT chart is simple. And don't worry about the way the changes will affect the Gantt chart. Microsoft Project is keeping records for you. Any changes to a task or a link in the PERT Chart view appear also in the Gantt Chart view and are recorded in relevant tables.

Adding a task

In this section, you add a task to the sample project file. Suppose that the customer has decided to install a geothermal heat system. This requires the digging of a well. So, you need to add a well-digging task:

1. **Select one of the noncritical tasks on the far middle left part of the chart.**

   The noncritical tasks are ones that can finish late and not mess up the project schedule. They are black nodes.

2. **Click the Zoom In button on the Standard toolbar three times.**

   The screen should look like Figure 10-5.

3. **Draw a task box next to the Plumbing lines task by clicking to the right of the task and dragging a box (Figure 10-6).**

   Another way to create a new task box next to an existing task is by selecting the existing task and then pressing the Insert key.

4. **Double-click the new task box.**

   The Task Information dialog box appears.

5. **In the Name text box, type** Geothermal Furnace.

6. **Give the task a 3-day duration.**

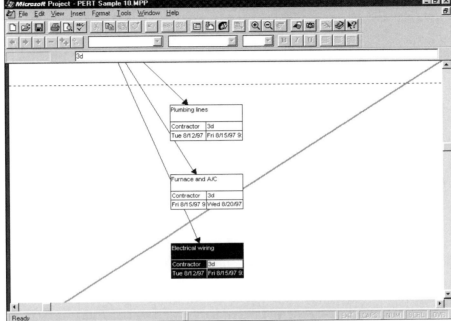

Figure 10-5:
If you first
select a
task, the
Zoom In and
Zoom Out
buttons
focus
on the
selection.

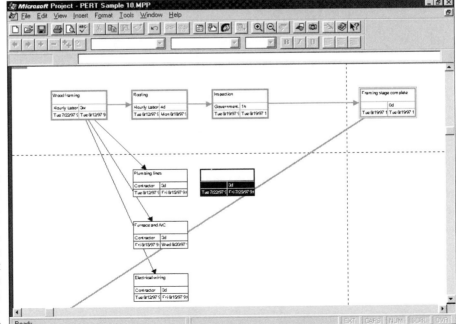

Figure 10-6:
An empty,
unlinked
task node
now exists
to the right
of the
Plumbing
lines task.

7. **Click the Resources tab.**

8. **In the Resource Name text box, type** Well Drilling Contractor.

9. **Click OK.**

The new task box should contain the task information.

Creating a link

To link a new task to its predecessor or its successor or both, you click in the middle of the predecessor task and drag to its new relationship. If you don't understand what I mean by linking, you might want to connect with Chapter 6.

Using the sample project file

1. **Click the Zoom Out button once.**

2. **Scroll to reveal Plumbing lines task successor.**

By *task successor,* I mean the task that precedes other tasks in the schedule. This, too, is described in Chapter 6.

3. **Place your mouse cursor over the Wood framing task.**

4. **Drag the mouse to the task you have just created and release the mouse button.**

See Figure 10-7. You've just created a relationship.

Changing the layout

You may find a different layout easier to read. Choose Format⇨Layout. The Layout dialog box appears. Two link format layout options are available. Select the link format on the right. (See Figure 10-8.)

Click OK. The task relationships are now shown in orthogonal lines. Sorry. I was just itching to use my big word. To make something orthogonal, you make it perpendicular with right angles. So now you can hang out your shingle as an orthogonist.

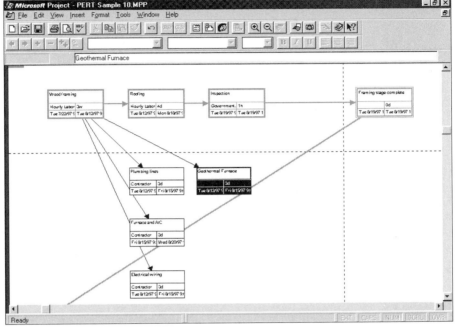

Figure 10-7:
The
relationship
between
the Wood
framing
task and
your new
task is
noncritical
and doesn't
have a
successor.

Figure 10-8:
For details
on the
Layout
options,
click the
Help button
in the
Layout
dialog box.

Chapter 11

The Calendar

*T*he beauty of the Calendar view is also its liability. On the positive side, the Calendar view lets you see and present your work in a familiar manner. On the minus side, the Calendar view limits how much information you can present at a time. Ah, life! You can, however, do lots of things with the Calendar view if you work within its limitations.

The Calendar view can be helpful in two major ways. First, the Calendar view is a whiz at creating simple projects. Second, the Calendar view is a great tool for viewing, segregating, and reporting more complex projects. Accordingly, this chapter is divided into two major sections. The first focuses on how to create a simple project using the Calendar view. The second section deals with using the Calendar view for existing, more complex projects. If you want to skip the first section and go right into the second section, have at it!

Making a Simple Schedule with the Calendar View

The planner industry has nothing to worry about with Microsoft Project's Calendar view. Planners and Calendar view are for entirely different purposes. They're Appaloosas and orangutans.

Using the Calendar view, you can make a fully functioning project. You can create and track a schedule of tasks and establish their resources. After you create a project in the Calendar view, you can view it in the Gantt Chart view, resource views, graphs, and in combination views. You can also make reports from projects you create in Calendar view.

Creating a project using the Calendar view

Creating a project in Calendar view is fun in a project manager sort of way. To begin, you need to switch views:

1. **Start Microsoft Project.**

   The program opens in the Gantt Chart view.

2. **Choose View⇔Calendar.**

   Welcome to the Calendar view.

Here's the project: Simultaneously begin to develop a Web page and a company brochure. Then simultaneously contact trade associations, send mailers, distribute flyers, perform Web-search sign-ups, and amend database forms. For the date, assume that today is February 3, 1997.

Microsoft Project uses the current date as the default project start date if you don't specify a start date. To specify a start date, choose File⇔Project Info. The Project Info dialog box appears. To set a new project date, change the Start Date.

Here's how you can plan the project in the Calendar view: Begin by pressing the Insert key seven times. This creates seven tasks. The task boxes stack on top of each other in the start date box on the calendar (Figure 11-1).

Notice that the task boxes take up more space than is allowed in the date window. A down arrow in the date's shaded areas tells you that some tasks are hidden. You can access the hidden task boxes by zooming or by exploding the date window. Zooming magnifies the entire calendar. Exploding the date window magnifies only one date.

You access the hidden tasks by exploding the date window. Double-click the gray date bar of the date that holds the task boxes. A task list box appears, as shown in Figure 11-2. The check marks indicate the tasks that are visible in the window.

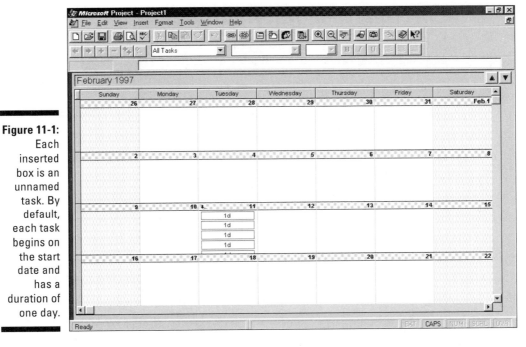

Figure 11-1:
Each inserted box is an unnamed task. By default, each task begins on the start date and has a duration of one day.

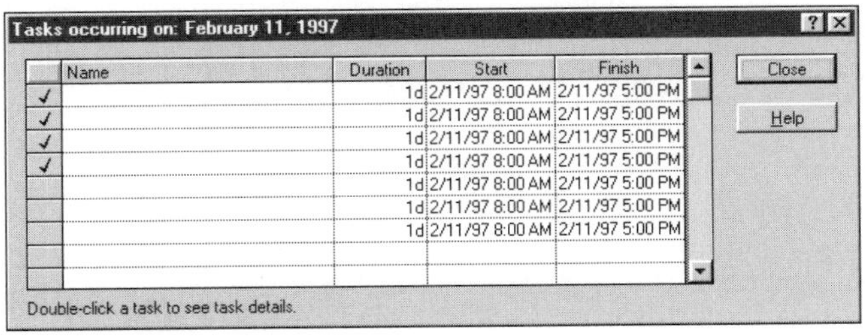

Figure 11-2:
Another way to access the task list box is by right-clicking the date bar and then selecting Task List.

Entering task information

Now that you have the task list on the screen, I'll show you a shortcut for entering task information. You'll use this method to enter the following tasks:

Develop Web Page

Publish Brochure

Contact Trade Associations

Send Mailers

Distribute Flyers

Web Page Search Sign-ups

Amend Database Forms

To enter these task names

1. Double-click the first empty task name box in the Name column.

2. In the box, type Develop Web Page **(Figure 11-3).**

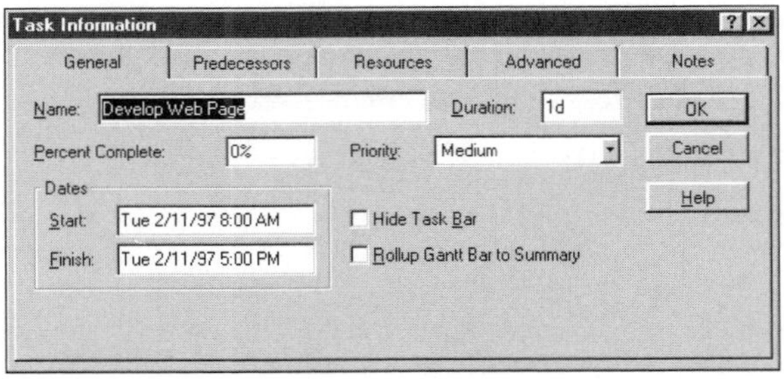

Figure 11-3:
The Task
Information
box used
in the
Calendar
view is
identical to
the Task
Information
box used in
the Gantt
Chart view.

3. Click OK.

4. Double-click in the next empty name box.

5. Type the next task name.

6. Click OK.

7. **Repeat steps 4 through 6 for the remaining tasks.**

   After you are finished, you will have named all seven task boxes. The result looks like Figure 11-4.

8. **Close the task list box.**

Figure 11-4:
Using the
task list
box, you
can see
and modify
all tasks
occurring
on a certain
date,
including
the ones
hidden from
view.

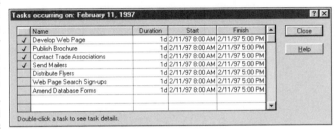

Zooming the calendar

The default Calendar view shows four successive weeks. You can change that view from four weeks to two weeks with the Zoom In button.

 Click the Zoom In button on the Standard toolbar once. The view changes to a two-week interval. If your start date is in one of the latter two weeks on the calendar (as in the example), the tasks disappear. That's because the Zoom In command focused on the first two weeks of the calendar. To expose your start date, press the Page Down key once. The calendar should now look like Figure 11-5.

If you want, you can open the task list box again to see all tasks with checks. To do so, simply double-click the date bar of the date that holds the task boxes.

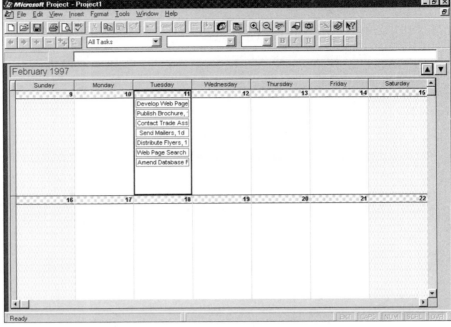

Figure 11-5:
The Zoom In button enlarges the view size of each date box and exposes all the tasks in the project start date.

Adding duration in the Calendar view

You can add durations to the seven tasks you entered in two ways: using the Task Information dialog box and by dragging. In this section, you try out both ways. It'll be fast and fun. Well, kind of fun anyway.

Here are the durations you need to add:

Develop Web Page: 2 weeks

Publish Brochure: 3 weeks

Contact Trade Associations: 3 days

Send Mailers: 3 days

Distribute Flyers: 3 days

Web Page Search Sign-ups: 3 days

Amend Database Forms: 3 days

To add these durations, do the following:

1. **Click the Zoom Out button on the Standard toolbar once.**

   You're back in the four-week view.

2. **Double-click the first task, Develop Web Page.**

   The Task Information dialog box appears.

3. **Type 2w in the Duration box.**

4. **Click OK.**

   You've just entered a two-week duration for the Develop Web Page task using the Task Information dialog box.

5. **Move the mouse cursor to the right edge of the second task, Publish Brochure.**

   The cursor changes to a vertical bar and a right arrow.

6. **Click and drag downward.**

   A task information caption balloon appears. In the balloon is a duration reading.

7. **Drag down and back and forth until the duration reading is 15d (three work weeks).**

8. **Release the mouse button.**

   You've entered a duration using the drag method. The second task, Publish Brochure, should now show a 15d duration.

 9. **Click the Zoom In button on the Standard toolbar once.**

   The screen returns to the two-week view.

10. **If necessary, press the Page Up key to expose the starting date.**

11. **Using the dragging technique, give each of the remaining tasks a 3-day duration.**

   The resulting view should look like Figure 11-6.

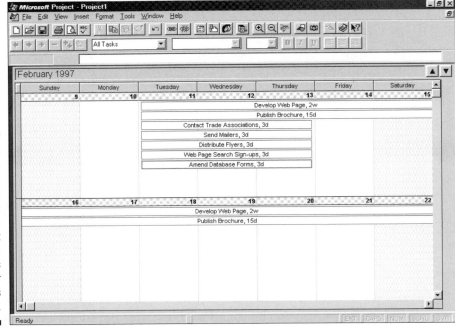

Figure 11-6:
The tasks appear in stacked order because they don't have predecessors or successors yet.

Linking tasks in the Calendar view

Linking tasks is simple in the Calendar view: You select the tasks and use the Link button. In the Calendar view, like the Gantt Chart view, the default relationship type is finish to start.

Using this example, change a number of relationship types. Here are the relationships:

ID	Task Name	Predecessor	Type
1	Develop Web Page		
2	Publish Brochure	1	Start to start
3	Contact Trade Associations	2	Finish to start
4	Send Mailers	3	Finish to start
5	Distribute Flyers	3	Finish to start
6	Web Page Search Sign-ups	3	Finish to start
7	Amend Database Forms	3	Finish to start

You can use the Task Information dialog box to enter this information. To get you started, I show you how to add information for the Publish Brochure task:

1. **Double-click the Publish Brochure task.**

   The Task Information dialog box appears.

2. **Click the Predecessors tab.**

3. **Select the first empty box under the Task Name column.**

   A small down arrow becomes active next to the text entry box.

4. **Click the down arrow.**

   A list box of all the tasks appears (Figure 11-7).

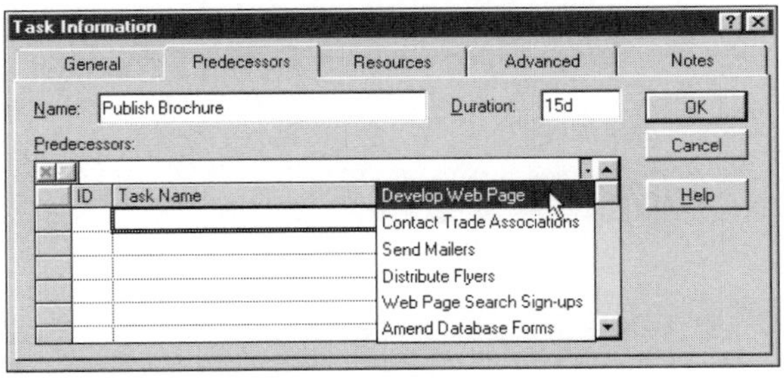

Figure 11-7:
You can type the information in the box, but selecting from the list box is usually faster and safer.

5. **Select Develop Web Page.**

6. **Click in the Type box.**

   A small arrow becomes active next to the entry box.

7. **Click the down arrow.**

   A list box of all the relationship types appears.

8. **Select Start-to-Start.**

9. **Click OK.**

10. **If necessary, press the Page Up key.**

Now complete the information for the tasks using these steps and the table preceding them as a guide.

Fitting the information to the calendar

After you've finished entering task information, click the Zoom Out button on the Standard toolbar once to change the screen to month view. Then press the Page Up or Page Down key until the month of March is in view. Notice that some tasks are partially or totally hidden (Figure 11-8). Tasks remain vertically hierarchical even though they are separated horizontally.

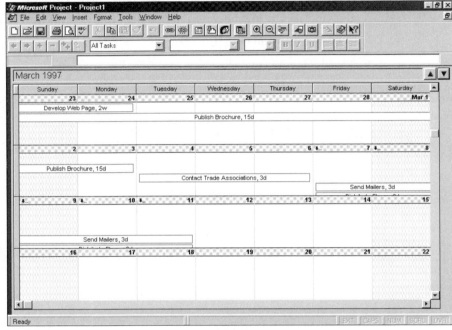

Figure 11-8:
Linked tasks don't have connecting lines in the Calendar view as they do in the Gantt Chart view and the PERT Chart view.

You can modify the task layout to better fit them in the calendar boxes. To do this:

1. **Choose Format⇨Layout.**

   The Layout dialog box appears.

2. **Select the Attempt to Fit as Many Tasks as Possible option.**

3. **Click OK.**

   The screen should now look like Figure 11-9.

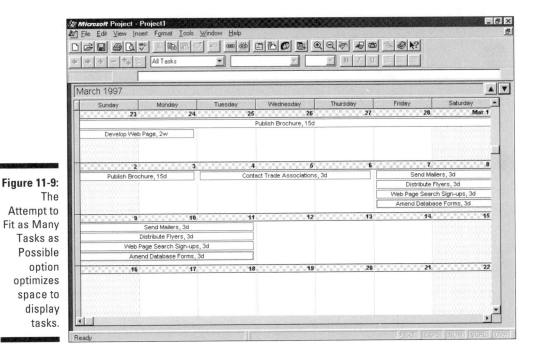

Figure 11-9:
The
Attempt to
Fit as Many
Tasks as
Possible
option
optimizes
space to
display
tasks.

Save this project file in your Practice Files folder as follows:

1. **Click the Save button on the Standard toolbar.**

2. **Change folders to the Practice Files folder.**

3. **Save the project using a name such as Small Calendar.**

4. **If you want, you may close the file by choosing File⇨Close.**

Using the Calendar View for Existing Projects

The Calendar view can also be used with existing projects. Sometimes it's a convenient tool for reviewing and reporting a portion of a project's schedule. As mentioned, though, the Calendar view has its strengths and weaknesses. It handles small amounts of information well, but quickly becomes unwieldy for more complicated projects.

If you're working with an existing project, adding or editing tasks in the Calendar view can be messy. For instance, if you add a task to the middle of a project in the Calendar view, it will be messed up in the Gantt view. The task will be linked as you indicated, but it will be listed as the lowest ID number. Who needs such problems! It's safer to add or edit the task in the Gantt view. Then come back to the Calendar view to see your task nestled safe and warm where you want it.

If you haven't copied the files from the sample disk to your hard drive, you might want to do so before proceeding with this chapter. See Appendix C for instructions.

In this section, you see how you can use the Calendar view to analyze an existing project. Open the sample project file called Calendar 11.MPP from the Practice Files folder. To do so:

1. **Click the Open button on the Standard toolbar.**

2. **Open the Practice Files folder.**

3. **Double-click Calendar 11.MPP.**

4. **If the file doesn't open in Calendar view, choose <u>V</u>iew⇨<u>C</u>alendar.**

Cruising the calendar

Notice that the calendar opens to the project start date (Figure 11-10). The month is in the upper-left corner. The default view displays four weeks. Nonworking days are shaded gray.

Try cruising around a bit. You can do so in four ways:

✔ Click the up and down arrows to move from month to month.

✔ Click the scroll bar to slide your calendar up or down. When you click the scroll box, an information box appears that alerts you to the dates visible on the screen.

✔ Press Page Up and Page Down to move from month to month. (This is the same as clicking the up and down arrows on the screen.)

✔ Press Alt+Home and Alt+End to jump to the start or the end of the project, respectively.

When you've finished cruising, press Alt+Home to return to the beginning of the project.

Month up and down buttons

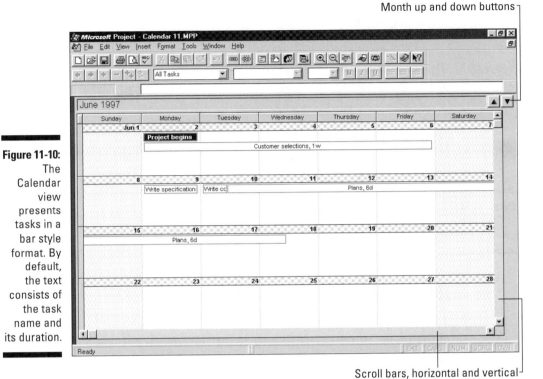

Figure 11-10:
The
Calendar
view
presents
tasks in a
bar style
format. By
default,
the text
consists of
the task
name and
its duration.

Scroll bars, horizontal and vertical

Zooming to make it fit

Using the down arrow, change the Calendar view to August. The entire month isn't showing. You can either scroll down to see the final week, or you can make the month fit on the screen by zooming.

You can zoom with the Zoom In and Zoom Out buttons on the Standard toolbar, but you'd get better results using the Zoom dialog box. Try this:

1. **Right-click anywhere in the white, unused portion of any date box.**

   A shortcut menu appears.

2. **Choose Zoom.**

   The Zoom dialog box appears (Figure 11-11).

3. **Select Custom.**

4. **In the Weeks box, type** 5.

5. **Click OK.**

The Calendar view shows five weeks.

The default zoom in and zoom out increments are 1, 2, 4, and 6 weeks. You can customize your view in weeks, or you can set a view based on specific start and finish dates.

Figure 11-11:
The Zoom
dialog box.

Making it fit with layout

You still have a problem. You can see all the weeks, but you can't see many of the tasks. Notice that beginning in the third week, down arrows are in each date box. This can be corrected using a layout command. But you have to make a decision. Do you want to see all the weeks of the month or all the tasks on each day?

For this example, you change the layout to display all the tasks on each day. First, return to a four-week view:

1. **Right-click anywhere in the white, unused portion of any date box.**

The shortcut menu appears.

2. **Choose Zoom.**

3. **Select the 4 Weeks option.**

4. **Click OK.**

To make the tasks all appear in their respective days, begin by changing the calendar layout. To do this:

1. Right-click anywhere in the white, unused portion of any date box.

The shortcut menu appears.

2. Choose Layout.

The Layout dialog box appears (Figure 11-12).

Figure 11-12:
You can use the Layout dialog box to modify the layout in three ways. For detailed information, press the Help button.

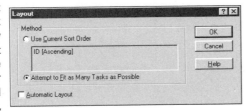

3. Select the Attempt to Fit as Many Tasks as Possible option.

4. Click OK.

Some of the tasks have now appeared (Figure 11-13).

You have one more thing to do to maximize the view: Make the weeks fit as best as possible. To do this, you use the automatic resizing feature. To automatically resize the weeks:

1. Place the mouse cursor over any horizontal line at the bottom of a week row.

The cursor turns into a horizontal line with an up and down arrow.

2. Double-click.

Voilà! The tasks all fit into their date boxes.

Notice that Microsoft Project calculated the space necessary and pushed the weeks down slightly (Figure 11-14).

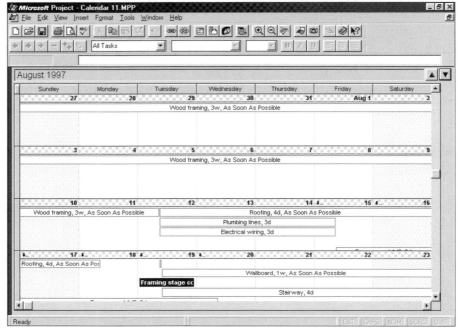

Figure 11-13:
The layout command fits as many tasks as it can into the date boxes.

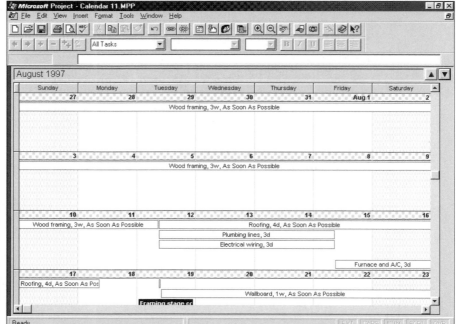

Figure 11-14:
The Calendar view is now maximized to show all the tasks.

Viewing a day

Notice that August 19 has a task so small there's no text identification. You can see what it is and simultaneously view all the other tasks on the day by double-clicking the day's date bar. When you do, you'll see that the short task is a one-hour inspection (Figure 11-15).

The check marks indicate that all the tasks are now visible.

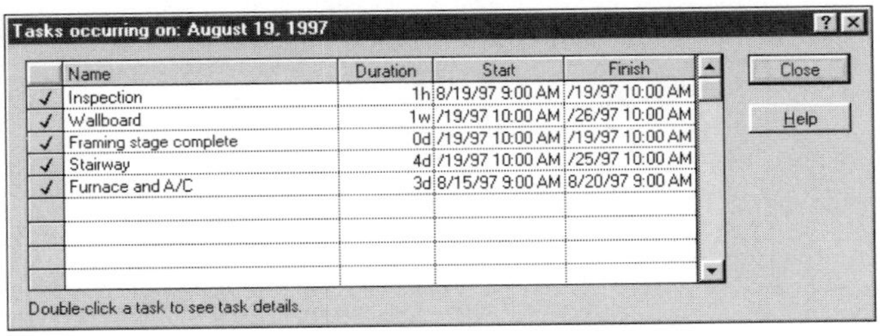

Figure 11-15:
The date
list box
shows all
the tasks
occurring
on that day.

	Name	Duration	Start	Finish
✓	Inspection	1h	8/19/97 9:00 AM	/19/97 10:00 AM
✓	Wallboard	1w	/19/97 10:00 AM	/26/97 10:00 AM
✓	Framing stage complete	0d	/19/97 10:00 AM	/19/97 10:00 AM
✓	Stairway	4d	/19/97 10:00 AM	/25/97 10:00 AM
✓	Furnace and A/C	3d	8/15/97 9:00 AM	8/20/97 9:00 AM

Tasks occurring on: August 19, 1997

Close
Help

Double-click a task to see task details.

If you want, save this file. Give it another name so that you can use the original file again.

Chapter 12

Resource Views

. . . .

In This Chapter

▶ Viewing the Resource sheet

▶ Viewing the Usage sheet

▶ Viewing Resource tables

▶ Viewing the Resource graph

. . . .

Chapter 8 explains the reasons for and importance of views, especially task views. Resource views have their place, too. Sometimes isolating resource information is helpful — such as when you have an overallocation problem. Each resource view displays information from a different perspective. Two of the views, Resource Sheet and Resource Usage, let you enter and edit resource information. The third view, the Resource Graph view, is for illustration.

If you haven't copied the files from the sample disk to your hard drive, you might want to do so before proceeding with this chapter. See Appendix C for instructions.

In this section, you use the sample project file called Smith Home 12.Mpp to view and manipulate resource information. Open the sample project file from the Practice Files folder, as follows:

1. **Click the Open button on the Standard toolbar.**

2. **Open the Practice Files folder.**

3. **Double-click Smith Home 12.MPP.**

   The file opens in the Gantt Chart view.

Resource Sheet View

The Resource sheet, like the Task sheet, is in spreadsheet form. The sheet lists resources and their related details such as initials, group designations, and maximum units (Figure 12-1). You can use the sheet to enter and edit resource details. To access the Resource Sheet view, choose View⇨Resource Sheet.

Figure 12-1: The Resource Sheet view is a handy way to review individual resources and groups of resources. And editing the sheet is usually a friendly experience.

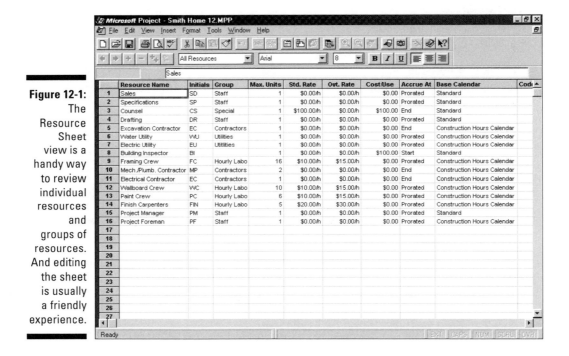

	Resource Name	Initials	Group	Max. Units	Std. Rate	Ovt. Rate	Cost/Use	Accrue At	Base Calendar	Cod
1	Sales	SD	Staff	1	$0.00/h	$0.00/h	$0.00	Prorated	Standard	
2	Specifications	SP	Staff	1	$0.00/h	$0.00/h	$0.00	Prorated	Standard	
3	Counsel	CS	Special	1	$100.00/h	$0.00/h	$100.00	End	Standard	
4	Drafting	DR	Staff	1	$0.00/h	$0.00/h	$0.00	Prorated	Standard	
5	Excavation Contractor	EC	Contractors	1	$0.00/h	$0.00/h	$0.00	End	Construction Hours Calendar	
6	Water Utility	WU	Utilities	1	$0.00/h	$0.00/h	$0.00	Prorated	Construction Hours Calendar	
7	Electric Utility	EU	Utitlties	1	$0.00/h	$0.00/h	$0.00	Prorated	Construction Hours Calendar	
8	Building Inspector	BI		1	$0.00/h	$0.00/h	$100.00	Start	Standard	
9	Framing Crew	FC	Hourly Labo	16	$10.00/h	$15.00/h	$0.00	Prorated	Construction Hours Calendar	
10	Mech./Plumb. Contractor	MP	Contractors	2	$0.00/h	$0.00/h	$0.00	End	Construction Hours Calendar	
11	Electrical Contractor	EC	Contractors	1	$0.00/h	$0.00/h	$0.00	End	Construction Hours Calendar	
12	Wallboard Crew	WC	Hourly Labo	10	$10.00/h	$15.00/h	$0.00	Prorated	Construction Hours Calendar	
13	Paint Crew	PC	Hourly Labo	6	$10.00/h	$15.00/h	$0.00	Prorated	Construction Hours Calendar	
14	Finish Carpenters	FIN	Hourly Labo	5	$20.00/h	$30.00/h	$0.00	Prorated	Construction Hours Calendar	
15	Project Manager	PM	Staff	1	$0.00/h	$0.00/h	$0.00	Prorated	Standard	
16	Project Foreman	PF	Staff	1	$0.00/h	$0.00/h	$0.00	Prorated	Construction Hours Calendar	

Adding information to the Resource sheet is similar to entering information in spreadsheet cells. You can insert rows and columns. You can also enter information at the first available open space at the bottom of the list.

Two of the greatest features of the Resource sheet are its sorting and filtering capabilities. I discuss sorting and filtering at length in Chapter 13. For now, experiment with a few options.

Sorting

You can increase the value of the Resource Sheet view through sorting. By default, the Resource sheet is ordered by ID. Microsoft Project automatically assigns an identification number to each resource. The order simply reflects the order in which the resources were entered. If there's a significance to this order, great. Often, however, the default order has no special value.

As an example of sorting, change the view to make the resources appear in alphabetical order. To do this:

1. **Choose Tools⇨Sort.**

   The Sort list box appears.

2. **Select by Name.**

   The view is now based on the alphabetical order of the resource names (Figure 12-2).

Figure 12-2: Each time you sort, Microsoft Project reassigns the ID number to the resource. This doesn't mess up your resource assignments to tasks. Phew!

	Resource Name	Initials	Group	Max. Units	Std. Rate	Ovt. Rate	Cost/Use	Accrue At	Base Calendar	Cod
1	Building Inspector	BI		1	$0.00/h	$0.00/h	$100.00	Start	Standard	
2	Counsel	CS	Special	1	$100.00/h	$0.00/h	$100.00	End	Standard	
3	Drafting	DR	Staff	1	$0.00/h	$0.00/h	$0.00	Prorated	Standard	
4	Electric Utility	EU	Utilities	1	$0.00/h	$0.00/h	$0.00	Prorated	Construction Hours Calendar	
5	Electrical Contractor	EC	Contractors	1	$0.00/h	$0.00/h	$0.00	End	Construction Hours Calendar	
6	Excavation Contractor	EC	Contractors	1	$0.00/h	$0.00/h	$0.00	End	Construction Hours Calendar	
7	Finish Carpenters	FIN	Hourly Labo	5	$20.00/h	$30.00/h	$0.00	Prorated	Construction Hours Calendar	
8	Framing Crew	FC	Hourly Labo	16	$10.00/h	$15.00/h	$0.00	Prorated	Construction Hours Calendar	
9	Mech./Plumb. Contractor	MP	Contractors	2	$0.00/h	$0.00/h	$0.00	End	Construction Hours Calendar	
10	Paint Crew	PC	Hourly Labo	6	$10.00/h	$15.00/h	$0.00	Prorated	Construction Hours Calendar	
11	Project Foreman	PF	Staff	1	$0.00/h	$0.00/h	$0.00	Prorated	Standard	
12	Project Manager	PM	Staff	1	$0.00/h	$0.00/h	$0.00	Prorated	Standard	
13	Sales	SD	Staff	1	$0.00/h	$0.00/h	$0.00	Prorated	Standard	
14	Specifications	SP	Staff	1	$0.00/h	$0.00/h	$0.00	Prorated	Standard	
15	Wallboard Crew	WC	Hourly Labo	10	$10.00/h	$15.00/h	$0.00	Prorated	Construction Hours Calendar	
16	Water Utility	WU	Utilities	1	$0.00/h	$0.00/h	$0.00	Prorated	Construction Hours Calendar	

Filtering

In addition to sorting, you can also change the filter of the Resource Sheet view. Whether you realize it or not, Microsoft Project is always filtering your information — not like your mother, but more like an administrative assistant. Microsoft Project isn't hiding anything from you; it's controlling the amount of information it thinks you want to see at any given time.

The default filter for the Resource Sheet view is All Resources. You can see this designation in the Filter box on the Formatting toolbar (Figure 12-2). Here's an example of using a filter:

1. **Click the down arrow next to the Filter box on the Formatting toolbar.**

2. **Select the Group option.**

   A Group entry box appears.

3. **In the entry box, type** Staff.

4. **Click OK.**

   The Resource Sheet view is now filtered to show only the Staff group (Figure 12-3).

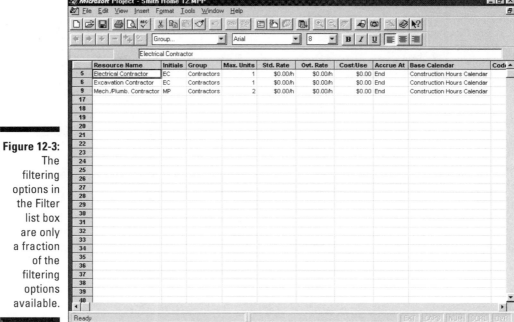

Figure 12-3: The filtering options in the Filter list box are only a fraction of the filtering options available.

If you want, play with the Resource Sheet view, sorting and filtering all you want. After you're finished and before you turn out the lights, please put the Resource Sheet view back the way you found it.

To return the Resource Sheet view to its original order:

1. **In the Filter list box, select the All Resources filter.**

2. **Choose Tools⇨Sort.**

   The Sort list box appears.

3. **Select Sort By.**

   The Sort dialog box appears.

4. **In Sort By, click the down arrow, and scroll to select Unique ID (not ID). See Figure 12-4.**

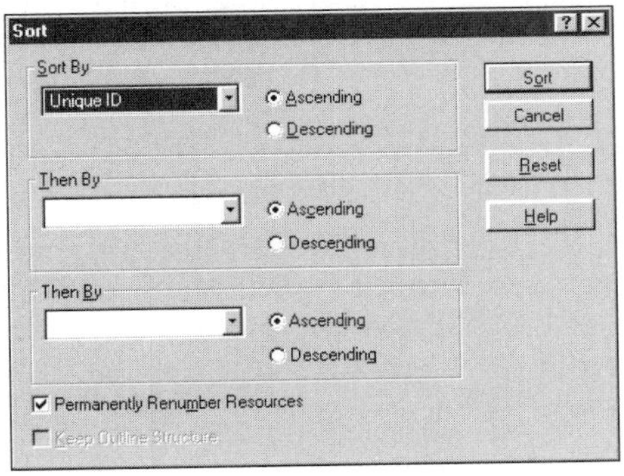

Figure 12-4: Be careful when using the Sort dialog box. Before you perform a sort, decide whether you want to permanently renumber resources.

5. **Click the Sort button.**

   The Resource Sheet view is back to its original condition.

Now you can turn out the lights! Return to the Gantt Chart view.

Resource Usage View

From the Gantt Chart view, change to the Resource Usage view by choosing View⇨Resource Usage. The Resource Usage view displays a combination view (Figure 12-5).

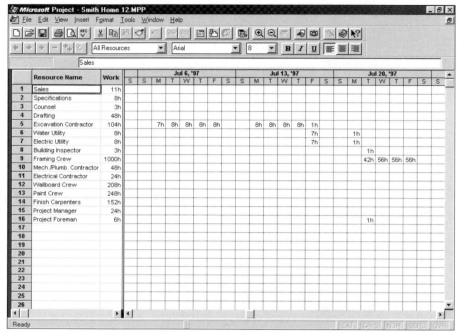

Figure 12-5:
You can
scroll
information
in either
window
with the
scroll bars.

The right window is a timeline depiction of the date and the amount of work performed by individual resources. The left screen can be any of five tables. To change tables, choose View⇨Table. If you want, drag the vertical bar between the timeline and the table to the right until you expose all the table details. Five of the tables follow:

Table	Does This
Entry Resource table	Shows the resource's initials, group, maximum units, rate, overtime rate, cost per use, accrual method, and relevant calendar.
Cost Resource table	Shows information about resources, including cost, baseline cost, variance, actual cost, and amount remaining.
Summary Resource table	Displays the assignment of resources, including the group name, the maximum units, the peak unit usage, the rates, the cost, and the work performed in hours.

Usage Resource table	Lists your project's resources.
Work Resource table	Shows various calculations about work, including percent completed, overtime, baseline, variance, actual, and remaining calculations.

A useful way to make resourceful usage of the Resource Usage view is by splitting — not as in leaving the scene, but as in splitting the screen into two views. To do this, choose Window⇨Split. A Resource Usage form appears in the lower view (Figure 12-6).

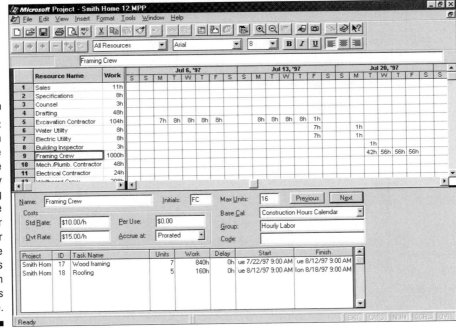

Figure 12-6:
You can change the active view by pressing F6. The blue bar on the far left of the screen tells you which view is active.

To try out the split view, highlight the Framing Crew resource name in the upper view. The form in the lower view reports the task information related to this resource.

After you've finished checking out this split view, unsplit it by choosing Window⇨Remove Split. You are unsplitted. Then return to the Gantt Chart view.

Resource Graph View

The Resource graph shows information about the allocation or cost of resources in measurements of time. Use it for reviewing allocations for a single resource or a group of resources.

The best way to use this graph is in a split view with the Resource Usage view. To do this:

1. **Choose View⇨More Views.**

   The More Views dialog box appears.

2. **Select Resource Allocation.**

3. **Click the Apply button.**

   The Resource Allocation split window appears (Figure 12-7).

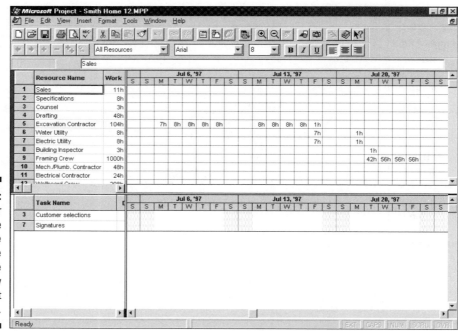

Figure 12-7: The upper view is the Resource Usage view. The lower view is a Gantt Chart view.

You can change to the Resource Allocation view also by accessing the Resource Management toolbar:

1. **Right-click anywhere in the toolbar area.**

   A shortcut menu appears.

2. **Select Resource Management.**

   The Resource Management toolbar appears.

3. **Click the Resource Allocation View button, which is on the far left.**

   You've changed to the Resource Allocation view.

4. **After you're finished with the Resource Management toolbar, right-click anywhere in the toolbar area and select Resource Management.**

   The toolbar disappears.

Now it's time to show your innovative genius. Add the Resource graph to the lower view, as follows:

1. **Press F6 to select the lower view.**

2. **Choose View⇨Resource Graph.**

   The Resource graph appears in the lower window (Figure 12-8).

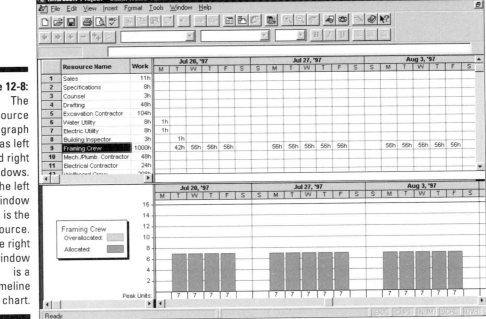

Figure 12-8: The Resource graph has left and right windows. The left window is the resource. The right window is a timeline chart.

3. **Select the Framing Crew resource name in the upper view.**

4. **Using the horizontal scroll bars in the right pane of either view, scroll to the week of July 20.**

   The Resource Usage view shows the hours used by the Framing Crew resource. The Resource Chart view shows the allocation and the number of units still available.

After you're finished with the Allocation view, remove the split window. If you've modified the file, you can save it — but use the Save as command and give it another name. This way, you can use the original Smith Home 12.MPP file again.

Chapter 13

Using Filters

So you've got this beautiful, huge project. Tasks are in order and resources are assigned. Relationships are set and durations are as tight as a drum. You know how to look at the project from about every view the human brain could imagine.

Life is good — at least for an hour or so. Then you get a memo from a stakeholder requesting a listing of all resources whose tasks will occur on Tuesdays in odd weeks of all summer months. While you're still trying to figure out what an odd week is, you get a call from a contractor wanting to know whether there could be any slippages of other tasks and, if so, how they will affect his start date. Oh, and he's got to know right now. And while your ear is still ringing from that one, your boss rushes in wanting a list of all tasks that cost more than $1,500, starting with the most expensive and ending with the least expensive.

Big deal! Why don't they ask for something complicated? All they want you to do is some filtering and sorting. So what are you going to do the second half of this hour?

Filtering and sorting are two of the best reasons for using software programs in project management. Quite often, you need to establish criteria for relating and finding certain details. In such situations, the least important project information might be what you needed the most just a few minutes ago.

A measurement of the worth of a project-management software program is its capability to solicit, associate, and interpret a group of facts from a mass of project information. With Microsoft Project, you can perform this with surprising ease and creative freedom.

A *filter* segregates information using predetermined criteria. A helpful analogy is the use of filters in photography. Choose a particular color filter, and all blue color is eliminated from a picture. In contrast, by choosing a saturation filter, all colors are screened from a picture by a predetermined percentage. As long as you use the same filter, you establish temporary group relationships that include some classes of visual information and exclude others. Using the same filter, you get the same visual relationships no matter where you point the camera.

In Microsoft Project, filters work in much the same way. For instance, you can choose a filter that allows the display of only unfinished tasks. Or you can choose a filter that displays all tasks with a duration greater than three days.

Sorting doesn't filter information; it does something else. A *sort* sets a task order based on your criteria. Unlike filtering, you don't segregate information. Instead, with a sort, you order the information in a different way. For instance, you can sort the tasks in alphabetical order by task name.

It's possible to both filter and sort. For example, you can use a filter that lists only tasks whose costs are based on hourly rates. Then you can sort the filtered tasks by the amount per hour in ascending or descending order.

If you haven't copied the files from the sample disk to your hard drive, you might want to do so before proceeding with this chapter. See Appendix C for instructions.

By the end of this chapter, you'll be able to filter and sort like a first-class detail sleuth. To begin sleuthing, you use the sample project file called Smith Home 13.MPP:

1. **Click the Open button on the Standard toolbar.**

2. **Open the Practice Files folder.**

3. **Double-click Smith Home 13.MPP.**

   The file should open to the Gantt Chart view.

Using Standard Filters

A filter segregates and associates project information to provide you with the specific facts you need. The underlying ingredients of a filter are test and value criteria. When you select a filter, you're saying you want to see all the tasks or resources with values that meet the conditions of a certain test.

For example, the test may be that you want to see all tasks with a duration value greater than one week. Microsoft Project then searches the project databases and finds and displays all tasks with values that conform to that test criterion.

Microsoft Project provides a bunch of standard filters — 31 in all. These filters will probably meet most of your needs. But if you're like most project managers, sooner or later you'll need to create a new filter or two. Fortunately, creating a new filter is almost as easy as using a standard one. As you might guess, though, finding out how the standard filters work before you jump into the creative mode is best.

Whatever view your file happens to be in, you're looking at information provided through a standard filter. The only exception to this is the PERT chart. For example, if your file is in the Gantt Chart view, you are looking at tasks through a filter. The default filter is All Tasks. Knowing which filter is active is easy. Just look at the Filter list box on the Formatting toolbar (Figure 13-1).

In most views, you can access standard filters and new filters in three ways: using the Filtered For command, the Filter list box, or the More Filters command. Although all three choices provide access to filters, they each offer distinct ways to use those filters.

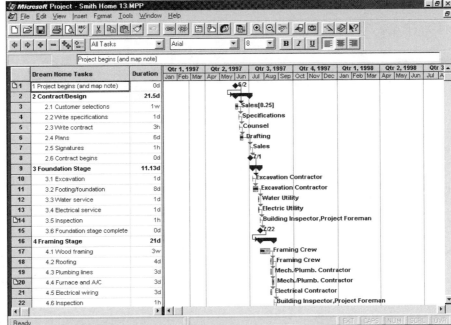

Figure 13-1:
The Filter list box displays the current filter selection, Completed Tasks.

The Filtered For command

The Filtered For command changes the active task or resource view to display information that meets the selected filter criterion. In the following, you use the Filtered For command to display all completed tasks:

1. **Choose Tools➪Filtered for: All Tasks.**

   The Filtered For submenu appears (Figure 13-2). The submenu lists nine commonly used filters.

2. **Choose Completed Tasks.**

   The Gantt chart displays all tasks that have met the test of completion (Figure 13-3).

The view you just selected from the submenu can be referred to as an isolated filter view. An *isolated filter view* shows only those tasks or resources that meet the criterion of the selected filter.

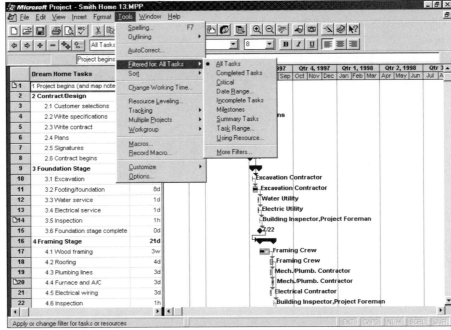

Figure 13-2:
In addition
to the nine
most
commonly
used filters,
the
submenu
can display
any filter
created by
you.

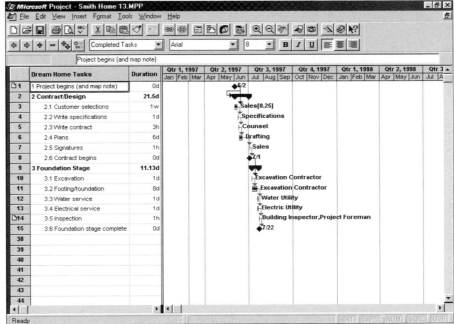

Figure 13-3:
The Gantt
Chart view
displays
only those
tasks
containing
values that
equal the
test of
completion.

In the Filtered For command, you can show either an isolated filter view or a highlighted filter view. A *highlighted filter view* is different from the isolated filter view in one major way. It identifies the tasks or resources that meet the filter criterion and displays them in a highlighted manner among all the other tasks or resources.

Using the Filtered For command, select a filter in the highlighted filter view:

1. **Hold down the Shift key.**

2. **Choose Tools➪Filtered for: Completed Tasks.**

   The submenu appears.

3. **Choose Incomplete Tasks.**

   The Gantt chart displays all the tasks, but highlights all incomplete tasks (Figure 13-4).

In summary, the Filtered For command lists a submenu of commonly selected filters. It can also list filters created by you. Later, I show you how to create a filter and list it in this submenu. The maximum number of filters that can be listed in the submenu is 20.

You can revert to the default filter by pressing F3.

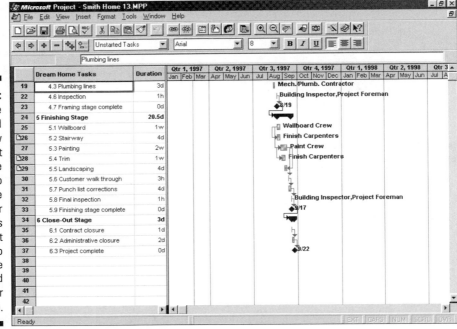

Figure 13-4:
The
highlighted
filter view
uses a font
difference
to
designate
the tasks or
resources
that
conform to
the
selected
filter
criterion.

The Filter list box

The Filter list box serves two purposes. It displays the current filter and it provides a list of all task filters in task views or all resource filters in resource views. To use the Filter list box:

1. **Click the down arrow next to the Filter list box.**

2. **Scroll and select the Unstarted Tasks filter.**

   Two things happen. The highlighted filter disappears and is replaced by an isolated view of the Unstarted Tasks filter.

The Unstarted Tasks view displays all tasks meeting the test of the Actual Start Date equaling NA (not applicable). By comparison, any started or completed task has an Actual Start Date not equaling NA because a date has been entered into the Microsoft Project database field. If you would like to view and compare this field:

1. **Press F3.**

   The filter returns to the All Tasks filter.

2. **Choose View➪Table: Tracking.**

   The view changes to the Tracking table.

3. Drag the vertical separator bar to the right to expose the full Tracking table.

Look at the Act. Date (Actual Start Date) column. Tasks whose Act. Date field is NA are the tasks that appeared when you chose the Unstarted Tasks Filter.

When you are finished with the Tracking table:

1. Choose View➪Table➪Entry.

2. Drag the vertical separator bar back to the left so that it rests on the right edge of the Duration column.

Remember, the Filter list box always displays the current filter. The Filter list box also contains all available task or resource filters as well as any filters you created.

You can't use the Filter list box to access the highlighted filter view.

The More Filters command

The More Filters command is a misleading name. The command displays a dialog box that is like a command central for filters—it provides a number of options for selecting, highlighting, editing, creating, and organizing filters. To access the dialog box:

1. Choose Tools➪Filtered for: All Tasks.

The Filtered For submenu appears.

2. Choose More Filters.

The More Filters dialog box appears (Figure 13-5).

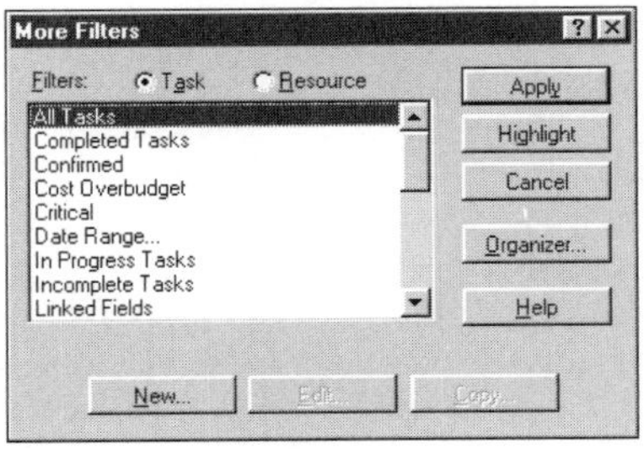

Figure 13-5:
The More
Filters
dialog box.

More Filters	? X
Filters: ⊙ Task ○ Resource	Apply
All Tasks	Highlight
Completed Tasks	
Confirmed	Cancel
Cost Overbudget	
Critical	Organizer...
Date Range...	
In Progress Tasks	
Incomplete Tasks	Help
Linked Fields	
New... Edit... Copy...	

Using the More Filters dialog box, you can perform many functions. (These are described later in this chapter.) In addition to these creative opportunities, you can select either an isolated filter view or a highlighted filter view.

To select the isolated filter view, choose a filter and then click the Apply button. To select a hightlighted filter view:

1. **Select the In Progress Tasks filter.**

2. **Click the Highlight button.**

   The In Progress Tasks filter identifies the tasks that meet this criterion.

Customizing the highlighted display

Sometimes fixing up your project view is necessary or simply more enjoyable. The default text style for the highlighted filter is normal blue text.

For easier reading, change the text style of the highlighted filter:

1. **Choose Format⇨Text Styles.**

2. **In the Item to Change list box, select Highlighted Tasks.**

3. **Select the Underline option.**

4. **In the Font Style list box, select Bold Italic.**

5. **In the Color text box, choose Red.**

   The Text Styles dialog box should look like Figure 13-6.

6. **Click OK.**

   The highlighted filter view displays the modified highlighted text (see Figure 13-7).

Figure 13-6:
Use this dialog box to modify the default settings for all text categories on the Gantt chart.

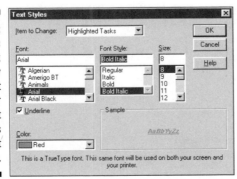

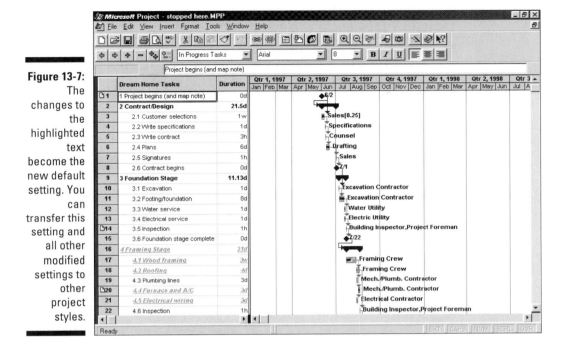

Figure 13-7:
The changes to the highlighted text become the new default setting. You can transfer this setting and all other modified settings to other project styles.

Types of filters

The two major classifications of standard filters in Microsoft Project are task filters and resource filters. The task filters are accessible in all task views except the PERT Chart view. The resource filters are accessible in all resource views. Tables 13-1 and 13-2 describe the filters available in each type.

In split views, filters work only for the upper view. And filters always apply to an entire project file. If you select a filter and then select a second filter, the second filter reviews the entire file, not just the product of the first filter.

Table 13-1	Types of Task Filters
Task Filter	**Description**
All Tasks	Shows all the tasks. The default filter.
Completed Tasks	Shows all tasks that are completely finished.
Confirmed	Shows tasks that have been agreed upon by requested resources.
Cost Overbudget	Shows all tasks that have a cost greater than their baseline amount.

(continued)

Table 13-1 *(continued)*

Task Filter	Description
Critical	Shows all critical tasks.
Date Range	Shows all tasks between the two dates you specify. This is an interactive filter.
In-Progress Tasks	Shows all tasks that have started but haven't finished.
Incomplete Tasks	Shows all tasks that aren't finished (including those that haven't started).
Linked Fields	Shows all tasks with text linked to other applications.
Milestones	Shows all milestones.
Resource Group	Shows all tasks associated with resources belonging to the group you specify. This is an interactive filter.
Should Start By	Shows all the tasks that should have started by the date you specify, but haven't started. This is an interactive filter.
Slipping Tasks	Shows all the tasks that aren't finished and are behind schedule.
Summary Tasks	Shows all the tasks that have subordinate tasks.
Task Range	Displays all tasks within a range of task IDs that you specify. This is an interactive filter.
Tasks with Attachments	Shows all the tasks that have objects or notes in the note box.
Tasks with Fixed Dates	Shows all tasks that have any constraint other than As Soon As Possible and tasks that have already started.
Top Level Tasks	Displays the uppermost-level summary tasks. This filter is for projects with summary tasks within summary tasks.
Unconfirmed	Shows tasks that have requested but unconfirmed commitment.
Unstarted Tasks	Shows the tasks that haven't started yet.
Update Needed	Shows tasks that have experienced change and need to be sent for update or confirmation.
Using Resource	Shows all the tasks that use the resource you specify. This is an interactive filter.
Work Overbudget	Shows all tasks with scheduled work greater than their baseline work.

Table 13-2	Types of Resource Filters
Resource Filter	*Description*
All Resources	Shows all resources in your project file.
Cost Overbudget	Shows all resources with scheduled cost greater than the baseline cost.
Group	Shows you the resources associated with the group you specify. This is an interactive filter.
Linked Fields	Shows all resources with text linked to other applications.
Overallocated Resources	Shows all overallocated resources.
Resource Range	Shows you the resources within the range of ID numbers that you specify. This is an interactive filter.
Resources with Attachments	Shows the resources that have objects attached or notes in the note box.
Work Overbudget	Shows all resources with scheduled work that's greater than the baseline work.

Using interactive filters

An *interactive filter* is one that asks you a question or questions and then goes hunting for the information you want. You can tell many of the interactive filters in the filter list boxes by the ellipsis marks following a filter name, such as Should Start by. . . .

Using the Smith Home example, find all the tasks whose resource is the Framing Crew. Then you use the highlighted filter option to display those tasks among all the others. To do this:

1. **Press and hold down the Shift key.**

   You should continue holding down the Shift key until the last step.

2. **Choose Tools⇨Filtered for: In-Progress Tasks.**

3. **Choose Using Resources.**

   The interactive question box appears.

4. **Use the down arrow to scroll to the Framing Crew resource.**

5. **Select Framing Crew.**

6. **Click OK and release the Shift key.**

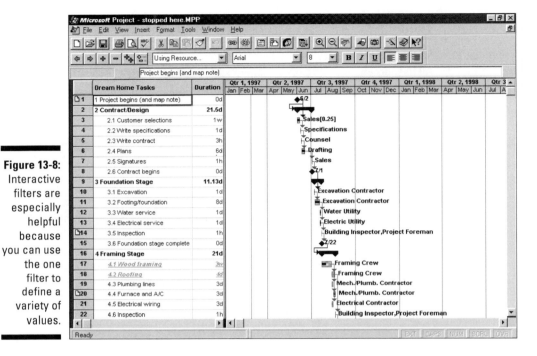

Figure 13-8:
Interactive
filters are
especially
helpful
because
you can use
the one
filter to
define a
variety of
values.

The Using Resource filter displays in the highlighted option. The filtered tasks display in the new default text style. In addition, the filter box on the Formatting toolbar displays the Using Resource selection (Figure 13-8).

Creating Your Own Filters

So you've given Microsoft Project the benefit of the doubt. You've checked out all the task and resource filters, but none of them scratches the precise itch you have for details about your project. You're not a vanilla kind of project manager. You want some flavor and characteristics in your work. No problem — create your own filter.

Just follow a few rules, and Microsoft Project will help you make your project as up front and personal as you want. The neat thing is that you don't have to tell anybody it's easy. Go ahead, impress the "gazingies" out of your stakeholders!

Creating a filter by editing an existing one

The easiest way to create a new filter is by editing an existing one — most of the work has already been accomplished. A slight change to an existing filter can make it work differently and look unique.

Using the Smith Home example, you can edit an existing filter to create a new one that shows a map to the Smith property. To do this:

1. **Choose Tools⇨Filtered for: Using Resource.**

   The Filtered For submenu appears.

2. **Choose More Filters.**

   The More Filters dialog box appears.

3. **Select Task Range, and then click the Copy button.**

   The Filter Definition dialog box appears (Figure 13-9). Copy of Task Range is a temporary name for the copy of the Task Range filter. All the changes you make will be to the copy; the original filter remains intact.

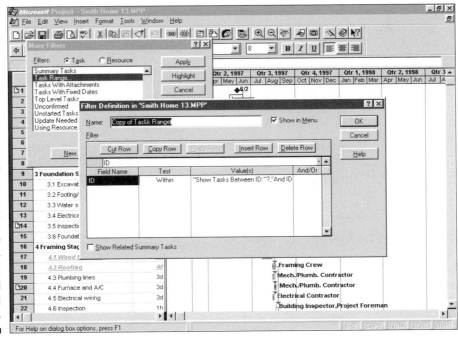

Figure 13-9:
This dialog box provides a number of options for customizing and applying filters.

4. **In the Name box, type** Smith Property.

The Field Name is already ID, so leave it alone.

5. **In the Test column, select Within.**

A small down arrow appears next to the text box.

6. **Click the small down arrow.**

The Test list box appears. (See Figure 13-10.)

Figure 13-10:
The Test list box contains 11 choices that make up the basis for choosing filter criteria.

7. **Select Equals.**

8. **In the Values column, select "Show Tasks Between ID:"?,"And ID:"?**

9. **Drag across the text box, and then press the Delete key.**

10. **Type** 37 **in the text box.**

Notice that the Show in Menu check box is selected. By leaving this box checked, your new filter will appear in the Filtered For submenu.

11. **Click OK.**

Your new filter Smith Property appears in the More Filters dialog box (Figure 13-11).

12. **Click the Apply button.**

The Smith Project map appears. The map is a graphic object associated with task 37. In Chapter 9, I describe how you can paste a graphic image in your Gantt chart.

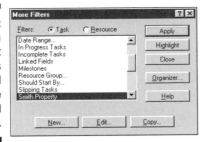

Figure 13-11:
Your Smith
Project
filter is
added to all
the
standard
filters.

13. Scroll down to expose the entire map (Figure 13-12).

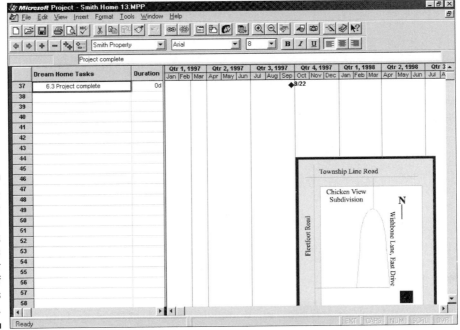

Figure 13-12:
The filter
displays the
sole task
that meets
the filter
criterion of
all task IDs
equaling 37.

Creating a filter from scratch

You create a new filter the same way you edit one, except you choose New rather Edit in the More Filters dialog box. Using the Smith Home example, create a filter that lists all tasks that have the Building Inspector resource. To do this

1. **Press F3 to return to the All Tasks filter.**

   This step isn't really necessary; it simply cleans the slate back to the default setting.

2. **Choose Tools⇨Filtered for: All Tasks.**

   The Filtered For submenu appears.

3. **Choose More Filters.**

   The More Filters dialog box appears.

4. **Click the New Button.**

   The Filter Definition dialog box appears (Figure 13-13).

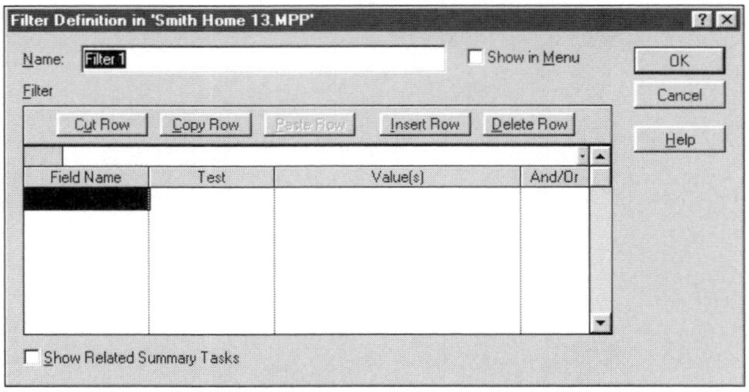

Figure 13-13:
When you use the Filter Definition dialog box to create a filter from scratch, all the columns are empty.

You use the Filter Definition dialog box to set the criteria for selecting tasks or resources. After you create your filter, you'll be able to use it for both isolated and highlighted views. To create the Building Inspector filter:

1. **In the Name text box, type** Building Inspector Schedule.

   This becomes the filter's name.

2. **Select the Show in Menu option.**

   This way, your new filter will appear in the Filtered For submenu.

3. **Select the Field Name text box.**

   A down arrow appears to the right of the text edit box.

4. **Click the down arrow.**

5. **Scroll to select Resource Names.**

   You could have simply typed the field name, but this way you ensure that the name is accurate.

6. **Select the Test text box.**

7. **Click the down arrow to the right of the text edit box.**

8. **Scroll to select Contains.**

   The Contains test displays or highlights tasks and resources that contain a value. The value is the next thing to set.

9. **Select the Value(s) text box.**

10. **Click the text edit box.**

    You know it's active when a red *x* and a green ☑ appear to the left of the box.

11. **Type** Building Inspector **in the text edit box.**

12. **Click the green arrow to accept the text.**

13. **Check your work; it should look like Figure 13-14.**

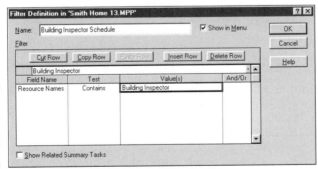

Figure 13-14:
Does your
work look
like this?

14. **After you are satisfied, click OK.**

    The More Filters dialog box contains your nifty new filter.

15. **Click the Highlight button.**

    All the tasks that meet the criteria of your new filter are highlighted.

Multiple criteria

One of the most muscular tools of Microsoft Project is a multiple criteria filter. A multiple criteria filter uses And conditions and Or conditions. For example, an And condition might be all the tasks that begin after June 15 and involve the project foreman. Two conditions are involved in this example. Condition one is all tasks beginning after June 15. Condition two is all tasks that involve the project foreman. The filter searches for all tasks that meet both conditions.

In the following, you look at an existing filter to see how multiple criteria works:

1. **Choose Tools⇨Filtered for: Building Inspector Schedule.**

   The Filtered For submenu appears.

2. **Choose More Filters.**

   The More Filters dialog box appears.

3. **Select In Progress Tasks.**

4. **Click the Edit button.**

   The Filter Definition dialog box appears (Figure 13-15).

The Filter Definition dialog box shows two rows of conditions. The first row looks for tasks whose Actual Start field doesn't equal NA. This means it looks for all tasks that have a date entered in the Actual Start field. The row ends with the And condition. The second row looks for tasks that have an Actual Finish date equaling NA, which means completion has not occurred. Together, the two conditions equal a filter that displays or highlights tasks in progress.

After you've finished kicking the tires on the In Progress Tasks filter, click the Cancel button.

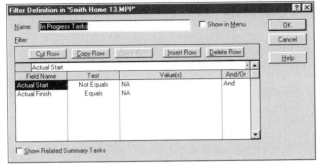

Figure 13-15:
Each task
has many
fields
whose
contents
are NA.
These fields
await
actions.

Sorting Your Project

Sorting tasks and resources is another way to control the display of project information. Sorting, unlike filtering, doesn't isolate or single out information. Instead, it changes the order of tasks in a descending or ascending manner based on the criteria of a particular field or fields. Is that confusing enough? Actually, it's not that bad.

By default, Microsoft assigns ascending ID numbers to tasks as you enter them into a project file. Task ID 1 is 1 simply because you entered it first. The same is true for task ID 2, 3, and so on. By using the sort option, you can use other criteria for ordering tasks.

This Sort feature works with whatever is in the active display. If you've already applied a filter to a project, the Sort feature will work with the tasks or resources that resulted from the filter criteria.

Before you resort to sorting, be sure that you know whether or not you want to maintain the original task ID relationships. The dialog box offers you the option of permanently renumbering tasks. If you choose to let the sort renumber tasks, it can do some strange and not-so-wonderful things to your task relationships. (In fact, allowing tasks to be renumbered might have been the inspiration for the invention of spaghetti.)

Types of sorting

In this section, using the Smith Home 13.MPP example, you play with the ways Microsoft Project can sort your information. You practice sorting by name and duration.

First, you can see the information in another way. So change to the Task Sheet view by choosing View⇨More Views. Scroll and select the Task Sheet view. Click the Apply button.

Now, to use the Sort command:

1. **Choose Tools⇨Sort.**

   The Sort submenu appears.

2. **Choose Sort By.**

   The Sort dialog box appears (Figure 13-16).

Figure 13-16:
The Sort dialog box lets you order tasks or resources based on as many as three fields.

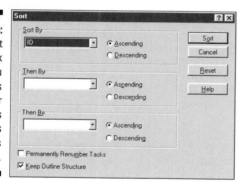

3. **Click the down arrow next to the Sort By text box.**

   The Sort By list box appears.

4. **Highlight Name.**

5. **Make sure that the Permanently Renumber Tasks check box is unchecked.**

6. **Click the Sort button.**

   The project is sorted to show all names in alphabetical order while maintaining summary task and subtask relationships (Figure 13-17).

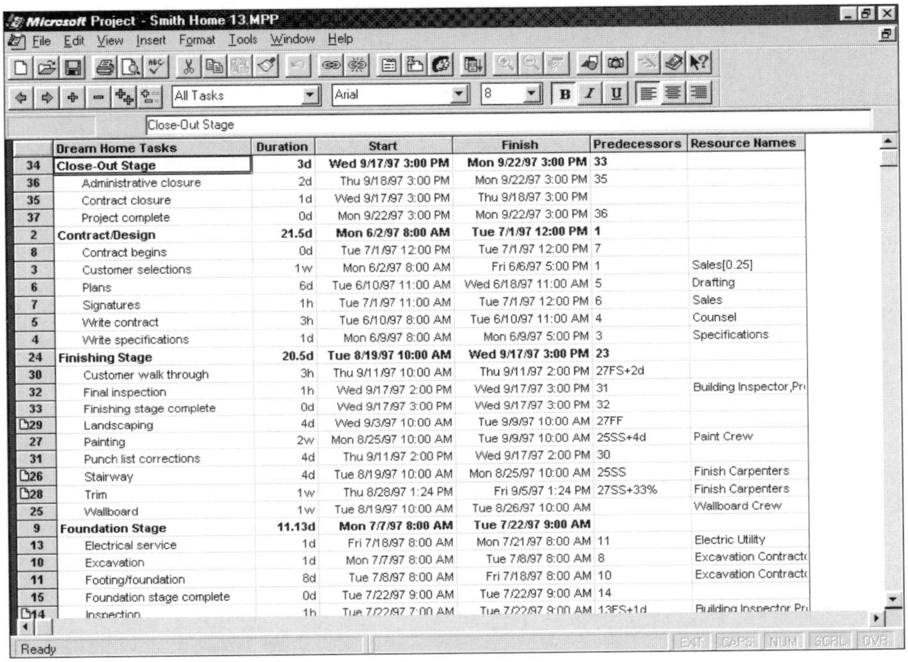

Figure 13-17:
The Sort command ordered the names in ascending order.

At the bottom of the Sort dialog box are two check boxes. The first is unchecked by default. The second is checked by default. With these defaults, Microsoft Project will not reassign ID numbers to tasks when you sort them. And all sorts will keep subtasks within their summary tasks.

Press Shift+F3 to return to the default ascending ID order. This time, order all the tasks by their duration, from longest to shortest, without keeping the outline structure. To do so:

1. **Choose Tools⇨Sort.**

   The Sort submenu appears.

2. **Choose Sort By.**

   The Sort dialog box appears.

3. **In the Sort By list box, select Duration.**

4. **Select Descending next to the Sort By text box.**

5. **Uncheck the Keep Outline Structure check box.**

6. **Click the Sort button.**

   The display should look like Figure 13-18.

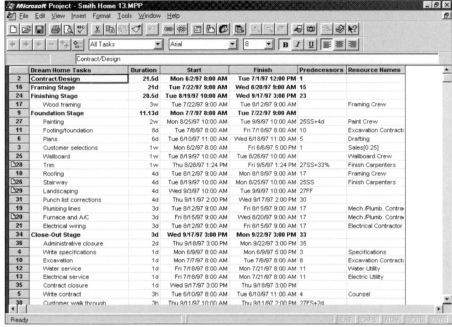

Figure 13-18: The Sort command sets all tasks in a descending duration order. The subtasks are freed from their summary tasks in this sort.

When you've finished reviewing the sort, press Shift+F3 to restore the default sort order.

Sorting with multiple fields

The Sort command lets you order materials by multiple criteria. An example of a multiple field sort is to order groceries by category and then by price. The first criterion is to order by category in ascending alphabetical order, such as fruit, produce, vegetable, and so on. The second is to order the items in each category by cost in descending order, such as bananas at 49 cents a pound, oranges at 39 cents a pound, and apples at 28 cents a pound. (You can tell how often I buy the groceries in my family!)

Using the Smith Home example, sort all the resource groups alphabetically in ascending order and sort all the individual resources by their standard rates in descending order. First, you need to change to the Resource Sheet view, so choose View⇨Resource Sheet.

To sort the resources:

1. Choose Tools⇨Sort.

The Sort submenu appears.

2. **Choose <u>S</u>ort By.**

   The Sort dialog box appears.

3. **In the Sort By text box, select Group.**

   Use the default Ascending order.

4. **In the Then by text box, select Standard Rate.**

5. **Select Descending next to the Then By text box.**

6. **Make sure that the Permanently Renumber Resources check box is unchecked.**

7. **Click the Sort button.**

   The sort should look like Figure 13-19.

Filtering and sorting are two of the most powerful tools that Microsoft Project has to offer you for mastering and controlling your project information. You touch on each of the basics — using standard filters, isolating and highlighting filters, editing filters, creating new ones, sorting, and multiple sorting—in this chapter.

Figure 13-19: The Sort command has ordered the resource groups in ascending alphabetical order. The resources within each group are ordered by standard rate in descending order.

	Resource Name	Initials	Group	Max. Units	Std. Rate	Ovt. Rate	Cost/Use	Accrue At	Base Calendar	Cod
1	Excavation Contractor	EX	Contractor	1	$0.00/h	$0.00/h	$0.00	Prorated	Construction Hours Calendar	
2	Mech./Plumb. Contractor	ME	Contractor	1	$0.00/h	$0.00/h	$0.00	Prorated	Construction Hours Calendar	
3	Electrical Contractor	EC	Contractor	1	$0.00/h	$0.00/h	$0.00	Prorated	Construction Hours Calendar	
4	Building Inspector	BU	Government	1	$0.00/h	$0.00/h	$100.00	Prorated	Standard	
7	Paint Crew	PA	Hourly Labo	1	$20.00/h	$30.00/h	$0.00	Prorated	Construction Hours Calendar	
8	Finish Carpenters	FI	Hourly Labo	1	$20.00/h	$30.00/h	$0.00	Prorated	Construction Hours Calendar	
5	Framing Crew	FC	Hourly Labo	16	$10.00/h	$15.00/h	$0.00	Prorated	Construction Hours Calendar	
6	Wallboard Crew	WA	Hourly Labo	1	$10.00/h	$15.00/h	$0.00	Prorated	Construction Hours Calendar	
13	Project Manager	PM	Office Staff	1	$40.00/h	$0.00/h	$0.00	Prorated	Standard	
11	Specifications	SP	Office Staff	1	$30.00/h	$45.00/h	$0.00	Prorated	Standard	
12	Project Foreman	PF	Office Staff	1	$30.00/h	$0.00/h	$0.00	Prorated	Construction Hours Calendar	
9	Sales	SL	Office Staff	1	$20.00/h	$30.00/h	$0.00	Prorated	Standard	
10	Drafting	DR	Office Staff	1	$20.00/h	$0.00/h	$0.00	Prorated	Standard	
14	Counsel	CO	Special	1	$75.00/h	$0.00/h	$0.00	Prorated	Standard	
15	Water Utility	WA	Utility	1	$0.00/h	$0.00/h	$0.00	Prorated	Construction Hours Calendar	
16	Electric Utility	EL	Utility	1	$0.00/h	$0.00/h	$0.00	Prorated	Construction Hours Calendar	

Part IV

Making Project 4.1 Work for You

In this part . . .

Now you focus on the endgame of the project plan, the final moments before project commencement. This involves a review of the original project scope and goals and a comparison of those early expectations with the current status. In this part, you learn to optimize your project plan, resolve cost and work overallocations, and level resource conflicts. You find out how to identify the critical path and how to crash the project's schedule.

This is where the fruit of all your efforts begins to show.

Chapter 14

Multiple Projects

· ·

· ·

So you're not a single-project kind of manager. You have a few balls in the air. It seems like there are more things to do than there are resources or time to do them. And worse yet, you're not really sure whether problems are lurking or whether everything is actually okay. Simplification sounds very attractive.

Microsoft Project can't make the world slow down, but it can reduce the chances of resource and time collisions. One way it does this is through the management of multiple projects. You are about to see some relatively simple ways to hold the reins on projects that would otherwise pull your attention and resources in conflicting directions.

If you haven't copied the files from the sample disk to your hard drive, you might want to do so before proceeding with this chapter. See Appendix C for instructions.

You work with multiple projects in the chapter, so you need to start by — you guessed it — opening a few project files. To do so:

1. **Click the Open button on the Standard toolbar.**

   The File Open dialog box displays the contents of the Winproj folder.

2. **Open the Practice Files folder.**

3. **Double-click Smith Home 14.MPP.**

   The file opens in the Gantt Chart view.

4. **Double-click Clark Home 14.MPP, and then double-click Office Remodel 14.MPP.**

   These project files open in the Gantt Chart view, too.

Using Multiple Open Project Files

Microsoft Project uses standard Windows conventions for displaying files. These simple standard Windows methods are the best way to begin using multiple projects.

Choose Window, and the Window menu appears (Figure 14-1). The menu lists four window choices. (Unhide appears dimmed because it is unavailable. It becomes available only after Hide is activated.) Next, the menu lists Split, which is the default combination view option.

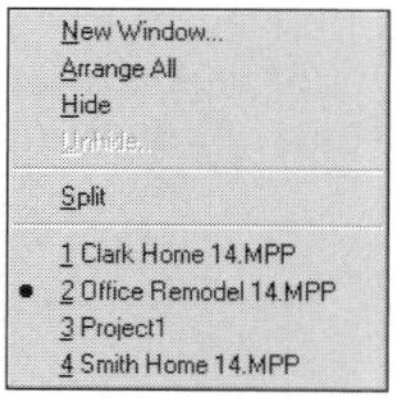

Figure 14-1:
The Window menu activates display relationships of open files.

Following these options is a list of the currently open project files. You can load as many project files as you want but only nine appear in this menu. The rest are accessible by a More command that becomes visible after you open the tenth file.

Hiding and unhiding

Hiding a file is not the same as closing it. By hiding a file, you remove its name from the Window menu, even though the file remains open. As an example, hide the Project1 window as follows:

1. **If you don't have an opened Project1 window, click the New button on the Standard toolbar.**

2. **Choose <u>W</u>indow⇨Project1.**

   The active window becomes Project1 in full expanded view.

3. **Choose <u>W</u>indow⇨<u>H</u>ide.**

   Project1 disappears.

4. **Choose <u>W</u>indow.**

   Project1 has disappeared from the menu and the Unhide option has become active. Exciting, huh?

5. **Choose <u>U</u>nhide.**

   The Unhide dialog box appears (Figure 14-2). This is where you can play magic and make the hidden file reappear. For our purposes, leave Project1 hidden. (By the way, you and I both know that you could have simply closed the Project1 file without saving it. But humor me for the sake of this example.)

Figure 14-2:
The Unhide
dialog box
holds
oodles of
files.

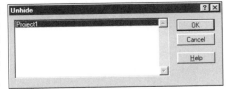

6. **Click the Cancel button.**

   This closes the Unhide dialog box.

Arranging all files

Once in a while, it's useful to simultaneously compare and edit information in a group of files. To do that, you need to put all the unhidden files on the screen at one time. Using the currently unhidden files

1. **Choose <u>W</u>indow⇨<u>A</u>rrange All.**

   A three-screen display appears (Figure 14-3).

2. **Alternately click in each of the three windows.**

   Each window becomes active as you click in it.

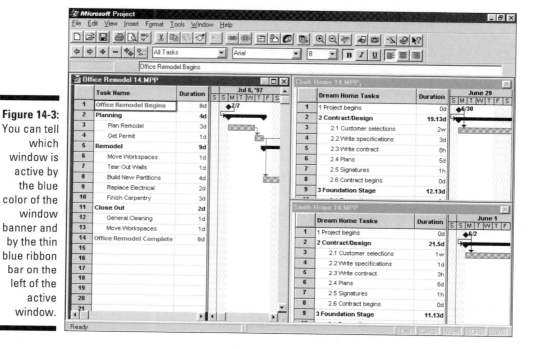

Figure 14-3:
You can tell
which
window is
active by
the blue
color of the
window
banner and
by the thin
blue ribbon
bar on the
left of the
active
window.

One example of information you can assess from this multiple window display is the start date for all three projects.

There's a limit to how many project files can be displayed at one time. The resolution of the windows doesn't change, so each window is only a portion of the full-screen display.

To replace the Arrange All display with a single project display, you use the Maximize button in the active window. For example, click in the Office Remodel window to make it active, and then click its Maximize button. The Office Remodel project is now full screen.

Instead of using the Window menu to flip through the full-screen display of unhidden project files, press Ctrl+F6. Each time you do, the screen displays the next project file (as listed in the Window menu).

Building a new window without pane, er, pain

Another nifty standard window feature is the New Window option. With it, you can create multiple views of the same project. In addition to acting as a shortcut to various views, this gives you the opportunity to customize combination views.

To illustrate the new window option, it would be helpful to hide two of the currently unhidden project files:

1. **Press Ctrl+F6 to display the Smith Home 14.MPP project file.**

2. **Choose Window⇨Hide.**

3. **Repeat Steps 1 and 2 to hide Clark Home 14.MPP.**

    The Office Remodel.MPP project file is the active display.

With all but one of the open project files hidden, use the New Window option to create a combination view of the Office Remodel project. To do this:

1. **Choose Window⇨New Window.**

    The New Window dialog box appears (Figure 14-4).

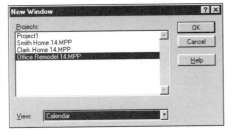

2. **In the View list box, select Calendar.**

    This tells Microsoft Project that you want a new window that displays the Calendar view of the Office Remodel project. Because the Gantt Chart view of the Office Remodel project is already loaded, you'll have two active displays of the same project. What a country!

3. Click OK.

The Calendar view of the Office Remodel project appears (Figure 14-5).

Now that you have two displays of the same project, and because all other open project files are currently hidden, you can create that special combination view you've always wanted! Well, at least you've wanted it for the last three minutes. Simply choose Window⇨Arrange All, and the combination view appears (Figure 14-6). The blue bar on the far left of the screen indicates which window is active. Press Ctrl+F6 to activate the other window.

Creating a workspace

You can create and save a file that remembers all the files you have opened. This can be helpful for picking up where you left off the day before or for guiding others to sets of information that you've grouped for some ingenious purpose.

Create a workspace file of the project files you currently have open. Before you do, though, unhide the Smith Home 14.MPP and Clark Home 14.MPP projects. Choose Window⇨Unhide to unhide Smith Home 14.MPP. Repeat the same steps to unhide Clark Home 14.MPP.

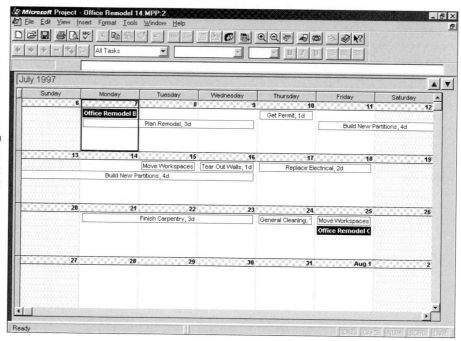

Figure 14-5:
Notice that the project name ends with 2, indicating that this is the project's second window display.

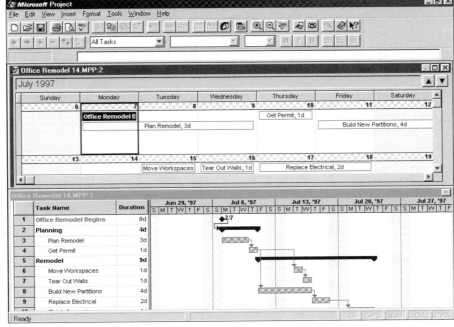

Figure 14-6:
The combination view uses the standard convention that allows one window to be active at a time.

Now you're ready to create the workspace. To do this:

1. **Choose File➪Save Workspace.**

   You're asked whether you want to save the changes to Office Remodel 14.MPP.

2. **Click Yes.**

3. **If you're asked the same question for either of the other two project files, click Yes for them, too.**

   The Save Workspace as: dialog box appears.

4. **In the File name text box, type** Building Projects.

   See Figure 14-7.

5. **Click the Save button.**

   Microsoft Project saves the workspace with the .MPW extension.

The .MPW file contains only a call to reopen the project files; it doesn't contain the project files themselves. If you make any changes to the project files individually, those changes will appear the next time you open the workspace.

Figure 14-7:
The
Workspace
file will be
stored in
the same
folder as
your project
files unless
you choose
otherwise.

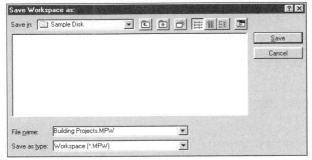

Consolidating Projects

Microsoft Project offers you the opportunity to consolidate individual project files into a single window. This makes it possible for you to manage a number of projects at once, as if they were a single project.

Consolidating a project differs from multiple windows in one big way. In a consolidated project file, you can use all the information from all the projects as if they were a single project. For instance, you can use a filter for the consolidated project that filters all the project files.

For the next example, close Smith Home 14.MPP, Clark Home 14.MPP, and Office Remodel.MPP. Unhide Project1 or click the New button on the Standard toolbar. A project, even an unsaved blank one, must be open to access the Microsoft Project menu options.

Now that the project files are closed, consolidate them as follows:

1. **Choose Tools⇨Multiple Projects.**

   The Multiple Projects submenu appears.

2. **Choose Consolidate Projects.**

   The Consolidate Projects dialog box appears.

3. **Click the Browse button to select Clark Home 14.MPP, Office Remodel 14.MPP, and Smith Home 14.MPP in the Sample Disk folder.**

   To do this, hold down the Ctrl key and select each of the files.

4. **Click the Add Files button.**

   The three files are loaded into the Consolidate Projects dialog box (Figure 14-8).

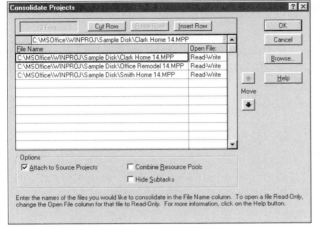

Figure 14-8:
The files
are listed in
the order in
which you
loaded
them.

After the files are loaded, you can change their order. This will directly affect the manner in which they are displayed in the consolidated view. For example, select the Office Remodel file name, and press the Move down arrow until the file name is third.

By default, Microsoft Project allows individual file edits to a consolidated file. Any edits in the consolidated file are automatically reflected in the source file or files. You can use the dialog box to protect the source files by designating them Read Only in the Open File column. In this way, someone can read but can't edit the consolidated files.

If you want, you can make some files Read Only and others Read Write. Be careful though — you can get a really big head masterminding all this consolidation stuff.

By default, Microsoft Project attaches source files to the consolidated file. If you want to edit information in the consolidated file without affecting the source file, clear the Attach to Source Project option.

After you've had a chance to look at the remaining options in the Consolidate Projects dialog box, click OK. The consolidated file loads.

Notice that the first project is identified by its project name, Clark Home 14.MPP. To see the consolidated view more easily:

1. **Click the Goto Selected Task button on the Standard toolbar.**

2. **Click the Zoom Out tool on the Standard toolbar twice to display the full summary tasks of each of the three projects.**

The consolidated file looks like Figure 14-9.

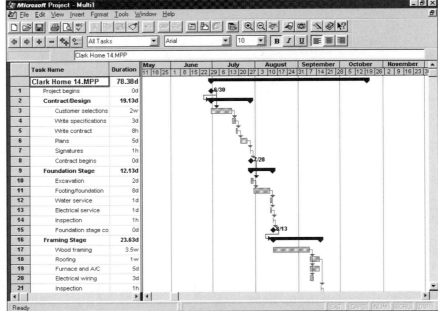

Figure 14-9:
The file displays the projects, even though you haven't loaded the individual source files.

Notice that all the project tasks maintain their ID numbers in their respective tasks. As far as Microsoft Project is concerned, you have each of these three files open and editable (unless you specified otherwise in the Consolidated Projects dialog box).

To save the consolidated project:

1. Click the Save button on the Standard toolbar.

2. If Microsoft Project asks whether you'd like to save the changes to the three projects, click the Yes button.

The File Save dialog box appears.

3. Give your consolidated project a name.

By default, Microsoft Project offers the name Multi1.MPP.

4. Click the Save button.

After you're finished, please close the file but don't turn out the lights.

Using Subprojects in Master Projects

If you were to list every single task in a really big project, the size of the project could become unmanageable. Sometimes creating master projects and subprojects is a good idea.

In a master project, each subproject is listed as a single task. If you open the task, you open the subproject. This way, you can leave the details to those responsible for them. Unopened, you see a start and finish date for the subproject task in the master project. Another advantage of subtasks is that you can use them in any number of projects.

For example, a number of details make up the Wood framing task in the Smith Home project. Assign a framing subproject to this task:

1. **Open Smith Home 14.MPP.**
2. **Scroll to the Wood framing task.**
3. **Double-click the Wood framing task.**

   The Task Information dialog box appears.

4. **Click the Advanced tab.**
5. **Click the Browse button next to the Subproject Filename text box.**

   The Subproject dialog box appears.

6. **In the Sample Disk folder, double-click Smith Framing 14.MPP.**

   The name appears in the Subproject Filename text box (Figure 14-10).

7. **Click OK.**

   The framing subproject is assigned.

To view the subproject, double-click the Wood framing task. The Smith Framing subproject appears (Figure 14-11).

The subproject is assigned to the Framing Task, but no notification of this appears. Attach a note to tasks in which subprojects are assigned. Using the Note button on the Standard toolbar, assign a note to the Wood framing task in Smith Home 14.MPP, explaining that a subproject is attached.

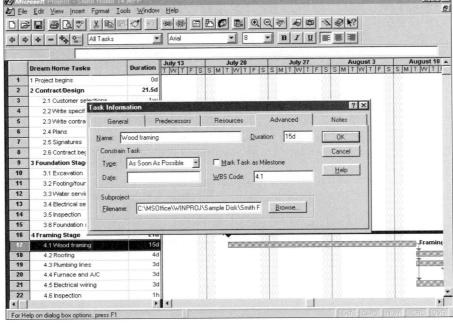

Figure 14-10:
The
filename
with its
entire
directory
structure is
entered
in the
Filename
box.

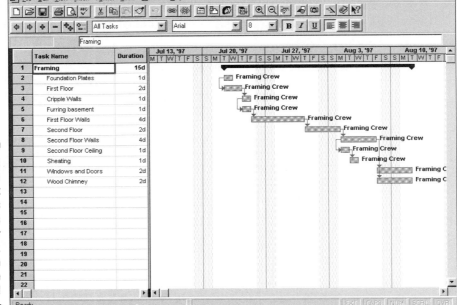

Figure 14-11:
The
subproject
can be as
complex as
any other
project.
And it can
have
subprojects!

Assigning Resources to Multiple Projects

A convenient feature of Microsoft Project is its capability to assign resources from one project to other projects. This allows you to use the same resource pool for a number of projects. If you want, you can keep the projects linked by the shared resources, which makes you less likely to overallocate people and equipment.

Using the Smith Home 14.MPP file, assign resources to another building project. The Smith Home project file is already open, but you need to open a file to which you'll assign resources. To do this:

1. Open Clark Home 14.MPP.

2. To assign resources, choose Tools➪Multiple Projects.

The Multiple Projects submenu appears (Figure 14-12).

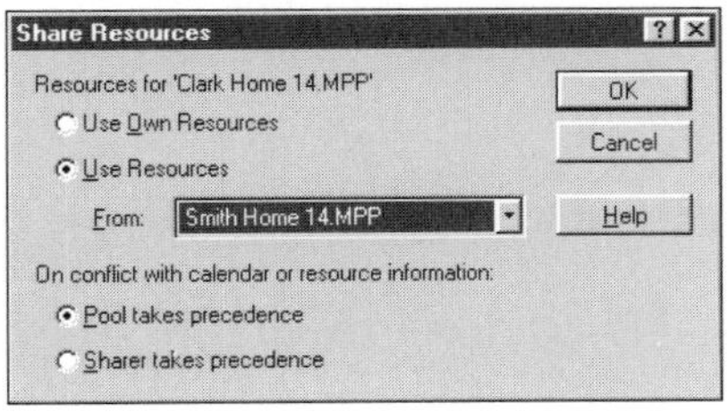

Figure 14-12:
The Share
Resources
dialog box
identifies
the name of
the file
where the
resources
will be
assigned.

3. Select the Use Resources option.

4. Use the down arrow in the text box to select the Smith Home 14.MPP project as the source of the resource pool.

5. Click OK.

Smith Home 14.MPP is now the source of the resource pool.

Now that Clark Home 14.MPP is a resource pool groupie of Smith Home 14.MPP, click the Resource Assignment button on the Standard toolbar. You'll see all your friends' sales and specifications. Project management is a very friendly profession!

Chapter 15

Setting and Viewing Costs

- -

In This Chapter

▶ Finding work and cost discrepancies

▶ Analyzing cost estimate problems

▶ Reducing costs

- -

You've determined the tasks, created the links, set the durations, and assigned the costs to your project. The start date of project tasks is about to occur. In this chapter and the next, you do the final tweaking of your project to prepare for the onset of reality.

If you haven't copied the files from the sample disk to your hard drive, you might want to do so before proceeding with this chapter. See Appendix C for instructions.

In this section, you use the sample project file called Smith Home 15.MPP to make last-minute cost and work improvements to a project before its project start date. To open the sample project file called Smith Home 15.MPP from the Practice Files folder:

1. **Click the Open button on the Standard toolbar.**

2. **Open the Practice Files folder.**

3. **Double-click Smith Home 15.MPP.**

   The file opens in the Gantt Chart view.

Cost and Work

You should check the pulse of your project occasionally, even before it's born. One of the quickest ways to get an overall summary view of the project is by viewing project statistics. To do so:

1. **Right-click anywhere on the toolbar.**

   The toolbar menu appears.

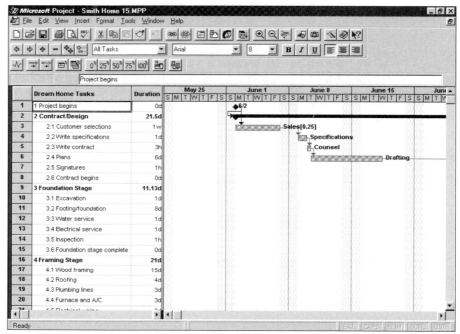

Figure 15-1:
The
Tracking
toolbar is
one of nine
available
toolbars.

2. Select the Tracking toolbar.

The Tracking toolbar appears (Figure 15-1).

3. Click the Statistics button.

The Project Statistics dialog box appears (Figure 15-2).

Another way to access this dialog box is by choosing File⇨Project Info⇨Statistics.

Figure 15-2:
Check out
the Project
Statistics
dialog box
to see
statistics
about your
project.

Project Statistics for 'Smith Home 15.MPP'

	Start	Finish
Current	Mon 6/2/97 8:00 AM	Mon 9/22/97 3:00 PM
Baseline	Mon 6/2/97 8:00 AM	Mon 9/22/97 3:00 PM
Actual	NA	NA
Variance	0d	0d

	Duration	Work	Cost
Current	78.75d	1908h	$59,175.00
Baseline	78.75d	1708h	$56,375.00
Actual	0d	0h	$0.00
Remaining	78.75d	1908h	$59,175.00

Percent Complete:

Duration: 0%   Work: 0%

Close   Help

The Project Statistics dialog box shows statistics about your project, such as the start date, the finish date, and the cost. The area in the lower left marked Percent Complete indicates that none of the project's duration has been used and none of its work has been performed. The middle section shows that the project's baseline duration was set at 78.75 days. Since the setting of the baseline, the latest estimated duration remains the same.

The Work and Cost columns are another story. The baseline estimate of work was 1708 hours. The estimate has escalated to 1908 hours. The baseline cost was $56,375.00 and the latest estimate is $59,175.00. This tells you that the project plan is overbudget. You need to find out which tasks are the culprits, and modify them if possible.

After you've finished checking out the Project Statistics dialog box, click the Close button. Then close the Tracking toolbar by right-clicking anywhere in it and choosing the Tracking toolbar again from the menu that appears.

View detailed work and cost estimates

Finding the overages of work and costs is probably easiest in the Task Sheet view. Switch to that view now:

1. **Choose View➪More Views.**

   The More Views dialog box appears.

2. **In the list box, select the Task Sheet view.**

3. **Choose View➪Table: Entry.**

   The Table submenu appears.

4. **Choose Work.**

   The Work Table Sheet view appears. Scroll down to fully display the Framing Stage and the Finishing Stage and their subtasks. (Figure 15-3).

To simplify the work of viewing the Work view, use a filter. To highlight overbudget tasks, choose Tools➪Filter for: All Tasks➪More Filters; select the Work Overbudget filter, and then select Highlight. Or in the Filter list box on the Formatting toolbar, select the Work Overbudget filter. Now, two tasks and their summary tasks remain (Figure 15-4).

The Wood framing task estimate has 120 hours more labor than was originally predicted. The Painting task estimate has 80 hours more labor.

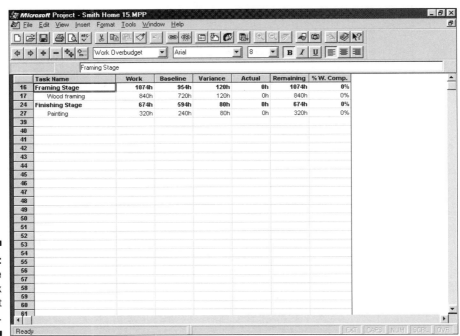

Figure 15-3:
The Work
table lists
all the tasks
and the
work
assigned to
them, the
work
performed
and the
work
remaining,
plus
calculations
of the
percentage
of work
completed.

Task Name	Work	Baseline	Variance	Actual	Remaining	% W. Comp.
9 **Foundation Stage**	**90h**	**90h**	**0h**	**0h**	**90h**	**0%**
10 Excavation	8h	8h	0h	0h	8h	0%
11 Footing/foundation	64h	64h	0h	0h	64h	0%
12 Water service	8h	8h	0h	0h	8h	0%
13 Electrical service	8h	8h	0h	0h	8h	0%
14 Inspection	2h	2h	0h	0h	2h	0%
15 Foundation stage comple	0h	0h	0h	0h	0h	0%
16 **Framing Stage**	**1074h**	**954h**	**120h**	**0h**	**1074h**	**0%**
17 Wood framing	840h	720h	120h	0h	840h	0%
18 Roofing	160h	160h	0h	0h	160h	0%
19 Plumbing lines	24h	24h	0h	0h	24h	0%
20 Furnace and A/C	24h	24h	0h	0h	24h	0%
21 Electrical wiring	24h	24h	0h	0h	24h	0%
22 Inspection	2h	2h	0h	0h	2h	0%
23 Framing stage complete	0h	0h	0h	0h	0h	0%
24 **Finishing Stage**	**674h**	**594h**	**80h**	**0h**	**674h**	**0%**
25 Wallboard	200h	200h	0h	0h	200h	0%
26 Stairway	32h	32h	0h	0h	32h	0%
27 Painting	320h	240h	80h	0h	320h	0%
28 Trim	120h	120h	0h	0h	120h	0%
29 Landscaping	0h	0h	0h	0h	0h	0%
30 Customer walk through	0h	0h	0h	0h	0h	0%
31 Punch list corrections	0h	0h	0h	0h	0h	0%
32 Final inspection	2h	2h	0h	0h	2h	0%
33 Finishing stage complete	0h	0h	0h	0h	0h	0%
34 **Close-Out Stage**	**0h**	**0h**	**0h**	**0h**	**0h**	**0%**
35 Contract closure	0h	0h	0h	0h	0h	0%

Figure 15-4:
Use the
Work
Overbudget
filter.

Task Name	Work	Baseline	Variance	Actual	Remaining	% W. Comp.
16 **Framing Stage**	**1074h**	**954h**	**120h**	**0h**	**1074h**	**0%**
17 Wood framing	840h	720h	120h	0h	840h	0%
24 **Finishing Stage**	**674h**	**594h**	**80h**	**0h**	**674h**	**0%**
27 Painting	320h	240h	80h	0h	320h	0%

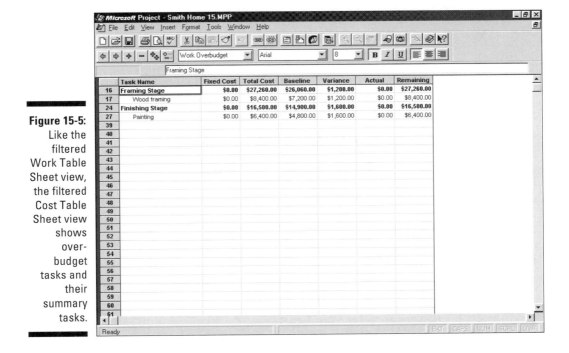

Figure 15-5:
Like the
filtered
Work Table
Sheet view,
the filtered
Cost Table
Sheet view
shows
over-
budget
tasks and
their
summary
tasks.

While in the Work Overbudget filter, change to the Cost Table Sheet view. Choose View⇨Table⇨Cost. The filtered Cost table appears (Figure 15-5).

The Wood framing task is estimated to cost $1,200.00 more than was set as the baseline. The Painting task is estimated to cost $1,600.00 more than its baseline.

You've found the problems. Now it's time to attempt a fix. If you want, press F3 to return to the All Tasks filter.

Reducing Costs

Change to the Gantt view. Using Microsoft Project, you can resolve cost discrepancies any number of ways. In this section, I show you one way. Use the Task form in a split view to make the correction:

1. In the Gantt view, choose Window⇨Split.

The Split view appears.

2. **Choose <u>V</u>iew⇨Table: Entry.**

   The Table submenu appears.

3. **Choose <u>C</u>ost.**

   The Cost table replaces the Entry table in the upper window.

4. **Drag the vertical separator bar to expose the Cost table so that it includes Variance.**

5. **Scroll and select the Wood framing task.**

6. **Click the Goto Selected Task button on the Standard toolbar.**

7. **If necessary, click the Zoom Out button on the Standard toolbar to show the entire Wood framing task's Gantt bar.**

   The screen should look like Figure 15-6.

To reduce the Wood framing task's cost, change the makeup of resources as follows:

1. **In the lower-left pane, select the units associated with the Framing Crew resource.**

2. **Change the units from 7 to 4.**

3. **In the Work column, replace 840h with 480h.**

4. **To add a resource, select the space below the Framing Crew resource.**

5. **In the text editing box on the Formatting toolbar, click the down arrow.**

6. **Scroll and select Day Labor. Click the green ☑check to accept your choice.**

7. **In the lower-left pane, type** 3 **in the Units column for Day Labor.**

8. **In the Work column for Day Labor, type** 360h.

9. **In the lower pane Task Detail form, click OK.**

   The screen should look like Figure 15-7.

The changes appear in the Cost table. The added resources are registered next to the Gantt bar. (If necessary, scroll the Gantt chart horizontally to expose the resource names.)

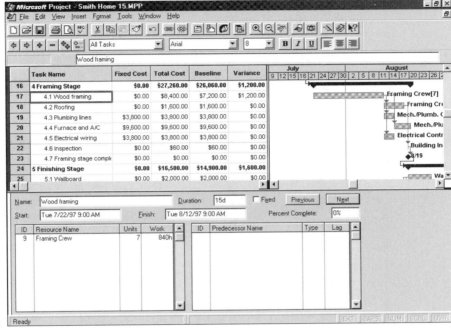

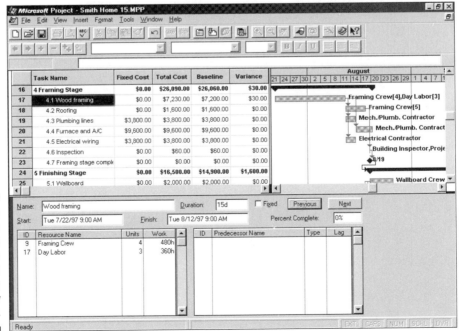

For some more practice, try correcting the Painting task yourself by assigning 2 units at 160h for the Paint Crew and 3 units at 240h for Day Labor. The result should look like Figure 15-8.

You can reduce costs in more ways than I've mentioned here. For example, another way to reduce costs is to reschedule work. By changing the work calendar, you avoid paying overtime. I discuss rescheduling work in Chapter 16.

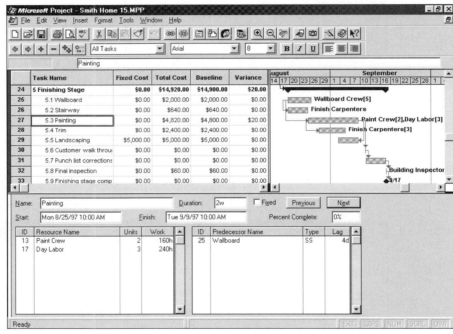

Figure 15-8:
The
Variance
for the
Painting
task is now
$20.00.

Chapter 16

Optimizing Your Plan

In This Chapter

▶ Correcting scheduling errors

▶ Finding overused resources

▶ Crashing the critical path

▶ Reconciling overallocations

O ne of the more fascinating stages of project management is the period of time just before the project start date. You have all the pieces fashioned in relative order. Some things are just as you had expected, others are slightly different, and some are out in left field.

In these predawn hours before your project meets the light of day, you have the opportunity to walk around it and look up close and from a few steps back to marvel at its strengths and to search for its potential weaknesses. And you have a final chance to make improvements that might make all the difference between success and something less than success.

Don't be too bothered if everything isn't trim and perfect. By the time you reach the project's start date, it's not unusual for the plan to have a little bulge around the belt. Perhaps the schedule has become longer than originally anticipated. Maybe some resources are overused and others are underused. And it shouldn't be a surprise if the task relationships had a bug or two.

Quite often, the most challenging task of project management is remembering and using your original goals — simply doing what you said you were going to do. Ninety-nine out of a hundred times, the best course of action is the one you spent all that time planning in the first place. In this chapter, you discover the many ways Microsoft Project can help you analyze and modify your schedule to best ensure that you achieve your project's goals and objectives.

The accompanying disk has a project sample for you to use throughout this chapter. But you can use your own project if you want. In either case, though, this stuff really is fascinating.

If you haven't copied the files from the sample disk to your hard drive, you might want to do so before proceeding with this chapter. See Appendix C for instructions.

You can use a sample project file called Smith Home 16.MPP to hone your optimizing skills. Open the sample project file from the Practice Files folder:

1. **Click the Open button on the Standard toolbar.**
2. **Open the Practice Files folder.**
3. **Double-click Smith Home 16.MPP.**

   The file should open in the Gantt Chart view.

Correcting Overallocated Resources

The term *overallocated* is very real to anyone who owns a checkbook. The term is usually associated with things like antacids and rapid heartbeat. In project management, overallocation is also very real and can cause some big headaches, mostly yours.

Maybe that's why Microsoft Project doesn't let you get very far into overallocation before it alerts you to problems. Look at the status bar at the bottom of the screen. Microsoft Project is alerting you about an overallocation and is recommending a solution (Figure 16-1). It's telling you that you probably need to level the Drafting resource.

In project management, to *level* means just what the word implies. A resource is all bunched up in task responsibilities — to the extent that the resource has more task responsibilities than hours to do them in. Microsoft Project is suggesting that you might stretch out the tasks associated with the resource so that it can be more evenly allocated over time.

A common example of an overallocated resource is an employee who is assigned two full-time jobs at the same time. Something has to give. The employee can

- ✔ Take work home evenings and weekends (overtime or change working time or both)
- ✔ Request extra assistance (additional resources)
- ✔ Ask to be relieved of some of the duty (task reduction)
- ✔ Ask for extended deadlines (resource leveling)

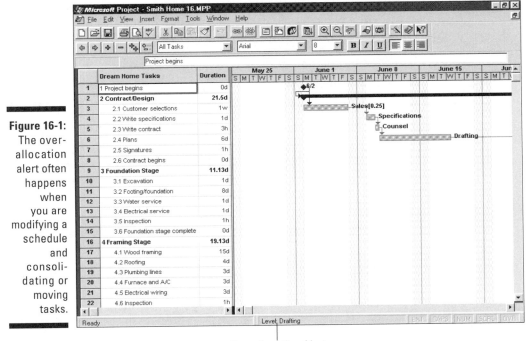

Overallocation Alert

Figure 16-1:
The over-
allocation
alert often
happens
when
you are
modifying a
schedule
and
consoli-
dating or
moving
tasks.

All these are common solutions to overallocation. Only the last, requesting an extended deadline, is leveling. When Microsoft Project suggests leveling an overallocation, it's offering this solution because it can do the leveling for you automatically. (You have to work out all the other solutions.) Leveling is often the least desirable solution to an overallocation problem. You don't want deadlines extended if, for instance, your project has to be ready on a certain date.

A Gantt Chart View of Overallocation

The status bar alerts you to a single overallocation. That doesn't mean the project doesn't have other overallocations — Microsoft Project is telling you about the first one it encounters. You need to find out how many resources are having this problem and the severity of the problem. The best way to do your sleuth work is with a combination view.

Maybe the easiest and fastest way to get the bead on resource allocation problems is with (you guessed it) the Resource Allocation view. You can access this view with the Resource Management toolbar:

1. **Right-click in the toolbar area**.

   The toolbar menu appears.

2. **Click the Resource Management toolbar.**

3. **On the far left, click the Resource Allocation View button**.

   Guess what appears (Figure 16-2). In the Resource Allocation view, the Resource sheet is in the upper pane and a delayed Gantt chart is in the bottom pane. The delayed Gantt chart shows only the taskbars related to the task selected in the upper pane.

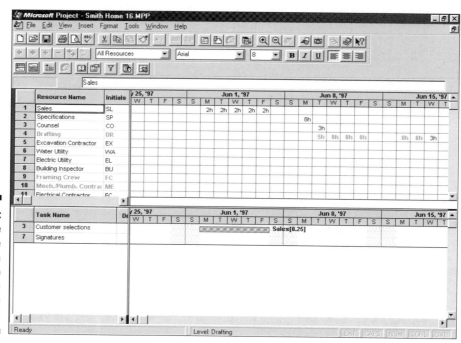

Figure 16-2: Use the Resource Allocation View to analyze resource problems.

The Resource Allocation view is a pretty sharp way to analyze resource problems. Overallocated resources are designated by red text. As you can see, drafting isn't the only resource with problems — the framing crew and the mechanical/plumbing contractors have difficulties, too. Analyze the problems one at a time. To do so:

1. Select the Drafting resource in the upper pane.

The delayed Gantt chart displays the task associated with the resource.

2. Press F6 to activate the lower pane.

3. Click the Goto Selected Task button on the Standard toolbar.

The chart and the table jump to the task dates (Figure 16-3).

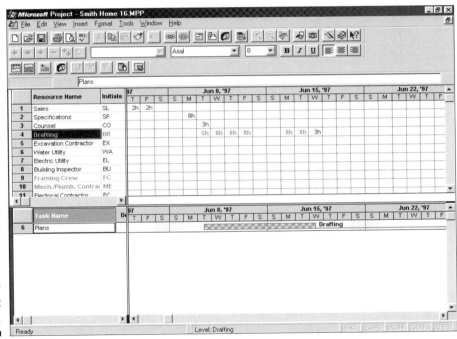

Figure 16-3:
The Goto Selected Task button works only in the Gantt chart.

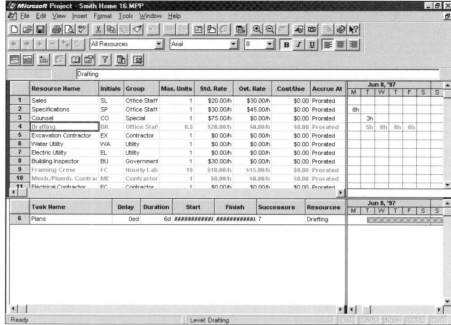

Figure 16-4:
The
Resource
sheet holds
all the
information
entered
about each
resource.

So what's the problem? The Resource sheet shows that the draftsman is working no more than eight hours a day. Maybe the resource information has the answer. Check it out by dragging the vertical bar to the right until it exposes the Accrue At column (Figure 16-4).

The problem is evident. The maximum units for the draftsman resource is .5. This means the draftsman is allocated a maximum of four hours per day (assuming an eight-hour day) for each of the six days of the drafting task. The original assumption was that the draftsman would be available for eight hours per day.

Before you correct this overallocation problem, check out the other two trouble resources. To do this:

1. **Drag the vertical bar back to its original position (showing the Resource Name and Initials columns).**

2. **Select the Framing Crew resource.**

   The lower pane displays the two tasks associated with the resource (Figure 16-5).

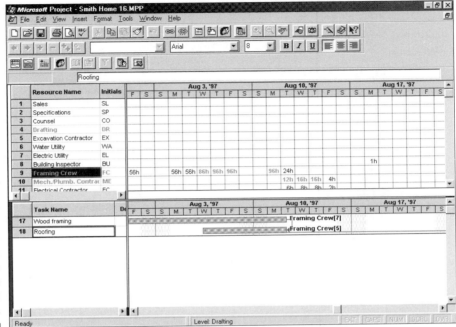

Figure 16-5:
The over-
allocated
resources
shown in
the upper
pane align
with the
days in
which the
crew is
performing
two tasks.

3. In the lower pane, select the Roofing task.

4. Click the Goto Selected Task button on the Standard toolbar.

Notice that the framing crew is responsible for 7 units for the Wood framing task and 5 units for the Roofing task. Drag the vertical bar to the right until it exposes the Accrue At column. The maximum units for the framing crew is 10 (Figure 16-6). That's the reason for this overallocation.

While you're looking at the Resource sheet details, select Mech./Plumb. Contractor. The problem with this resource is that it is currently assigned 1 maximum unit. The contractor works for a fixed fee. It doesn't matter to you how many people the contractor uses as long as the job is accomplished according to the contract. But because only 1 unit is assigned to the re-source, Microsoft Project interprets that the contractor can't perform two tasks at the same time.

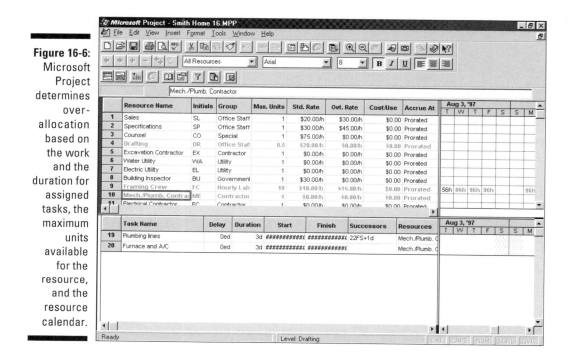

Figure 16-6:
Microsoft Project determines over-allocation based on the work and the duration for assigned tasks, the maximum units available for the resource, and the resource calendar.

Correcting Resource Overallocations

You can correct resource overallocations in more than one way. You use three solutions with the resource problems in this project. You extend duration for the draftsman, add units for the framing crew, and delete a task for the mechanical/plumbing contractor. Each solution is the best one for the circumstances of the resource.

The best way to perform this work is manually, rather than through automatic leveling. To do so:

1. **Choose Window⊅Remove Split.**

2. **Choose View⊅Gantt Chart.**

3. **Right-click anywhere in the toolbar area.**

4. **Choose Resource Management to close the Resource Management toolbar.**

5. **Choose Tools⇨Resource Leveling.**

   The Resource Leveling dialog box appears.

6. **Under Leveling, select Manual (Figure 16-7).**

   This turns off the automatic leveling option.

Figure 16-7:
The
settings in
this dialog
box remain
intact until
you change
them again.

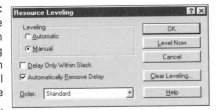

7. **Click OK.**

8. **Choose Window⇨Split.**

9. **In the upper pane, select the Plans task.**

   The Drafting Resource appears in the lower pane.

10. **In the Units column, change 1 to .5.**

11. **Click OK.**

12. **Scroll the Gantt chart to expose the entire Plans taskbar and its resource designation.**

The task has leveled to 12 days (Figure 16-8). The Drafting resource limitation is maintained as 0.5 units. The solution was acceptable because adding six days to the task doesn't conflict with the successor date. And that's because the successor task is a fixed date later than the 12-day period.

The Level: Drafting alert has been replaced by Level: Framing Crew. One pesky little problem solved, two to go.

Instead of leveling, you use another method to correct the Framing Crew overallocation. You add resources to the Framing Crew:

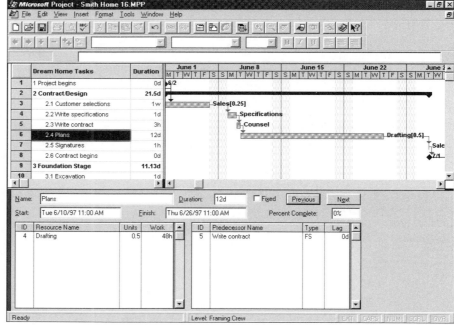

Figure 16-8:
The number
of hours
worked
by the
draftsman
remains the
same but is
extended
over 12
days. The
resource is
leveled.

1. **With any task highlighted, click the Resource Assignment button on the Standard toolbar.**

   The Resource Assignment dialog box appears.

2. **Scroll the list and double-click the Framing Crew resource.**

   The Resource Information dialog box appears.

3. **Change Max Units from 10 to 12 (Figure 16-9).**

4. **Click OK.**

Now the Level: Framing Crew alert has been replaced by Level: Mech./ Plumb. Contractor. You're almost finished.

Last, you remove the Mechanical/Plumbing Contractor resource overallocation by removing one of the two identical tasks. This schedule error comes from an earlier decision to grant both the plumbing and mechanical contracts to the same contractor. You aren't changing anything by removing a task because the contractor is responsible for all the crew and related resources. To remove a task:

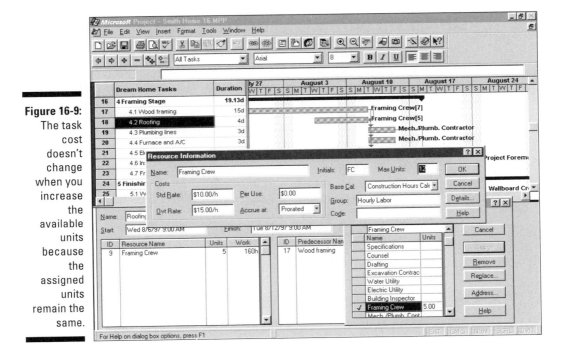

Figure 16-9:
The task
cost
doesn't
change
when you
increase
the
available
units
because
the
assigned
units
remain the
same.

1. **Highlight the Furnace and A/C task.**

2. **Press the Delete key**.

   The resource overallocation is gone.

3. **Choose Window⇩Unsplit.**

Crashing the Critical Path

The term *crashing* has a few common uses, but none have anything to do with project management. One common meaning is to run into something, such as crashing a milk cart into a cow. Another meaning was spawned in the '60s as a term for what you do after a night of partying — not running into a cow but falling on a couch or a floor and sleeping, usually at someone else's pad.

When a project manager crashes, a higher and nobler action is happening (I hope). In project management, *crashing* is doing what's necessary to decrease the total project duration.

Understanding the critical path

So what's a critical path, you ask? Good question. A *critical path* is the series of tasks that determines the completion date of a project. Project management differentiates tasks that are on the critical path from those that aren't.

The critical path of the project includes only tasks that have not been performed. For that reason, as the project progresses, the critical path becomes smaller.

All the tasks in the Smith Home project, for example, are necessary for its completion. Ignore any of them, and the Smiths will be quick to inform you that the project isn't complete. Even so, some Smith Home tasks are part of the critical path and some aren't.

To view the current Smith Home critical path:

1. **Switch to the Gantt Chart view (if necessary) by choosing View⇨Gantt Chart.**

   The screen should also be unsplit.

2. **Click the Zoom Out button on the Standard toolbar twice.**

   This will make viewing the whole project easier.

3. **Hold down the Shift key and choose Tools⇨Filter for: All Tasks.**

   The Filtered For submenu appears.

4. **Continue holding down the Shift key and choose Critical in the Filter for submenu.**

   The screen now displays the entire project with the critical path highlighted in underlined red text (Figure 16-10).

An example of a noncritical task is the Stairway task. The stairway needs to be completed by the end of the project, but it can float around a little bit without affecting the start or completion of other tasks. To a lesser degree, the same is true of the Roofing task. Its start can be delayed a little bit as long as its finish date doesn't go past the finish date of the Plumbing Lines task.

An example of a critical task is the Excavation task. The start date and finish date of the house excavation directly affect the continuance and timing of successor tasks and, ultimately, the completion date of the project. In another way, the Wallboard task is critical in that its duration has a direct outcome on the completion date of the project. If you could find a way of decreasing the Wallboard task's duration without increasing the cost, you would be crashing the critical path.

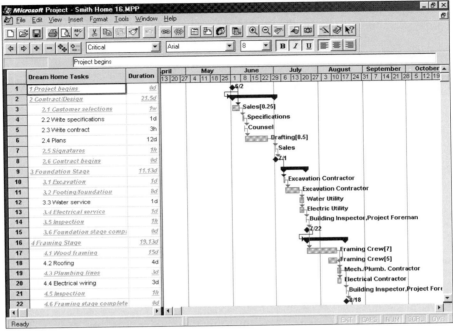

Figure 16-10:
Can you spot the critical path?

Scroll the Gantt chart to expose the final task. The Project complete milestone is September 19. That's a problem. For the sake of the example, suppose that your boss would like to have the house finished by September 1. Hey man, ya wanna crash at the Smith pad? Let's go!

One, two, three — crash!

Crashing a schedule requires some tough analysis and some pencil sharpening. Ask yourself these three questions:

- ✔ Is time being used most efficiently?
- ✔ Are there ways in which resources can be changed without increasing costs?
- ✔ Does the project have any unnecessary finish-to-start relationships?

Using time efficiently

Starting with time efficiency, there is a very noticeable way to crash the Smith Home critical path. You can change the construction working calendar. In the construction trades, it's common to work six days a week without incurring overtime. This is especially true in parts of the country with harsh winters. To change the construction calendar:

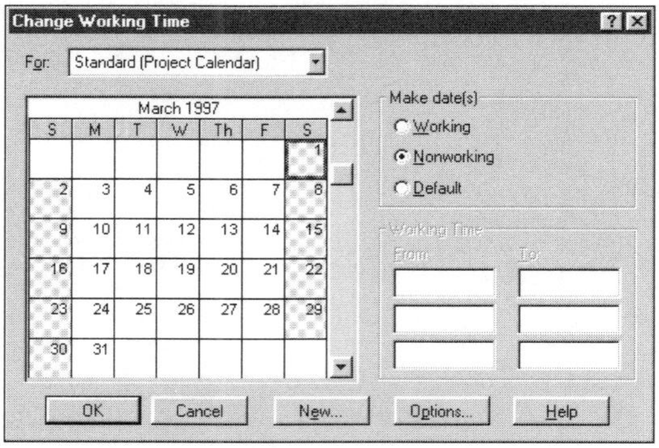

Figure 16-11:
The Change Working Time dialog box is the place for editing the default calendar and resource calendars.

1. **Choose Tools⇨Change Working Time.**

   The Change Working Time dialog box appears (Figure 16-11).

2. **In the For text box, select the Construction Hours Calendar.**

3. **Select the heading of the Saturday column.**

4. **Under Make date(s), select Working.**

   The Working Time editing area becomes active.

5. **Change the working times from the default settings to the normal construction hours as set on the other days.**

   Times should be From 7:00 AM To 11:00 AM and From 11:30 AM To 3:30 PM. The Change Working Time dialog box should now look like Figure 16-12.

6. **Click OK.**

   The Project complete milestone has changed to September 12. You're making progress (Figure 16-13).

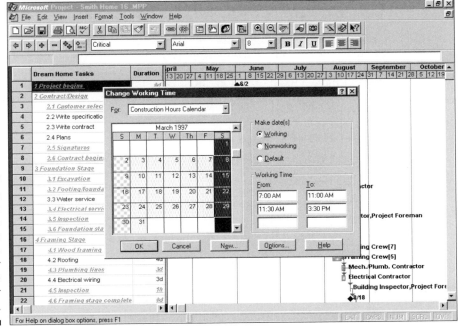

Figure 16-12:
When you change one month's setting, the settings for the entire calendar change.

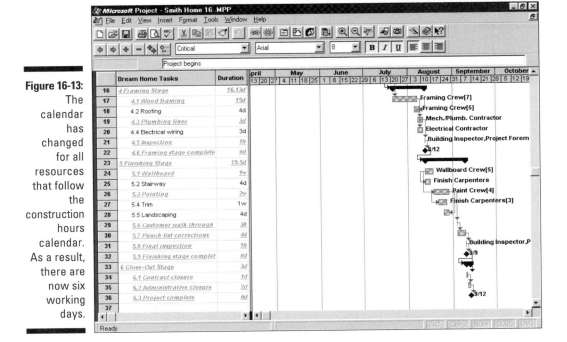

Figure 16-13:
The calendar has changed for all resources that follow the construction hours calendar. As a result, there are now six working days.

Changing resources

Another way to crash the plan is by changing resources. Sometimes this is the simplest and most straightforward solution to too much work and too little time. For example, in our Smith Home 16 project, the Painting task doesn't have a fixed duration. Increasing resource units won't increase costs but will reduce the duration. You can further crash the critical path by adding resources to the Painting Crew, as follows:

1. **Select the Painting task.**

2. **Click the Resource Assignment button on the Standard toolbar.**

   The Resource Assignment dialog box appears.

3. **Scroll and double-click the Paint Crew resource.**

   The Resource Information dialog box appears (Figure 16-14). Changes to this dialog box affect the amount of resource units available for a task.

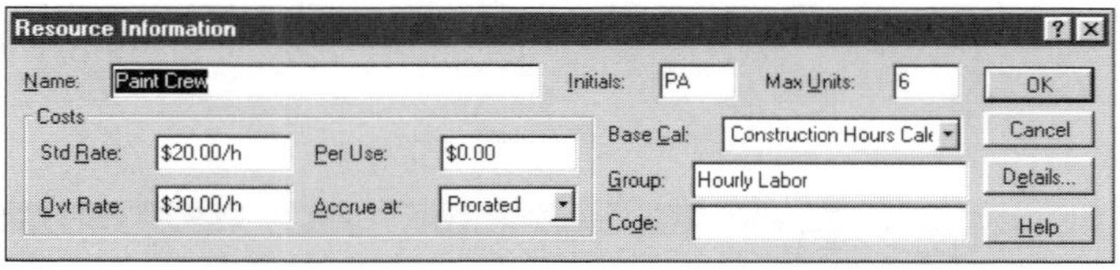

Figure 16-14:
The
Resource
Information
dialog box.

Resource Information						? ✕
Name:	Paint Crew		Initials:	PA	Max Units:	6	OK

Costs
Std Rate: $20.00/h   Per Use: $0.00   Base Cal: Construction Hours Cal ▾   Cancel
Ovt Rate: $30.00/h   Accrue at: Prorated ▾   Group: Hourly Labor   Details...
Code: _____   Help

4. **Change Max Units to 8.**

5. **Click OK.**

6. **In the Resource Assignment dialog box, change the number of assigned units from 4.00 to 8.00.**

   The Gantt chart changes and shows that the Painting task has been reduced from two weeks to one week (Figure 16-15). In addition, the Project complete milestone is now September 8.

7. **Click the Close button.**

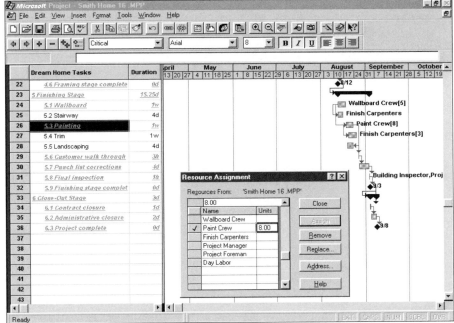

Figure 16-15:
The Gantt
bar for the
Painting
task
shows the
assignment
of eight
units.

Changing task relationships

Another thing you can do to crash the critical path is to change some task
relationships. Some are unnecessarily of the Finish-to-Start variety. The
Plumbing lines task and the Electrical wiring tasks can be made to finish
with their predecessor Wood framing task. To do so:

1. **Click the Zoom Out button on the Standard toolbar twice.**

   This makes working on the Gantt chart easier.

2. **Select the Plumbing lines task.**

3. **Click the Goto Selected Task button on the Standard toolbar.**

4. **On the Gantt chart, double-click the arrow that touches the Plumbing
   lines task**.

   The Task Dependency dialog box appears (Figure 16-16).

5. **Change the task dependency to Finish-to-Finish (FF).**

6. **Click OK**.

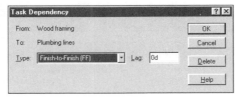

Figure 16-16:
The task dependency should be from Wood framing to Plumbing lines.

7. **Repeat Steps 2 to 6 for the Electrical wiring task.**

8. **Drag the Roofing task until it has the same Finish date as the Wood framing task (8/7/97).**

   The Gantt chart now looks like Figure 16-17. If you make a mistake, choose Edit⇨Undo. Drag.

9. **Scroll to the last task and click the Goto Selected Task button on the Standard toolbar.**

   The Project complete milestone says September 3. You're almost there.

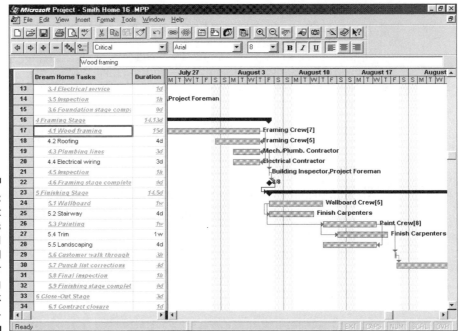

Figure 16-17:
The Gantt chart offers point and click, visual tools for optimizing task relationships.

Two quick changes will complete the crash. Delete the Contract closure task — it's redundant with Administrative closure. Then change Administrative closure to a one-day duration. The result should look like Figure 16-18.

Last, update the baseline. To do so:

1. Choose Tools⇨Tracking.

The Tracking submenu appears.

2. Choose Save Baseline.

The Save Baseline dialog box appears. Make sure that the Save Baseline option is selected.

3. Click the OK button.

You've optimized your plan. Everything is as ready as it can be. Take a break and relax. Come your project's start date, you can walk into the office with a little swagger to your step. This baby's going to fly!

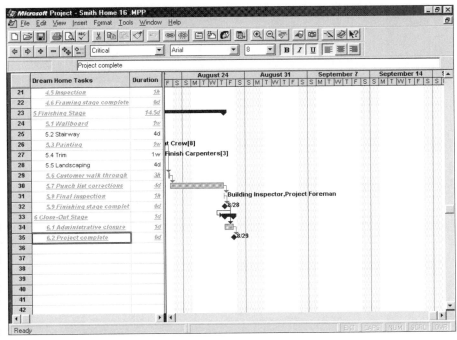

Figure 16-18: The project is within the contract time constraints.

Part V
Project Management

The 5th Wave   By Rich Tennant

IN A STROKE OF SELF-RELIANCE, RAY EXTENDS THE POWER ON HIS LAPTOP BY TAPPING INTO THE BATTERY ON HIS SLEEPING NEIGHBOR'S HEARING AID.

In this part . . .

*I*t probably seems odd that this part's title is "Project Management." Isn't that what the whole book is about? Yeah. It's sort of like calling a cylindrical piece of metal with a whole lot of gizmos a *spaceship*. It's a spaceship months before it ever lifts off the ground and forever after it reenters the atmosphere. During its entire life, it is only one thing — a spaceship. Yet only a brief period of its overall life is spent in space.

In all the previous chapters, you've been building a vehicle that exists solely for one purpose — project management. In this part, you launch. You study how to track your project and how to make midcourse corrections. And you learn how to modify your project environment after it starts showing some pesky anomalies.

Chapter 17

Tracking Your Project's Progress

*I*n this chapter, I assume that your project is beginning or has already begun. As you're about to see, Microsoft Project is an important asset in your project-management responsibilities. It's ready and waiting to help your project plan succeed in the cold test of reality. Although you'd like the project to go without a hitch, you know that's almost impossible. Besides, if the project had no problems, it would need only a project planner — not a project manager.

A project manager has to know what's going on to be proactive to the process of change. This requires keeping a close watch on the schedule, tasks, resources, and costs. Programs such as Microsoft Project provide a tremendous capability to analyze present circumstances against the original plan and to make adjustments to better ensure future success. The term for this is *tracking*.

Tracking has a double meaning. One meaning is keeping track, as in remaining informed. It also means to keep *on* track — to keep the project going where and how it is designed to progress.

Tracking has three major components:

- ✔ **The baseline plan.** The baseline is the fully developed plan that you save before the start date of the first project task. The baseline is like a set of completed blueprints and specifications. It's your best prediction of how the project should go. You use the baseline throughout the project to maintain goals and to get things back on track.

- ✔ **Current information.** After the project begins, Microsoft Project keeps a dynamic model of the project. This model may or may not be the same as the baseline. As you see in this chapter, Microsoft Project calculates upcoming start and finish dates based on the latest information. You use Current information to determine how upcoming tasks are being affected by the present and by what has already occurred.

- ✔ **Actual information.** Tasks that have already started or have finished are referred to as Actual. As you see in this chapter, the Actual start and finish dates for tasks are designated NA until they begin.

Using Microsoft Project, you can perform either minimal or detailed tracking. *Minimal tracking* refers to keeping records of the start and finish dates for each task. *Detailed tracking* isn't a specific action, but a range of possibilities. You can track start and finish dates plus percentage of task completion, duration, costs, and work. You can then use the information to maneuver your tasks through complicated situations.

In this chapter, using the Smith Home example, you track a project after it has begun. You work with baseline, current, and actual information.

If you haven't copied the files from the sample disk to your hard drive, you might want to do so before proceeding with this chapter. See Appendix C for instructions.

Open the sample project file called Smith Home 17.MPP from the Practice Files folder. To do so:

1. **Click the Open button on the Standard toolbar.**

2. **Open the Practice Files folder.**

3. **Double-click Smith Home 17.MPP.**

   The file should open in the Gantt Chart view.

Viewing the Baseline

You've put a lot of time and effort into creating your baseline. Wouldn't it be nice to see it? Get ready to meet your baseline:

1. **Choose View⇨More Views**.

   The More Views dialog box appears.

2. **Double-click Task Sheet.**

   The screen changes to Task Sheet view.

3. **Choose View⇨Table: Cost.**

   The Table submenu appears.

4. **Choose More Tables.**

   The More Tables dialog box appears.

5. **Choose Baseline.**

   Baseline, meet your project manager. Project manager, this is your baseline (Figure 17-1).

Figure 17-1: The baseline is ground zero for your project. It's your best estimate of your project's duration, resource usage, and cost.

	Task Name	Baseline Dur.	Baseline Start	Baseline Finish	Baseline Work	Baseline Cost
1	Project begins	0d	Mon 6/2/97 8:00 AM	Mon 6/2/97 8:00 AM	0h	$0.00
2	**Contract/Design**	**21.5d**	**Mon 6/2/97 8:00 AM**	**Tue 7/1/97 12:00 PM**	**70h**	**$1,645.00**
3	Customer selections	1w	Mon 6/2/97 8:00 AM	Fri 6/6/97 5:00 PM	10h	$200.00
4	Write specifications	1d	Mon 6/9/97 8:00 AM	Mon 6/9/97 5:00 PM	8h	$240.00
5	Write contract	3h	Tue 6/10/97 8:00 AM	Tue 6/10/97 11:00 AM	3h	$225.00
6	Plans	12d	Tue 6/10/97 11:00 AM	Thu 6/26/97 11:00 AM	48h	$960.00
7	Signatures	1h	Tue 7/1/97 11:00 AM	Tue 7/1/97 12:00 PM	1h	$20.00
8	Contract begins	0d	Tue 7/1/97 12:00 PM	Tue 7/1/97 12:00 PM	0h	$0.00
9	**Foundation Stage**	**10.13d**	**Mon 7/7/97 8:00 AM**	**Mon 7/21/97 9:00 AM**	**90h**	**$13,770.00**
10	Excavation	1d	Mon 7/7/97 8:00 AM	Tue 7/8/97 8:00 AM	8h	$3,700.00
11	Footing/foundation	8d	Tue 7/8/97 8:00 AM	Thu 7/17/97 8:00 AM	64h	$9,200.00
12	Water service	1d	Thu 7/17/97 8:00 AM	Fri 7/18/97 8:00 AM	8h	$250.00
13	Electrical service	1d	Thu 7/17/97 8:00 AM	Fri 7/18/97 8:00 AM	8h	$500.00
14	Inspection	1h	Sat 7/19/97 7:00 AM	Mon 7/21/97 9:00 AM	2h	$120.00
15	Foundation stage comple	0d	Mon 7/21/97 9:00 AM	Mon 7/21/97 9:00 AM	0h	$0.00
16	**Framing Stage**	**14.13d**	**Mon 7/21/97 9:00 AM**	**Fri 8/8/97 10:00 AM**	**1050h**	**$17,660.00**
17	Wood framing	15d	Mon 7/21/97 9:00 AM	Thu 8/7/97 9:00 AM	840h	$8,400.00
18	Roofing	4d	Sat 8/2/97 9:00 AM	Thu 8/7/97 9:00 AM	160h	$1,600.00
19	Plumbing lines	3d	Mon 8/4/97 9:00 AM	Thu 8/7/97 9:00 AM	24h	$3,800.00
20	Electrical wiring	3d	Mon 8/4/97 9:00 AM	Thu 8/7/97 9:00 AM	24h	$3,800.00
21	Inspection	1h	Fri 8/8/97 9:00 AM	Fri 8/8/97 10:00 AM	2h	$60.00
22	Framing stage complete	0d	Fri 8/8/97 10:00 AM	Fri 8/8/97 10:00 AM	0h	$0.00
23	**Finishing Stage**	**14.5d**	**Fri 8/8/97 10:00 AM**	**Thu 8/28/97 3:00 PM**	**674h**	**$16,500.00**
24	Wallboard	1w	Fri 8/8/97 10:00 AM	Thu 8/14/97 10:00 AM	200h	$2,000.00
25	Stairway	4d	Fri 8/8/97 10:00 AM	Wed 8/13/97 10:00 AM	32h	$640.00
26	Painting	1w	Thu 8/14/97 10:00 AM	Wed 8/20/97 10:00 AM	320h	$6,400.00
27	Trim	1w	Sat 8/16/97 7:00 AM	Thu 8/21/97 3:30 PM	120h	$2,400.00

For the rest of your project, this information doesn't change unless you need to modify it for some reason. (For example, you might need to modify the baseline so that you can add a task to the project.)

You probably won't have a reason to use this specific table in your project, but you'll be using various parts of this information on an ongoing basis. For now, change back to the Gantt Chart view by choosing View➪Gantt Chart.

The Baseline in Other Tables

The baseline shows up in some of the most important places. For instance, it's in the Work table, the Cost table, and the Variance table. To see the baseline in these tables:

1. **Choose View➪Table: Entry.**

   The Table submenu appears.

2. **Choose Work.**

   The Work table appears.

3. **Drag the vertical bar to the right until the entire table is exposed (Figure 17-2).**

Figure 17-2:
The Work table shows work information.

	Task Name	Work	Baseline	Variance	Actual	Remaining	% W. Comp.
1	1 Project begins	0h	0h	0h	0h	0h	0%
2	2 Contract/Design	70h	70h	0h	0h	70h	0%
3	2.1 Customer selections	10h	10h	0h	0h	10h	0%
4	2.2 Write specifications	8h	8h	0h	0h	8h	0%
5	2.3 Write contract	3h	3h	0h	0h	3h	0%
6	2.4 Plans	48h	48h	0h	0h	48h	0%
7	2.5 Signatures	1h	1h	0h	0h	1h	0%
8	2.6 Contract begins	0h	0h	0h	0h	0h	0%
9	3 Foundation Stage	90h	90h	0h	0h	90h	0%
10	3.1 Excavation	8h	8h	0h	0h	8h	0%
11	3.2 Footing/foundation	64h	64h	0h	0h	64h	0%
12	3.3 Water service	8h	8h	0h	0h	8h	0%
13	3.4 Electrical service	8h	8h	0h	0h	8h	0%
14	3.5 Inspection	2h	2h	0h	0h	2h	0%
15	3.6 Foundation stage cor	0h	0h	0h	0h	0h	0%
16	4 Framing Stage	1050h	1050h	0h	0h	1050h	0%
17	4.1 Wood framing	840h	840h	0h	0h	840h	0%
18	4.2 Roofing	160h	160h	0h	0h	160h	0%
19	4.3 Plumbing lines	24h	24h	0h	0h	24h	0%
20	4.4 Electrical wiring	24h	24h	0h	0h	24h	0%
21	4.5 Inspection	2h	2h	0h	0h	2h	0%
22	4.6 Framing stage comple	0h	0h	0h	0h	0h	0%

The Work table provides you with resource information about each task. The Work column is the total amount of work scheduled to be performed by all resources assigned to the task. The Variance column is a calculation of the difference between Baseline and (Current) Work. Actual is the amount of work that has been performed by all resources on the task. Remaining is the total amount of work that has yet to be performed. Percent of Work Completed (% W. Comp.) is the percentage of each task's work that has been performed.

The Cost table performs the same kind of function as the Work table except it tracks — you guessed it — cost. To see this table:

1. **Choose View⇨Table: Work.**

   The Table submenu appears.

2. **Choose Cost.**

   The Cost table appears (Figure 17-3).

Figure 17-3: The Cost table shows resource cost information regarding project tasks.

	Task Name	Fixed Cost	Total Cost	Baseline	Variance	Actual	Remaining
1	1 Project begins	$0.00	$0.00	$0.00	$0.00	$0.00	$0.00
2	2 Contract/Design	$0.00	$1,645.00	$1,645.00	$0.00	$0.00	$1,645.00
3	2.1 Customer selections	$0.00	$200.00	$200.00	$0.00	$0.00	$200.00
4	2.2 Write specifications	$0.00	$240.00	$240.00	$0.00	$0.00	$240.00
5	2.3 Write contract	$0.00	$225.00	$225.00	$0.00	$0.00	$225.00
6	2.4 Plans	$0.00	$960.00	$960.00	$0.00	$0.00	$960.00
7	2.5 Signatures	$0.00	$20.00	$20.00	$0.00	$0.00	$20.00
8	2.6 Contract begins	$0.00	$0.00	$0.00	$0.00	$0.00	$0.00
9	3 Foundation Stage	$0.00	$13,770.00	$13,770.00	$0.00	$0.00	$13,770.00
10	3.1 Excavation	$3,700.00	$3,700.00	$3,700.00	$0.00	$0.00	$3,700.00
11	3.2 Footing/foundation	$9,200.00	$9,200.00	$9,200.00	$0.00	$0.00	$9,200.00
12	3.3 Water service	$250.00	$250.00	$250.00	$0.00	$0.00	$250.00
13	3.4 Electrical service	$500.00	$500.00	$500.00	$0.00	$0.00	$500.00
14	3.5 Inspection	$60.00	$120.00	$120.00	$0.00	$0.00	$120.00
15	3.6 Foundation stage cor	$0.00	$0.00	$0.00	$0.00	$0.00	$0.00
16	4 Framing Stage	$0.00	$17,660.00	$17,660.00	$0.00	$0.00	$17,660.00
17	4.1 Wood framing	$0.00	$8,400.00	$8,400.00	$0.00	$0.00	$8,400.00
18	4.2 Roofing	$0.00	$1,600.00	$1,600.00	$0.00	$0.00	$1,600.00
19	4.3 Plumbing lines	$3,800.00	$3,800.00	$3,800.00	$0.00	$0.00	$3,800.00
20	4.4 Electrical wiring	$3,800.00	$3,800.00	$3,800.00	$0.00	$0.00	$3,800.00
21	4.5 Inspection	$0.00	$60.00	$60.00	$0.00	$0.00	$60.00
22	4.6 Framing stage comple	$0.00	$0.00	$0.00	$0.00	$0.00	$0.00

The Fixed Cost column contains the fixed cost for a task, such as contractor fees. Total Cost is the total projected cost for the task. The remaining columns are set up in the same way as the Work table.

The Variance table compares the difference, if any, between the project's baseline start and finish dates and the scheduled start and finish dates after the project has begun. For example:

1. **Choose View⇨Table: Cost.**

   The Table submenu appears.

2. **Choose Variance.**

   The Variance table appears (Figure 17-4).

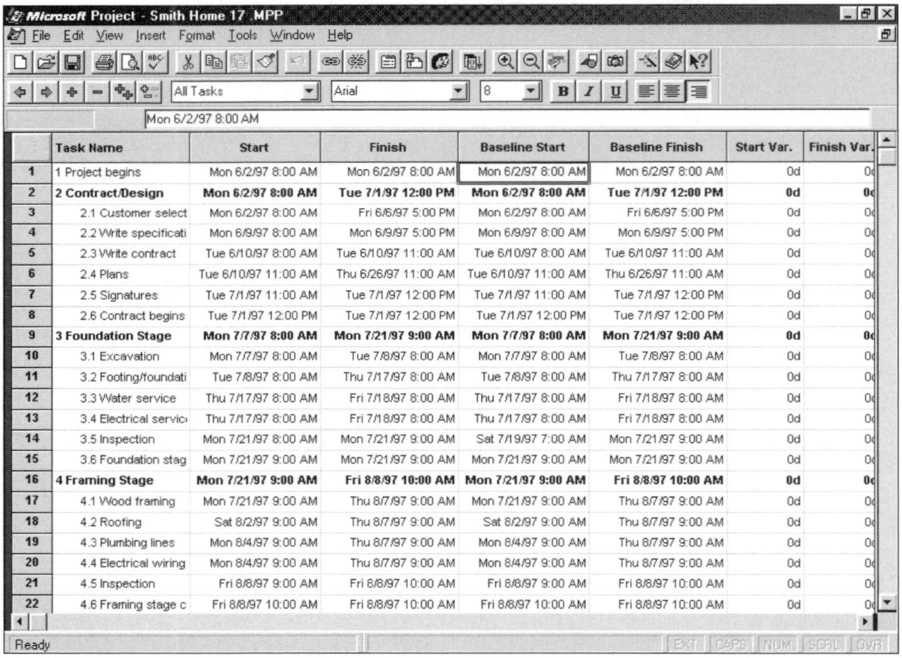

	Task Name	Start	Finish	Baseline Start	Baseline Finish	Start Var.	Finish Var.
1	1 Project begins	Mon 6/2/97 8:00 AM	Mon 6/2/97 8:00 AM	Mon 6/2/97 8:00 AM	Mon 6/2/97 8:00 AM	0d	0(
2	**2 Contract/Design**	**Mon 6/2/97 8:00 AM**	**Tue 7/1/97 12:00 PM**	**Mon 6/2/97 8:00 AM**	**Tue 7/1/97 12:00 PM**	**0d**	**0(**
3	2.1 Customer select	Mon 6/2/97 8:00 AM	Fri 6/6/97 5:00 PM	Mon 6/2/97 8:00 AM	Fri 6/6/97 5:00 PM	0d	0(
4	2.2 Write specificati	Mon 6/9/97 8:00 AM	Mon 6/9/97 5:00 PM	Mon 6/9/97 8:00 AM	Mon 6/9/97 5:00 PM	0d	0(
5	2.3 Write contract	Tue 6/10/97 8:00 AM	Tue 6/10/97 11:00 AM	Tue 6/10/97 8:00 AM	Tue 6/10/97 11:00 AM	0d	0(
6	2.4 Plans	Tue 6/10/97 11:00 AM	Thu 6/26/97 11:00 AM	Tue 6/10/97 11:00 AM	Thu 6/26/97 11:00 AM	0d	0(
7	2.5 Signatures	Tue 7/1/97 11:00 AM	Tue 7/1/97 12:00 PM	Tue 7/1/97 11:00 AM	Tue 7/1/97 12:00 PM	0d	0(
8	2.6 Contract begins	Tue 7/1/97 12:00 PM	Tue 7/1/97 12:00 PM	Tue 7/1/97 12:00 PM	Tue 7/1/97 12:00 PM	0d	0(
9	**3 Foundation Stage**	**Mon 7/7/97 8:00 AM**	**Mon 7/21/97 9:00 AM**	**Mon 7/7/97 8:00 AM**	**Mon 7/21/97 9:00 AM**	**0d**	**0(**
10	3.1 Excavation	Mon 7/7/97 8:00 AM	Tue 7/8/97 8:00 AM	Mon 7/7/97 8:00 AM	Tue 7/8/97 8:00 AM	0d	0(
11	3.2 Footing/foundati	Tue 7/8/97 8:00 AM	Thu 7/17/97 8:00 AM	Tue 7/8/97 8:00 AM	Thu 7/17/97 8:00 AM	0d	0(
12	3.3 Water service	Thu 7/17/97 8:00 AM	Fri 7/18/97 8:00 AM	Thu 7/17/97 8:00 AM	Fri 7/18/97 8:00 AM	0d	0(
13	3.4 Electrical servic	Thu 7/17/97 8:00 AM	Fri 7/18/97 8:00 AM	Thu 7/17/97 8:00 AM	Fri 7/18/97 8:00 AM	0d	0(
14	3.5 Inspection	Mon 7/21/97 8:00 AM	Mon 7/21/97 9:00 AM	Sat 7/19/97 7:00 AM	Mon 7/21/97 9:00 AM	0d	0(
15	3.6 Foundation stag	Mon 7/21/97 9:00 AM	Mon 7/21/97 9:00 AM	Mon 7/21/97 9:00 AM	Mon 7/21/97 9:00 AM	0d	0(
16	**4 Framing Stage**	**Mon 7/21/97 9:00 AM**	**Fri 8/8/97 10:00 AM**	**Mon 7/21/97 9:00 AM**	**Fri 8/8/97 10:00 AM**	**0d**	**0(**
17	4.1 Wood framing	Mon 7/21/97 9:00 AM	Thu 8/7/97 9:00 AM	Mon 7/21/97 9:00 AM	Thu 8/7/97 9:00 AM	0d	0(
18	4.2 Roofing	Sat 8/2/97 9:00 AM	Thu 8/7/97 9:00 AM	Sat 8/2/97 9:00 AM	Thu 8/7/97 9:00 AM	0d	0(
19	4.3 Plumbing lines	Mon 8/4/97 9:00 AM	Thu 8/7/97 9:00 AM	Mon 8/4/97 9:00 AM	Thu 8/7/97 9:00 AM	0d	0(
20	4.4 Electrical wiring	Mon 8/4/97 9:00 AM	Thu 8/7/97 9:00 AM	Mon 8/4/97 9:00 AM	Thu 8/7/97 9:00 AM	0d	0(
21	4.5 Inspection	Fri 8/8/97 9:00 AM	Fri 8/8/97 10:00 AM	Fri 8/8/97 9:00 AM	Fri 8/8/97 10:00 AM	0d	0(
22	4.6 Framing stage c	Fri 8/8/97 10:00 AM	Fri 8/8/97 10:00 AM	Fri 8/8/97 10:00 AM	Fri 8/8/97 10:00 AM	0d	0(

Figure 17-4: The Variance table shows schedule variance from the baseline start and finish dates of project tasks.

The Variance table displays current start and finish dates. As mentioned, the term *current* refers to calculated information based on the latest changes or lack of changes to the project. The project is only beginning, so no variances exist between current dates and baseline dates.

Tracking Project Progress

Enough of the baseline stuff already! It's time to do some project tracking:

1. **Change back to the Entry table by choosing View⇨Table: Variance.**

   The Table submenu appears.

2. **Choose Entry.**

   The Entry table appears.

3. **Drag the vertical bar back until it is to the right of the Duration column.**

4. **Click the Zoom Out button on the Standard toolbar.**

   This makes the Gantt chart easier to use.

Suppose that the project has been progressing for a number of days. Everything was going according to plan until the construction ran into a rain day. This not only delayed construction, but also affected the availability of some upcoming resource commitments.

You need to make some changes to the project. This won't affect the baseline. Instead, the baseline will tell you how the changes affect the overall project.

For this example, today is July 15, 1997. You need to inform Microsoft Project of this, as follows:

1. **Choose File⇨Project Info.**

   The Project Info dialog box appears.

2. **In the Current Date text box, type** 7/15/97 **(Figure 17-5).**

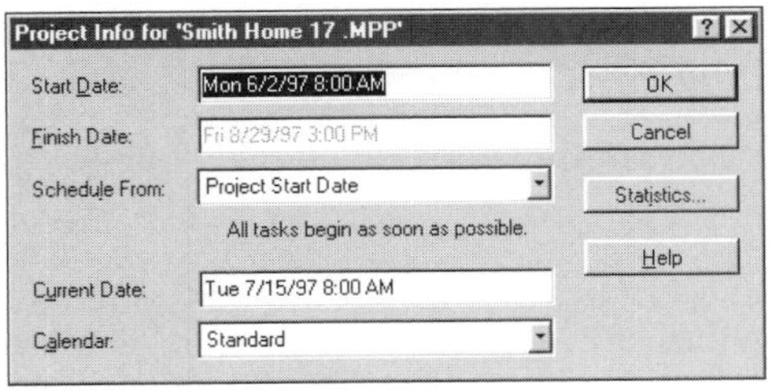

Figure 17-5:
Changing the current date in the Project Information dialog box doesn't affect your computer's clock.

3. **Click OK.**

4. **Choose Edit⇨Go To.**

   The Go To dialog box appears.

5. **In the Date box, type** 7/15/97 **(Figure 17-6).**

6. **Click OK.**

   The chart jumps to July 15.

Figure 17-6:
You can
use the Go
To dialog
box to jump
to an ID or
a date.

Microsoft Project informs you of the current date, July 15, by inserting a vertical dotted line on the Gantt chart.

Updating the schedule

As work is performed on project tasks, you feed progress information into your project file. The term for this is *updating*. Updating the schedule adds a record of work performed. Microsoft Project provides some shortcuts to aid you in this task. Some of the most common shortcuts are grouped together on the Tracking toolbar:

1. **Right-click anywhere in the toolbar area.**

   The toolbar menu appears.

2. **Choose Tracking.**

   The Tracking toolbar appears.

Using these tracking tools and a few others, you'll make the following updates to the project.

Tasks 1-10 were completed on time and without difficulty. Task 11 is half finished and is one day behind schedule because of mud. The ground conditions aren't affecting just the Smith project. The Electrical service task is behind schedule and won't be performed until July 21. This affects the building inspector — the Foundation Stage inspection can't take place until electric service has been installed.

Update as scheduled

One of the friendliest tools on the Tracking toolbar is the Update as Scheduled button. Louis Armstrong should be singing "What a Wonderful World" in the background when you use it. To update as scheduled means that you're a genius — as of the current date, everything is going as planned. For example:

1. **Select the task Project begins, ID 1.**

2. **Hold down the Shift key, and select the task Excavation, ID 10.**

 3. **Click the Update as Scheduled button on the Tracking toolbar.**

   Microsoft Project updates the selected tasks. The black bar all the way through the tasks indicates completion.

Scroll the Gantt chart to expose Tasks 1 through 10. The chart should look like Figure 17-7.

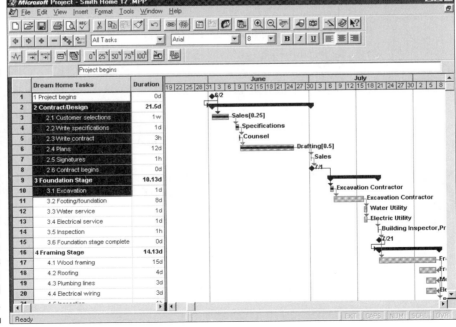

Figure 17-7: In addition to updating the Gantt Chart view, Microsoft Project has recorded the updated information to the tables. The ten tasks now have actual dates.

Update tasks

The Update Tasks button on the Tracking toolbar is a more specific tool than the Update as Scheduled button. The Update Tasks button updates schedule information for the task or tasks you select. With this button, you can do some detailed project management, as follows:

1. **Click the Zoom In button on the Standard toolbar.**

2. **Select the Footing/foundation task.**

3. **Click Goto Selected Task on the Standard toolbar.**

4. **Double-click the Footing/foundation task.**

    The Task Information dialog box appears. The task is 60 percent complete and one day behind schedule.

5. **In the Percent Complete text box, type** 60.

6. **In the Duration text box, type** 9d.

7. **Click OK.**

    The Footing/foundation task reflects your changes.

Another task needs your attention. The Electrical service task can't be performed until July 21. It's currently scheduled to start on July 18. To change the task's start date:

1. **Move the cursor to the Electrical service Gantt bar.**

2. **Drag to the right until the pop-up date box says that the start date is July 21.**

3. **Release the mouse button.**

    The Planning Wizard appears. It tells you that you might be creating a task relationship problem. You can turn off this option by selecting the Don't tell me about this again option. I suggest that you wait awhile before you choose this option.

    The Planning Wizard says that there's a problem because the link between tasks will not drive the start date of the later task. The Wizard is saying a task relationship exists between the two tasks (Electrical service task and Footing/foundation task) that requires the later task to begin upon the completion of the previous task. By moving the first task's start date, everything is getting messed up.

4. **Choose the first option, which lets Microsoft Project remove the link (Figure 17-8).**

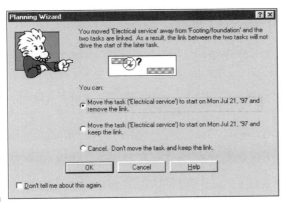

Figure 17-8:
The
Planning
Wizard
appears
automatically
when you
create a
possible
task
relationship
discrepancy.

5. Click OK.

The Electrical service task is moved to July 21.

Now you need to link the Electrical service task again. To do this:

1. Double-click the Electrical service task.

The Task Information dialog box appears.

2. Click the Predecessor tab.

3. In the text box below ID, type 11. **(See Figure 17-9.)**

4. Select the green ✔ **(check).**

5. Click OK.

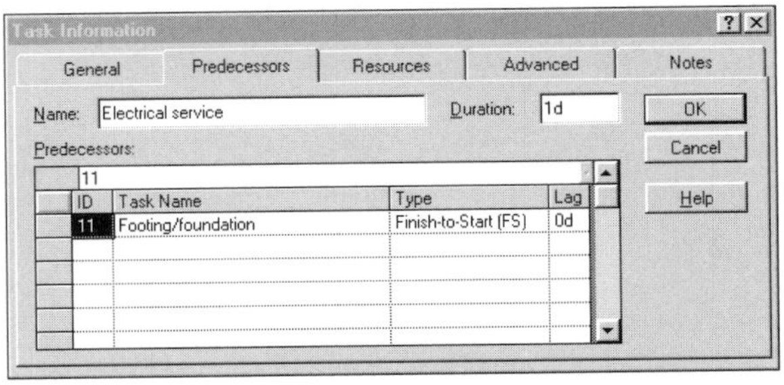

Figure 17-9:
The
Electrical
service task
is now the
successor
of the
Footing/
foundation
task.

One last thing. The Inspection task has a one-day lag from its Electrical service predecessor. You need to remove the lag. To do this:

1. **Double-click the arrow point touching the Inspection task.**

   The Task Dependency dialog box appears.

2. **In the Lag text box, type 0 to replace the 1d (Figure 17-10).**

3. **Click OK.**

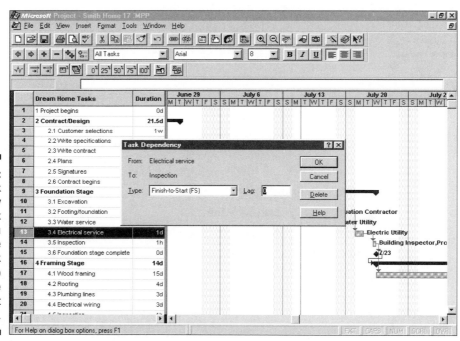

Figure 17-10:
The Task Dependency dialog box lets you change the type of task relationship and the amount of lag.

The Tracking Gantt table

One visually powerful view of tracking information is the Tracking Gantt table. It's best to access the view before you read the explanation. To access the Tracking Gantt table:

1. **Choose <u>V</u>iew⬚<u>M</u>ore Views.**

   The More Views dialog box appears.

2. **Double-click the Tracking Gantt view.**

   The Tracking Gantt view appears.

3. **Select the Footing/foundation task and click the Goto Selected Task button on the Standard toolbar.**

4. **Adjust the screen to match Figure 17-11.**

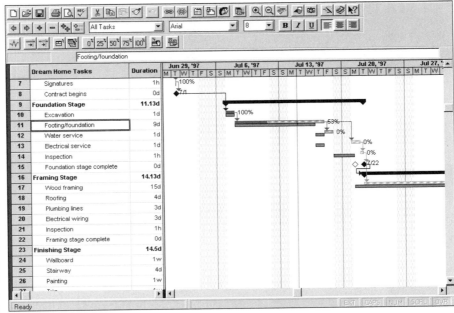

Figure 17-11:
The
Tracking
Gantt view
allows you
to compare
baseline
dates with
actual
dates.

A lot of visual messages are in this view, based mostly on changes of color:

- Dark gray bars are the baseline tasks.
- Dark blue bars are completed tasks or portions of tasks.
- Red bars are critical path tasks.
- Light blue bars are noncritical tasks.

The difference in horizontal location between the baseline bar and its partner is an indication of the schedule status. The more distance, the further the actual date is from the baseline date. The number at the end of each colored bar is the percentage of the task that is completed.

Tracking can be a blast as well as rewarding proof of your excellent planning. But all good athletes know that backslapping is for the end of the game, not during it. Tracking is your first defense against previously unforseeable problems. If you do it well, you'll be able to see to the horizon and — with your Microsoft Project tools — beyond.

Chapter 18

Personalizing Your Project Environment

In This Chapter

▶ Customizing tables

▶ Customizing bars

▶ Adding recurring tasks

▶ Changing default views

▶ Customizing toolbars

---

*T*elling you how to make your project environment unique is a self-contradictory task — something like my teenagers having to be themselves by conforming to all their peers. Ah, life! But I've never been accused of doing only sensible things, so here is an oxymoron chapter of standard ways to personalize your work environment.

This is written in question-and-answer format because, well, I needed to personalize my writing environment for writing a chapter about personal environments. Also, the only way this subject makes sense is by using some mini case studies. But don't think that someone actually wrote and asked me these questions — I asked the questions so that you might consider the answers as samples of what can be accomplished.

In this chapter, you do a bunch of stuff to make the workspace more personal. By using the same approach in other ways, you can truly make yourself at home with Microsoft Project.

If you haven't copied the files from the sample disk to your hard drive, you might want to do so before proceeding with this chapter. See Appendix C for instructions.

Open the workspace file called Chapter 18.MPW from the Practice Files folder. To do so:

1. **Click the Open button on the Standard toolbar.**

2. **Open the Practice Files folder.**

3. **Double-click Chapter 18.MPW.**

Customizing the Gantt Chart Entry Table

Question: *I want the resource names next to the task names in the Gantt chart. What do I do?*

Good idea! Why didn't I think of that? You need to do some column work to put resources next to tasks. Use the Office Remodel Project for this example. To customize columns:

1. **Choose <u>W</u>indow⇨Office Remodel 18.MPP.**

   The Office Remodel window becomes active.

2. **Select the Duration column head.**

3. **Right-click.**

   The shortcut menu appears.

4. **Choose Insert Column.**

   The Column Definition dialog box appears (Figure 18-1).

5. **In the Field Name box, select Resource Names.**

6. **In the Title text box, type something original, such as** Resources.

7. **In the Align box, select Left.**

8. **Rather than assign a character width, click Best Fit.**

   The column appears between the Task Name and Duration columns. You may have to scroll horizontally to bring the Duration column into view — but don't worry, it's there. (See Figure 18-2.)

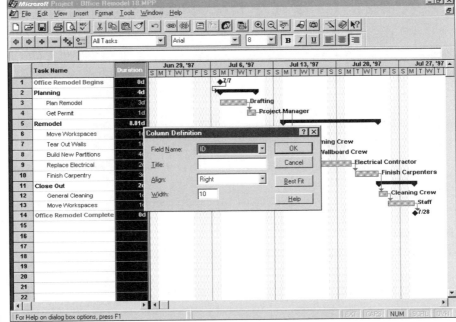

Figure 18-1:
Use the
Column
Definition
dialog box
to set
column
field
conditions.

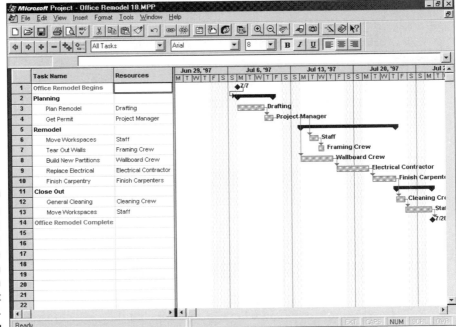

Figure 18-2:
Drag and
scroll to
bring the
information
into view on
the Gantt
chart.

Scheduling with the Gantt Chart

Question: *I get visually confused by nonworking time. When a task duration is going across a nonworking day, I can't tell if the nonworking time is applying toward the duration of a task. What can I do?*

Glad you asked. One good way to remove any doubt about tasks spanning nonworking time is to put the nonworking time on top. You can keep using the Office Remodel project for the example. To put the nonworking time on top:

1. **Double-click the open space representing nonworking time on the Gantt chart.**

   The Timescale dialog box appears (Figure 18-3).

Figure 18-3:
The Timescale dialog box provides options for customizing working and nonworking time.

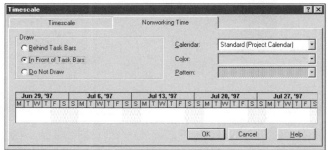

2. **Select the In front of Task Bars option.**

3. **Click OK.**

   The Gantt chart now hides tasks in nonworking times (Figure 18-4).

Question: *How do I change the look of bars on the Gantt chart?*

To change the format of all the bars, double-click the chart background to display the Bar Styles dialog box. You can change the format of one bar on the Gantt chart by double-clicking it. For the following example, switch to Jones Home 18.MPP.

1. **Choose Window⇨Jones Home 18.MPP.**

   The Jones Home project is now the active window.

2. **Double-click anywhere in the working time area of the Gantt chart.**

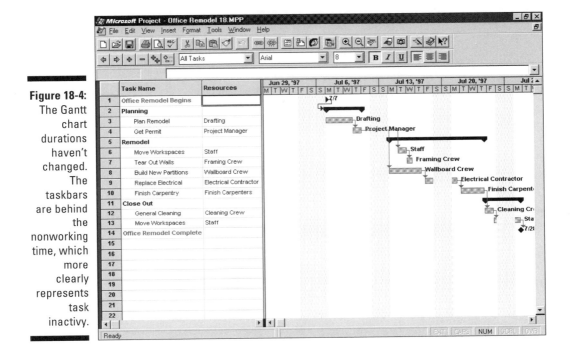

Figure 18-4:
The Gantt chart durations haven't changed. The taskbars are behind the nonworking time, which more clearly represents task inactivy.

The Bar Styles dialog box appears (Figure 18-5). The Bars tab has options for the Start Shape, Middle Bar, and End Shape for each task category. Feel free to use your imagination to change the settings any way you want.

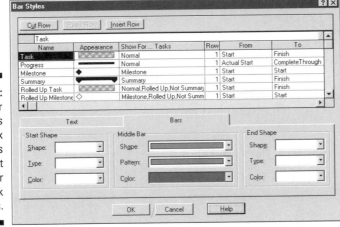

Figure 18-5:
The Bar Styles dialog box shows default settings for all task categories.

Question: *I get confused aligning task names with bars. What should I do?*

This one's simple. All you need to do is to add gridlines to the Gantt chart. To do this:

1. **Right-click anywhere in the Gantt chart.**

   The Gantt shortcut dialog box appears.

2. **Choose Gridlines.**

3. **In the Line To Change list, select Gantt Rows.**

4. **Under Normal, choose a line type, color, and interval (Figure 18-6).**

Figure 18-6:
Use this
dialog box
to specify
the pattern,
color, and
interval
spacing of
gridlines.

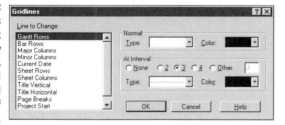

5. **Click OK.**

   The Gantt chart now has gridlines.

Recurring Tasks

Question: *I have to insert a bunch of weekly staff meetings into a project. How can I do this?*

Microsoft Project provides a shortcut for entering recurring tasks such as weekly staff meetings. Again, use the Jones Home project for an example. To do so:

1. **Choose Insert⇨Insert Recurring Task.**

   The Recurring Task Information dialog box appears (Figure 18-7).

2. **Enter the task name, the duration, and the frequency of occurrence.**

   If you select a recurring task that falls on a nonworking day, a dialog box will ask whether you want it rescheduled.

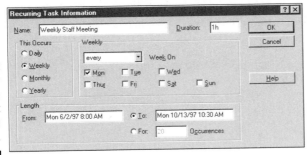

Figure 18-7:
The
recurring
task must
be a new
task; you
can't edit
an existing
one.

3. **Click OK.**

The Gantt chart now displays the weekly meetings.

Personalizing Your Workspace

Question: *Enough with this Gantt chart! How do I make something else the default view?*

Yeah, the Gantt chart gets tiring after awhile doesn't it? You can change the default view as follows:

1. **Choose Tools⇔Options.**

The Options dialog box appears.

2. **Select the View tab.**

3. **In Default View, choose another view.**

4. **Click OK.**

Customizing the Toolbar

Question: *Most of the time, I use only one button from the Tracking toolbar. Can I put it into the Formatting toolbar?*

Microsoft Project lets you make a toolbar longer by dragging buttons onto it. To do so:

1. **Right-click anywhere in the toolbar area.**

2. **Select the toolbar containing the button you want to move.**

3. **Hold down the Shift key and drag the button to the new toolbar.**

You can also place any button on any toolbar by right-clicking in the toolbar area and selecting Customize. The Customize dialog box instructs you on how to drag the button.

Thanks for all the tough questions. Play hard with your project files. The work will follow.

Part VI
Telling the World
How It's Going

UNDER PRESSURE TO INCREASE PRODUCTIVITY, THE SYSTEMS MANAGER AT MONDO CORP. READS THAT COMPUTER CHIPS RUN FASTER AT COLDER TEMPERATURES...

OK. BOB, THE PRINTER'S ONLINE!

In this part . . .

This is a bit much, you say. An entire part dedicated to printing? Why not just click the Print button? Yep. You can do that. If you want, skip this entire part. It's valuable only if you're interested in enhancing and customizing the look and effectiveness of your project communication. In this part, you use print preview and set margins, headers and footers, and legends. You also learn about how to customize a bunch of standard reports and how to create reports from scratch.

So, before you click that Print button, you may want to give this part at least a little consideration.

Chapter 19
Previewing and Printing Views

- -

In This Chapter

▶ Using Print Preview

▶ Setting margins

▶ Setting headers and footers

▶ Setting legends

- -

Congratulations! Your project is a masterpiece. It's rich with resources, tight on the tasks, realistic about risks, and correct about costs. Only one challenge remains. You need to make the plan a basis of understanding among everyone involved in the project.

In many ways, a project plan is only as valuable as your ability to communicate it. Unfortunately, this isn't always easy to do. Clear and simple communication can be a moving target. The kind and quantity of information needed varies dramatically from day to day and from one group to the next. Project team members need to know schedules and resource allocations. Accountants require access to cost information. Managers must be kept abreast of work. Stakeholders want to know how things are going.

Sometimes too much information is as disastrous as too little. Other times, information is proprietary or sensitive. In some circumstances, the back of a napkin is sufficient; other circumstances require a full-blown presentation. With Microsoft Project, you can dig in, find what you're looking for, determine what and how much you'll report, customize the manner of presentation, and print the results.

If you have your own project in the works, you might want to use it rather than the sample file provided for this chapter. Otherwise, open the sample project file called Smith Home 19.MPP from the Practice Files folder. To do so:

1. **Click the Open button on the Standard toolbar**.

2. **Open the Practice Files folder.**

3. **Double-click Smith Home 19.MPP.**

   The file should open in the Gantt Chart view.

Sending the World Your Views

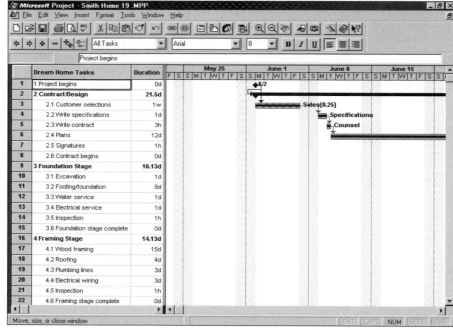

Printing a view can be as simple as clicking the Print button on the Standard toolbar. The value of this approach is also its deficiency. Click the button and the computer prints the view with a bunch of predetermined default settings. In many instances, this print option is exactly what the circumstances call for. But when you need a lot more control of the print function, a great alternative is just one button to the right on the Standard toolbar. Print Preview's the name, and functionality is its game. (Sorry.)

Getting around in Print Preview

For this example, make sure that the project is in Gantt view and set to the default timescale (Figure 19-1).

Figure 19-1: Print Preview is based on whatever screen you happen to be in when you choose it. Any filters or sorts are carried into the view.

Click the Print Preview button on the Standard toolbar. The Print Preview screen appears (Figure 19-2).

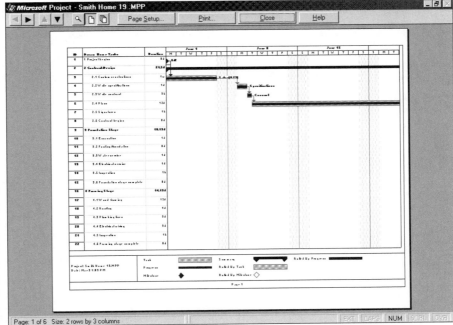

Figure 19-2:
The Print Preview command displays the view as it will be printed.

The toolbar at the top has directional arrows that enable you to jump from page to page of your view. The number of pages in Print Preview is Microsoft Project's calculation of how many pages it takes to see whatever was in view when you chose the Print Preview command. If you zoom out before clicking the Print Preview button, fewer pages are printed. If you zoom in, more pages are printed.

The status bar at the bottom of the window displays the current page number, the page count, and a description of the layout.

The toolbar also has a magnifying glass and a single page button. These buttons are copycats of mouse functions. As you move your mouse around the screen, the cursor turns into a magnifying glass. If you click somewhere on the screen, the information zooms to be readable and the window becomes scrollable. Click again, and it zooms back out. The same functions occur when you use the two corresponding toolbar buttons.

Big deal, you say! Project managers are renowned for their patience, so please humor me a little longer. Click the Multiple Pages button on the toolbar. Microsoft Project displays the whole view as it will appear in print (Figure 19-3).

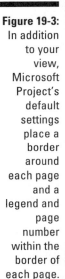

Figure 19-3: In addition to your view, Microsoft Project's default settings place a border around each page and a legend and page number within the border of each page.

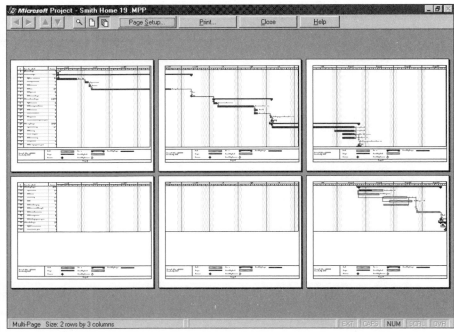

You can change some or all default settings and preview your work as you make the changes. That's what the next section is all about.

Using Page Setup

The Page Setup command controls certain aspects of the printed view. You can designate page orientation, margins, headers, footers, legends, and view options. In the Calendar view, you can also control units of time. Click the Page Setup button on the Print Preview toolbar. The Page Setup dialog box appears (Figure 19-4). The dialog box is divided into six sections, or tabs. (You can access the Page Setup dialog box also by choosing File⇨Page Setup.)

Figure 19-4:
When more
than one
project is
active, the
changes to
the Page
Setup dialog
box apply
only to the
file whose
view is
displayed.

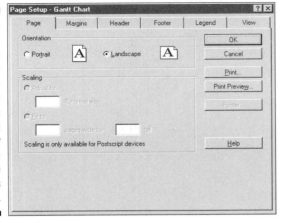

Setting the page

The Page tab offers two sets of options. The first, Orientation, permits Portrait (vertical) and Landscape (horizontal) selections. Microsoft Project defaults to the Landscape selection. The second set of options, Scaling, is available only for Postscript printers using Postscript printer drivers that support scaling.

Setting the margins

Now click the Margins tab. Two sets of options appear (Figure 19-5). If you want, in the first set of options, change the margins to see the effects of the change in the Sample box. You can further study the effect by clicking OK. The Print Preview screen adjusts to display your change. The second set of options, Borders Around, has two active selections in a Gantt view. You can turn off or turn on the borders around each page.

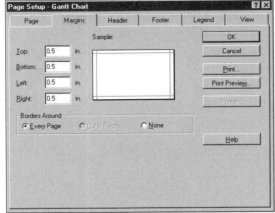

Figure 19-5:
The inactive
option,
Outer
Pages, is
available in
a PERT
Chart view.

Setting headers

The Header tab offers a number of options for creating a header. For the next example, you put the project manager's name and current date in the header on the right margin of each page:

1. **Click the Header tab.**

2. **In the Alignment area, select Right.**

3. **In the Code list box at the bottom of the screen, select Manager Name.**

   The Manager Name selection appears in the selection box.

4. **Click the Add button next to the Code list box.**

   The Manager Name code appears in the Selection box on the Right tab. The project manager's name appears in the Sample box.

5. **Press Enter.**

   The cursor in the Selection box on the Right tab drops to the next line.

6. **This time, instead of using the Code list box, click the Filename code button. (It's the one on the right of the Clock button.)**

   The Filename code appears on the second line in the Selection box.

7. **Add text to the first line of code in the Selection box by positioning your cursor in front of the code and typing** Manager: **(be sure to include a space after the colon).**

   The dialog box should now look like Figure 19-6.

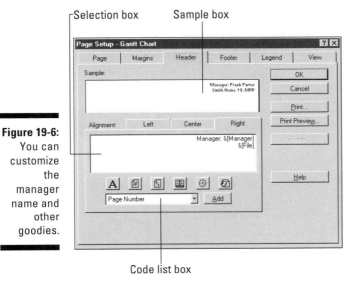

Selection box   Sample box

Figure 19-6:
You can
customize
the
manager
name and
other
goodies.

Code list box

One more thing before leaving the Header tab. Change the text style of the header. To do so:

1. Click the Text Styles button (the A).

The Text Styles dialog box appears.

2. In the Item to Change text box, select Header Right (Line 1).

This means the text style change will affect only the first line of the header.

3. In the Font list box, select Times New Roman.

4. In the Font Style list box, select Bold.

5. In the Font Size list box, select 16.

6. Click OK.

The Page Setup dialog box should now look like Figure 19-7.

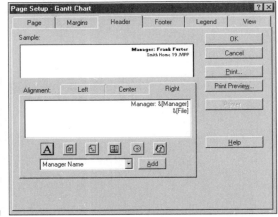

Figure 19-7:
The first line is now bold. The header is limited to a maximum of three lines.

To better see your work, click OK in the Page Setup dialog box. Then click the header once or twice to get a close-up view (Figure 19-8).

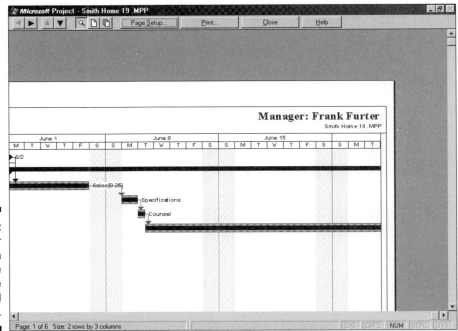

Figure 19-8:
The header appears on every page of the printed view.

Setting footers

Click the Page Setup tab to return to the Page Setup dialog box. Now click the Footer tab. The Footer tab has the same options as the Header tab. Because they're a repeat, I won't detail these options for you.

Setting the legend

You use the Legend tab to add text to the legend area of the printed view. The legend describes the meaning of the various bars and other symbols used in the Gantt chart or other charts.

Click the Legend tab in the Page Setup dialog box, and the screen shown in Figure 19-9 appears. The text options are the same in the Legend tab as they are in the Header and Footer tabs, with two additions. One additional option allows you to determine whether the legend should appear on every page, on its own page, or not at all. The other option lets you determine the width in inches for the text portion of the legend. After you have finished looking at the Page Setup features, click OK.

Figure 19-9:
The Width option allows a text box from 0 to 5 inches in the legend portion of the page.

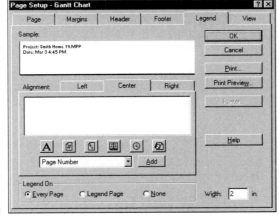

Printing Views

After you've determined the page setup, you can to move to the print options. Click the Print button in the Print Preview toolbar. The Print dialog box appears (Figure 19-10).

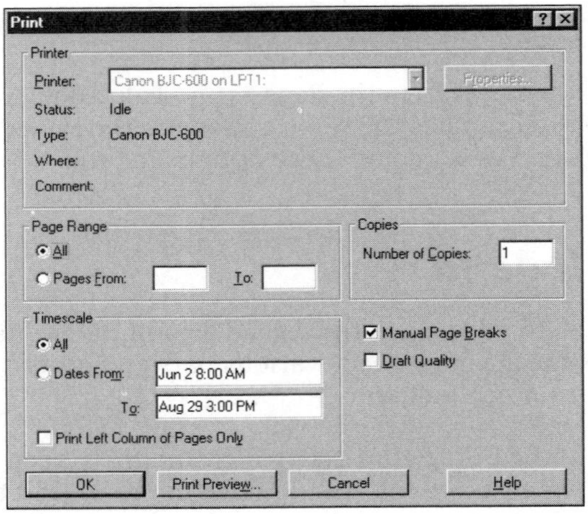

Figure 19-10:
The Print
dialog box
offers four
groups of
options.

From the Print Preview toolbar, the Print dialog box offers four groups of
options:

Option Group	Description
Page Range	Select All to print all pages of the view.
	Select Pages From to print a range of pages as listed in Print Preview.
Printer	Inactive in the dialog box shown in Figure 19-10. If you need to change your printer selection, do so by closing the Print Preview screen and choosing File⇨Print.
Timescale	Select All to print all pages of the view.
	Select Dates From to enter different start and finish dates in the From and To boxes.
Copies	Type the number of copies to be printed.

When you are finished with the Print dialog box, click OK to return to the
Gantt Chart view.

Chapter 20

Using and Customizing Reports

. . . .

In This Chapter

▶ Choosing from among 22 standard reports

▶ Customizing reports

▶ Creating reports

. . . .

*A*s much as you've come to love the Gantt Chart and PERT Chart views, you just can't take them to all the nice places. Some people will politely ask you to leave them at the door or in the car with the windows slightly rolled down. Fear not, Microsoft Project provides a solution — reports. You can take them anywhere.

Reports summarize and present specific information in an organized manner. They're designed to focus on trends or aspects of your project in a manner appropriate for the intended stakeholder or project team member.

Microsoft Project provides five kinds of reports as listed in the next section. A sixth category, Custom, is described later in the chapter.

If you have your own project in the works, you might want to use it rather than the sample file provided for this chapter. Otherwise, open the sample project file called Smith Home 20.MPP from the Practice Files folder. To do so:

1. Click the Open button on the Standard toolbar.

2. Open the Practice Files folder.

3. Double-click Smith Home 20.MPP.

The file should open in the Gantt Chart view.

Using Standard Reports

Five kinds of reports are ready-made and just waiting to be printed. You can use them as they are, or you can tweak them to meet your specific needs.

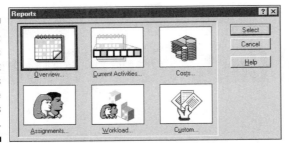

Figure 20-1:
The Reports
dialog box
provides
five
categories
of reports.

To access the five kinds of reports, choose View⟹Reports. The Reports dialog box appears (Figure 20-1).

Following is a description of each of the reports in their categories:

Report Category	Report Type	Display
Overview	Project Summary	The most important project information
	Top-Level Tasks	Information about top-level tasks
	Critical Tasks	Critical tasks for the project; includes summary tasks and successor tasks
	Milestones	Milestone tasks with their summary tasks
	Working Days	Working and nonworking times for resources
Current Activities	Unstarted Tasks	Tasks that haven't begun; includes predecessors and resources
	Tasks Starting Soon	Tasks that haven't started yet given the bookend dates you specify
	Tasks in Progress	Tasks in progress and their resources' schedules

Report Category	*Report Type*	*Display*
	Completed Tasks	Tasks completed in by-month breakdown
	Should Have Started Tasks	Tasks that should have started by a date you specify; includes summary tasks and successors
	Slipping Tasks	Tasks behind schedule; includes their summary tasks and successors
Costs	Weekly Cash Flow	Costs-per-task in one-week periods using a Crosstab Report
	Budget	The budget for all tasks
	Overbudget Tasks	Overbudget tasks for the project
	Earned Value	Earned value information for all tasks
Assignments	Who Does What	Task schedules for all resources
	Who Does What When	Tasks, their resources, and work using a Crosstab Report
	Weekly To-Do List	Weekly tasks for the resource you specify
	Overallocated Resources	Overallocated resources of the entire project
Workload	Task Usage	Resources assigned to tasks, including work information and totals, using a Crosstab Report
	Resource Usage	Tasks assigned to resources, including work information and totals, using a Crosstab Report

A good way to envision a crosstab report is to think of a mileage chart. In this type of chart, you find the distance between two cities by finding the box that is the crossing point between the horizontal line representing one city listing and the vertical line representing the other city listing.

For the next example, double-click Overview in the Reports dialog box. The Overview Reports dialog box appears (Figure 20-2).

Figure 20-2:
The Overview Reports dialog box doesn't offer an editing option.

Select the Critical Tasks report. The report is opened in Print Preview (Figure 20-3), which provides the opportunity to customize the orientation, the margins, and the header and footer.

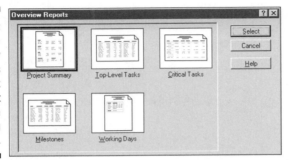

Figure 20-3:
The Print Preview of reports works in the same manner as the Print Preview of chart views.

Customizing a Report

Click the Close button in the Print Preview toolbar. You're back to the Reports dialog box. One special selection I haven't discussed yet is the Custom reports option. By choosing this option, you are telling yourself (and soon the world) that there is no fit like a tailored one. Good isn't enough. Unless it's pleated and tucked with your own aesthetic and intellectual insight, it's just not the very best you and your public have come to expect. My! You look *mahvelous.*

Double-click the Custom category. The Custom Reports dialog box appears (Figure 20-4).

Figure 20-4:
The Custom
Reports
dialog box
offers the
options of
editing,
copying,
and
creating
reports.

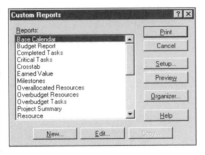

You'll customize the Critical Tasks report so that it presents the information in a highlighted format instead of an isolated format. To do so:

1. **Highlight the Critical Tasks report.**

   This is the report you access from the Reports dialog box, which I discuss earlier in this chapter.

2. **Click the Edit button at the bottom of the Custom Reports dialog box.**

   The Task Report dialog box appears (Figure 20-5). The Task Report dialog box offers highlighted (rather than isolated) reports, gray bands to separate tasks, and the opportunity to include summary tasks.

3. **Click the Definition tab if necessary.**

4. **Select the Highlight option.**

5. **Click OK.**

   You return to the Custom Reports dialog box.

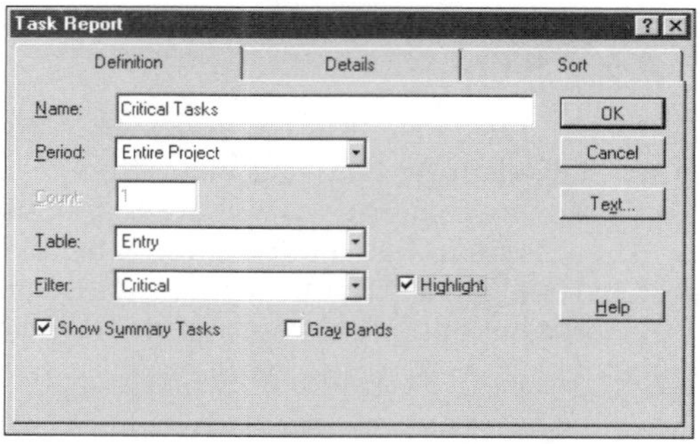

Figure 20-5:
The Task Report dialog box offers highlighted reports.

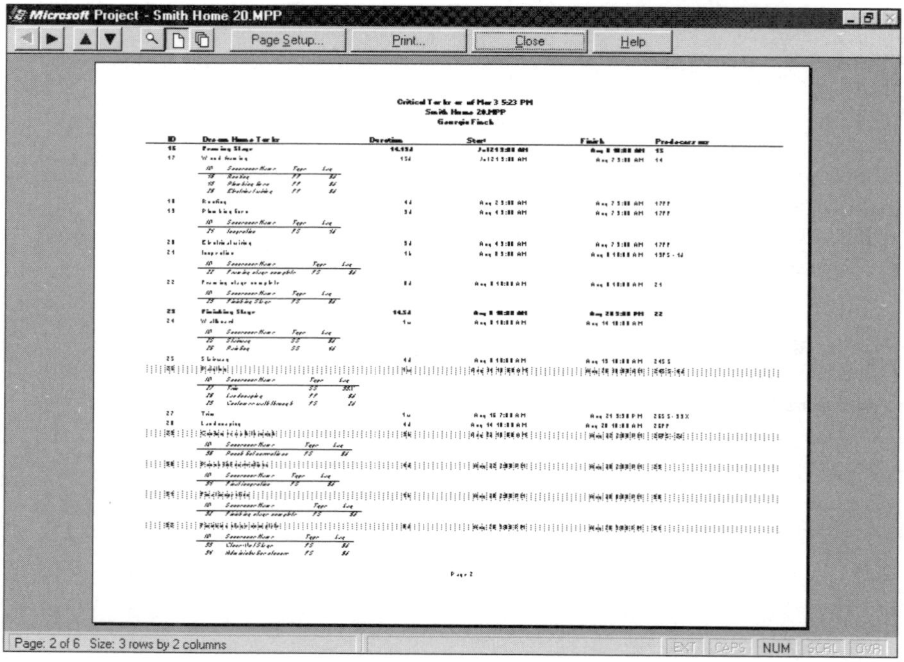

Task Report

| Definition | Details | Sort |

Name: Critical Tasks

Period: Entire Project

Count: 1

Table: Entry

Filter: Critical ☑ Highlight

☑ Show Summary Tasks ☐ Gray Bands

OK
Cancel
Text...
Help

Figure 20-6:
You can skip the Print Preview by choosing Print in the Custom Reports dialog box.

6. **Click the Preview button.**

   The revised report appears in Print Preview.

7. **Scroll to see the highlighted critical tasks (Figure 20-6).**

Creating a Report

To create a report from scratch, click the New button in the Custom Reports dialog box. The Define New Reports dialog box appears. The dialog box offers you four choices:

Report Type	*Displays*
Task	Schedule, cost, information about work, and task details
Resource	Schedule, cost, information about work, and task details
Monthly Calendar	Graphical representations of a calendar with tasks depicted as bars, lines, or start and finish dates
Crosstab	Information about tasks and resources over a period of time

For the next example, you create a Monthly Calendar report for the resources on the Construction Hours calendar. To do so:

1. **Click the New button in the Custom Reports dialog box.**

   The Define New Report dialog box appears.

2. **Select Monthly Calendar.**

   The Monthly Calendar Report Definition dialog box appears (Figure 20-7).

Figure 20-7: The Task, Resource, Monthly Calendar, and Crosstab Report options each have definition dialog boxes.

3. **In the Name text box, type** Construction Hours.

4. **In the Calendar list box, select Construction Hours Calendar.**

5. **In the Filter list box, select Date Range.**

6. **Click OK.**

You return to the Custom Reports dialog box.

7. **Click the Preview button.**

An interactive text box appears, asking you to designate tasks that start or finish after whatever you choose.

8. **In the text box, type** 8/1.

9. **Click OK.**

Another interactive text box appears, asking you to designate a date before. This may seem odd, but you're being asked what is the last date of the report. The interactive text box will use the date you enter as the parameter for showing all construction hour-related tasks before it. Sheesh.

10. **In the text box, type** 9/15.

The Monthly Calendar Report appears.

11. **Page down to August to view the filtered calendar report (Figure 20-8).**

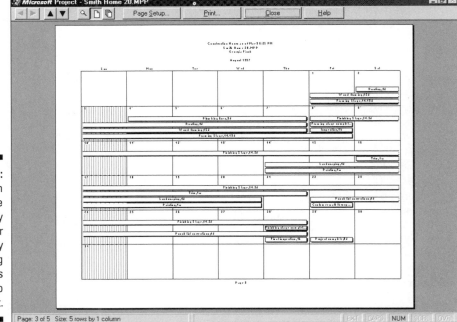

Figure 20-8:
You can skip the empty calendar pages by designating the pages you want to print.

Reports can be important to you as a project manager and to all the stakeholders of the project. They can also be powerful. An entire nation thought Mark Twain was dead, because of some false reports. The key to success in reporting is properly presenting correct information at the appropriate time to the right people. Just do that. And be sure to report to us how it goes!

Part VII
The Part of Tens

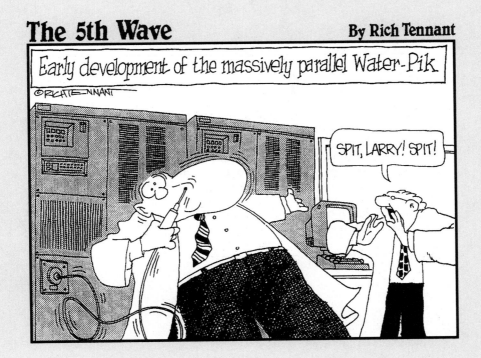

The 5th Wave — By Rich Tennant

Early development of the massively parallel Water-Pik.

SPIT, LARRY! SPIT!

In this part . . .

This part is an introduction to the rest of the world of Microsoft Project and project management. It presupposes that you have a modem and a connection to the World Wide Web. The material mentioned in this part suggests ways you can increase the efficiency of your project as well as your stature as a project manager. Here's betting that you're pleasantly surprised about all the things out there that are dedicated to making your project a success.

Chapter 21

Ten Terrific Templates

In This Chapter

▶ Finding templates to meet your need

▶ Templates for (almost) every occasion

A template is a helpful way to create something once and use it many times — something like sourdough. This chapter is devoted to sampling templates created for a wide variety of purposes. As you explore the templates, you're bound to get some great ideas for your own project-management design.

You can find the first nine of these templates on the Web at `http://www.microsoft.com/project/work.htm`. Select Templates, and then select General. To access these templates, download them into a template folder and self-extract them. (All these templates were available at the time this book was written.)

You'll notice that these files are saved as .MPP files instead of .MPT. They're still considered templates, though. When you access Microsoft's Web site, you might find additional templates.

The tenth template comes with the Microsoft Project software.

Happy Holidays!

The PRJHLDY1.MPP template is special for a few reasons. It's innovative and, for people like me, it has some nice ideas about organizing your holiday pageantry. See Figure 21-1.

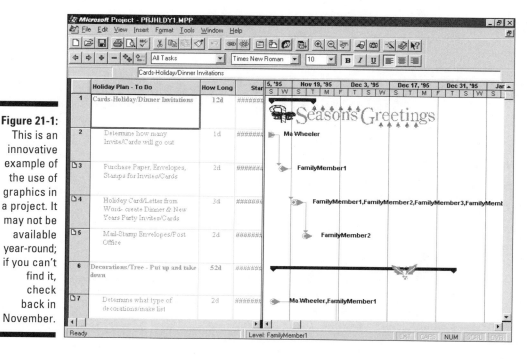

Figure 21-1:
This is an innovative example of the use of graphics in a project. It may not be available year-round; if you can't find it, check back in November.

3, 2, 1, Blastoff!

No, this doesn't mean that any of us will be sending a mission to the sun or anything in the near future. The AERO.MPP template shows the use of project management for a very large and long project. See Figure 21-2.

Just the Facts, Ma'am

The DATA.MPP template, shown in Figure 21-3, is a useful template of a project plan for anyone who's integrating a software program into a network.

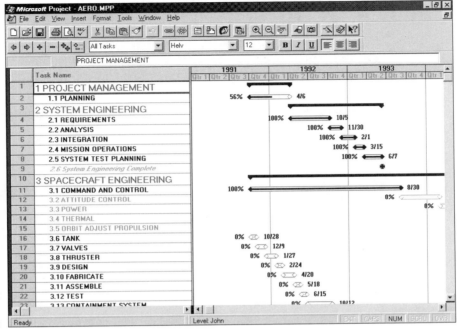

Figure 21-2:
Launch into this one with a critical eye to the use of layout techniques.

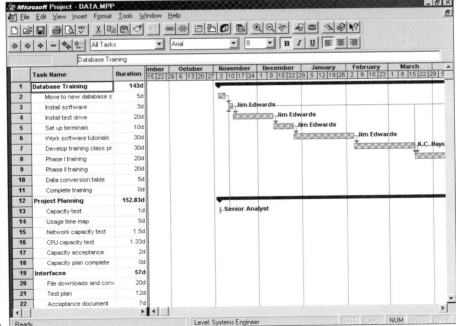

Figure 21-3:
A simple project design for software installation and training on a network.

Put It in Writing

Ready to start that newsletter or magazine you've always thought would turn your industry upside down? Here's a useful project template. It's called PUBLISH.MPP and is shown in Figure 21-4.

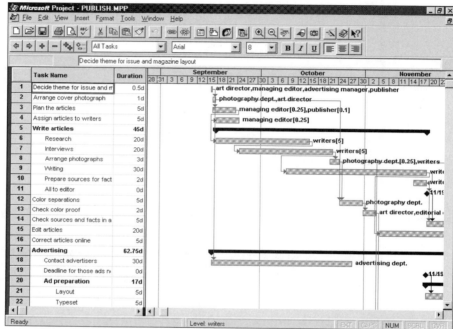

Figure 21-4:
A great outline for publishing a newsletter or magazine.

Engineering a Project

Maybe the construction of steam generation stations is a little removed from your area of expertise. Even so, the CAPITAL.MPP template might be worth checking out for its custom layout. See Figure 21-5.

Marketing Plan

The LAUNCH.MPP template, shown in Figure 21-6, offers some insightful summary group clusters for developing a marketing plan.

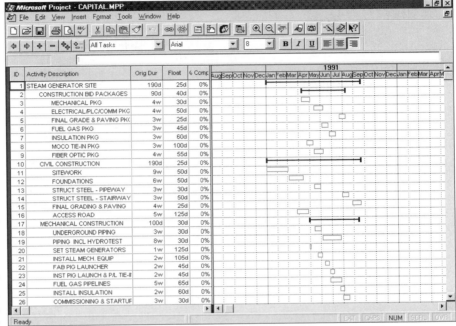

Figure 21-5:
An engineering project for steam generation.

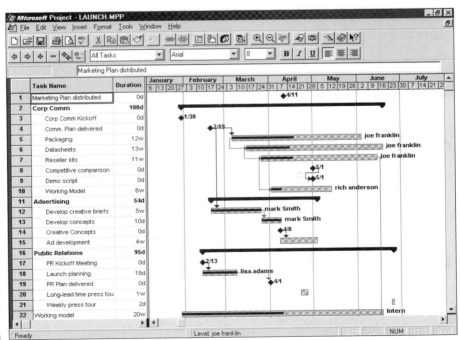

Figure 21-6:
A marketing project.

Designing a Lease

The LEGAL.MPP template (Figure 21-7) is useful for any organization planning a move or an expansion that involves a lease. That is, if the party of the first part is seriously considering tendering a counterproposal to the party of the second part. You know what I mean?

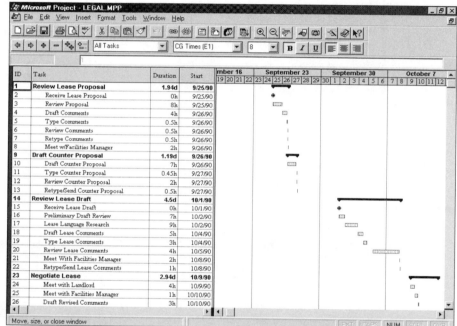

Figure 21-7:
A lease
project
plan.

A Rebuilding Project

Renovation anyone? Here's a template that covers much of the necessary planning of a remodeling of a corporate space. It's filename is RENOV.MPP, and it's shown in Figure 21-8.

Exploring for Oil

Oil be seeing you in all the old familiar places — like in OILEXPL.MPP, a petroleum company's exploration template. So this is a bit exotic, you say? I'm suggesting that you peruse it to see how complex a template can get. See Figure 21-9.

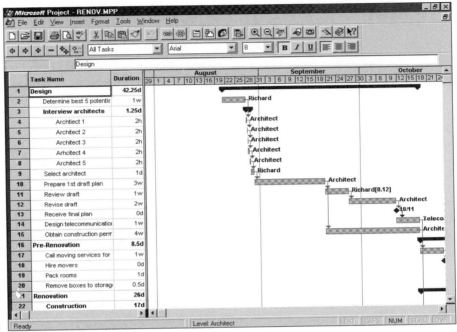

Figure 21-8:
A building renovation project.

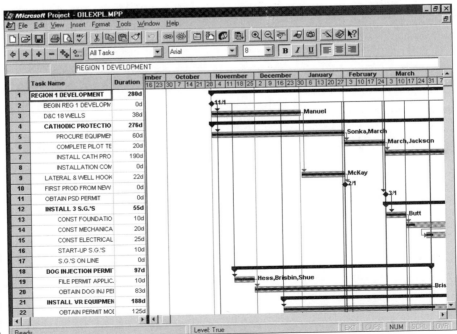

Figure 21-9:
An oil exploration project.

Understanding a Large Template

If all else fails, read the instructions. (Better yet, buy a ...*For Dummies* book.) Resident in your Winproj files is a tutorial for building a template. Although it's subject specific — software development — it's also filled with insightful ways to do your homework so that you can build a template of lasting value. The filename is SOFTDEV.MPT (Figure 21-10).

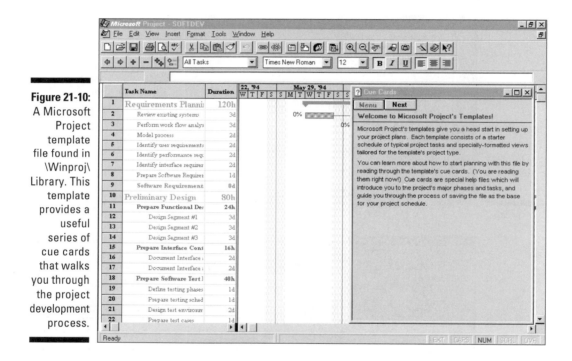

Figure 21-10: A Microsoft Project template file found in \Winproj\ Library. This template provides a useful series of cue cards that walks you through the project development process.

Chapter 22

Ten Innovative Things You Can Do for Your Project

In This Chapter

▶ Find out how to break the mold

▶ Different ways to see the world of project management

*T*he ten ideas in this chapter are all centered on you. They are assembled to help you discover new and better ways to accomplish your project-management tasks. When your responsibilities outweigh your skills and resources, you can get very lonely. But don't be too concerned — you're not alone! A plethora of resources is available to help you with your job.

The Project Management Institute

The recent extraordinary growth of project management and the number of practitioners is due, in part, to the Project Management Institute (PMI). This nonprofit professional association provides a wealth of written materials and training opportunities. Within this organization, you can associate with fellow project managers and tap into a network of expertise in your community, industry, and special area of interest. Considering what you get by belonging, membership is cheap (about $100 per year).

You can contact PMI at Project Management Institute, 130 South State Road, Upper Darby, PA 19082. The telephone number is 610-734-3330. The fax number is 610-734-3266.

Two of the most important resources available through PMI are the Project Management Body of Knowledge and the Project Management Professional certification, both of which I describe in this chapter.

Project Management Body of Knowledge

The basics of project management are universal. Over the years, professionals have synthesized project-management principles and practices into a standard, known as the Project Management Body of Knowledge. The 160-plus page document is available to you free of charge on PMI's Web site at `http://www.pmi.org`. This document is one of the best freebies you'll ever find.

Project Management Training

You can find a number of project-management training groups around the country. I know of one that is without question first class. It's called the International Institute for Learning (IIL). The IIL provides programs around the country at convenient locations. All programs are cosponsored with a major university or college, and all attendees receive a certificate of completion from that institution. Some program modules are

- Project Scope Management
- Project Time Management
- Project Cost Management
- Project Human Resource Management
- Project Risk Management
- Project Quality Management
- Project Procurement Management
- Project Communications Management

As of this writing, the cost for the program is about $2,200. You receive a comprehensive understanding of project management and the background to prepare yourself for certification.

Master of Project Management Degree

Project management degree programs are available at colleges and universities around the country. One that I can recommend is ITT Technical Institute's Master of Project Management (MPM) degree. The ITT objectives in the MPM program are to help students prepare for participation in project-management activities upon graduation; provide high-quality graduate instruction to help students prepare for advancement and professional development in their chosen career; and foster critical thinking, communication, and teamwork. Designed for working adults, the 21-month, 56 credit-hour MPM program emphasizes the practical issues of project management in a team-oriented format.

You can contact ITT Technical Institute at 9511 Angola Court, Indianapolis, IN 46268. The telephone number is 800-937-4488. Ask to speak to Lu Bruderly.

PMP Certification

Sooner or later, Project Management Professional (PMP) certification is a goal of all professional project managers. This may or may not be for you, but it's at least worth your investigation and consideration. Like other professions, such as law and accounting, project management is based on a recognized set of standards. The purpose of the PMP certification is to provide recognition of your abilities as a project manager. The certification is based on a combination of testing and proven experience and service in the field of project management. To find out more about it, contact PMI. See the "Project Management Institute" section at the beginning of this chapter for contact information.

Group Involvement

For a stimulating and challenging experience, you can't beat one-on-one contact with people who share common interests. You can accomplish this in project management with a PMI shared-interest group or through involvement in a local PMI chapter. Project managers throughout the world attend monthly chapter meetings. These self-governing chapters are great for exchanging ideas and information. Check your telephone directory for a local project management society, or contact PMI at 610-734-3330 or http://www.pmi.org.

Project-Management Newsgroups

A small number of project-management newsgroups are on the Web. One especially helpful newsgroup is the one you can access about Microsoft Project at http://microsoft.com/msproject. Select Support and then select Browse the Newsgroups.

Books and Periodicals

I don't mean to keep touting PMI, but the institute publishes an *Information Source Guide* that lists more than 100 books and periodicals about project management. The guide is free for the asking by calling 610-734-3330 or by faxing 610-734-3266.

Web Search

If you have a few hours, do a Web search of project management. A very large number of individuals and organizations offer services in project management. As is typical of such searches, a lot of your search will be marginal in value. However, some good sites are out there, too, such as http://www.projectmanagement.com/main.htm. It's great.

Microsoft Project

One of the least costly and most helpful study resources is the one you've been using — Microsoft Project. Microsoft Project's Help function is surprisingly helpful (ahem) in its organization and depth. One especially useful connection it offers is technical support.

At the time this book was written, Microsoft still offered limited free technical support. In the United States, no-charge support from Microsoft support engineers is available with a toll call between 6:00 a.m. and 6:00 p.m., Monday through Friday, except holidays. Call 206-635-7155. When you call, be sure to have your product ID number handy. You can find it by choosing Help⇨About Microsoft Project in the menu toolbar.

Part VIII
Appendixes

The 5th Wave   By Rich Tennant

EMPLOYEES MUST
WEAR OVEN MITTS

586
DEVELOPMENT
TEAM

In this part . . .

The appendixes in this part provide some basics about using Microsoft Project in workgroups and using data from other applications. The last appendix shows you how to load the sample project files.

Appendix A
Working with Workgroups

Microsoft Project is written for ease of sharing and updating project information. Through your use of the program's workgroup options, you can send and receive project file updates. The workgroup options are available to you if your system has e-mail capabilities.

You can access the workgroup options by choosing Tools⇨Workgroup or by using the Workgroup toolbar. To access the Workgroup toolbar, right-click anywhere in the toolbar area and choose Workgroup from the shortcut menu.

This appendix briefly describes each of the Workgroup options on the Workgroup toolbar. Some of the options in this toolbar, such as Consolidate Projects, are included for convenience as a preparation before electronic transmission.

Routing Slip

 The Routing Slip command permits you to route information to recipients. You can add to or delete from the routing list, reorder the recipients, choose whether the messages should be sent one after the other or all at once, and notify the originator when each recipient has forwarded the message.

Send Mail

 The Send Mail command attaches the project file to an electronic message.

Update Read Only

 The Update Read Only command changes the current file to read-only status as a basis for electronic transmission. *Read only* means that the project can be accessed and viewed, but cannot be resaved with changes.

Toggle Updates

 The Toggle Updates command switches the active project file between read-only and read-write status.

Consolidate Projects

 The Consolidate Projects command consolidates all unhidden project files into a single active file.

Open from Database

 The Open from Database command opens a file that has been saved to a database application.

Save to Database

 The Save to Database command saves a file to a database application.

Team Assign

 The Team Assign command alerts a resource or a team member that you are planning to assign the resource or the team member to a task.

Team Update

 The Team Update command informs resources or team members that you are about to modify their assigned tasks.

Team Status

 The Team Status command is a request to resources or team members for information about updates to tasks.

Set Reminders

 The Set Reminders command works with Microsoft Schedule+ to set reminders for selected tasks.

Appendix B

Working with Data from Other Applications

. . . .

Microsoft Project accommodates the addition of text, spreadsheet information, graphic objects, sound, movies, and animation. Using applications resident in Windows 95 or using more elaborate applications, such as Adobe Photoshop or Premiere, you can custom design your Project file to present product update discussions, customer interviews, project photos, or just about anything else you want. Microsoft Project can also send data to and receive data from databases.

Using the Clipboard

Using the clipboard might seem a little archaic at first, but it's actually pretty slick. Microsoft Project uses the Windows copy-and-paste features to place data from other applications into a project.

Pasting text

You can create a list of items in a word processor and, through pasting, cause the list to become tasks in Microsoft Project. The value of this is somewhat questionable, but it's good to know if you have already created lists in another application, such as in a proposal.

To perform this function, open a word processor such as Microsoft Word. Create a list of items or use an existing list. Select the list and copy it to the word processor's clipboard. In Microsoft Project, click the Paste button on the Standard toolbar. The items in the list appear as tasks.

Pasting graphics or multimedia

You can also paste a graphic, a sound, or another kind of object. When you paste it, the object or a representation of the object appears in the Gantt chart. After it appears, you can drag the object to an appropriate spot.

Using the Paste Special command

You can take advantage of object linking and embedding (OLE) through the Paste Special command. After you've created and copied something to the clipboard — for example, you've typed text in a word processor — you can paste the clipboard contents into a project in two ways. You can designate that you want to be able to activate the text by using the word processor, or you can paste a picture of the text into your document so that any changes to the text file are automatically updated in your project.

To place text in the Gantt chart, for example, open a word processor such as Microsoft Word. Create text or use an existing text file. Select the text and copy it to the word processor's clipboard. In Microsoft Project, choose Edit⇨Paste Special. The Paste Special dialog box appears. The dialog box provides choices of how you might want to display the contents of the clipboard. As you select each choice, a Result message appears below the highlighted item. The Result description explains the way that selection would affect the clipboard object.

The object of the clipboard can be text, spreadsheet information, graphics, or multimedia objects. If you want, rather than displaying the object in the Gantt Chart, you can choose Display as Icon. An icon appears that represents the originating application. When you place the icon in the Gantt chart, you can double-click the icon to display the object.

Inserting Objects

You can place objects in the Gantt chart not only with the clipboard but also by inserting them. To do this, choose Insert⇨Object. The Object dialog box appears.

The Create New option permits you to select an application from a list and open it. After you have created the object, you return to Microsoft Project. The object is embedded in the Gantt chart. The Create From File option permits you to embed or link an existing object file. In either case, Create New or Create from File, you can display an application icon rather than the object itself.

Using Project with Databases

You can open database information into Microsoft Project or save a project file to a database format. To open a database file, choose Tools⇨Multiple Projects⇨Open From Database.

To save a Microsoft Project file in a database file format, choose Tools⇨ Multiple Projects⇨Save To Database. Choose the drive and directory where you want to store the file. Select a database to save it into. Then click the Save button.

Appendix C

About the Disk

● ●

*I*f you want to practice your skills in Microsoft Project without making your hands hurt, the sample files disk is for you. The project files on the disk are used as a reference throughout the book. Imagine mastering the ins and outs of project management without all the keystroking agony of building projects! It's almost like hot fudge ice cream cake without guilt. Here's what you'll find on the *Microsoft Project For Dummies* disk:

✔ Sample Microsoft Project files you can use to master your project management skills

✔ Sample graphics to use with your projects

System Requirements

Make sure that your PC-compatible system meets the following system requirements for using this disk:

✔ Windows 95

✔ Microsoft Project for Windows 95

✔ A 486 or faster processor with *at least* 8MB of total RAM

✔ At least 2.1MB of hard disk space available to install all the files from this disk

Installing the Files

To install the sample practice files:

1. Insert the book's disk into your floppy disk drive.

2. Click the Start button, and then choose Run.

3. Type A:\PROJECTS.EXE **(substitute your floppy disk drive letter if it's different than A).**

The self-extractor window appears. The files will be copied to C:\MSOffice\Winproj\Practice Files by default. If you want to copy the files to a different location, type the new folder path in the Unzip To Folder box.

4. In the self-extractor window, click the Unzip button.

What You'll Find

After you install the sample files, you'll find a bunch of files with an .MPP or an .MPW extension. These are project files that Microsoft Project reads. You use these files with various chapters in the book.

You'll also see a file with a .BMP extension. This is a graphics file you use when you practice placing objects in a project file.

If You've Got Problems (Of the Disk Kind)

I tried my best to include Microsoft Project files that will work on most computers that meet the minimum system requirements. Alas, all computers are not identical and programs may not work properly for some reason.

If you have a problem installing or running the practice files, please call the IDG Books Worldwide Inc., Customer Support phone number: 1-800-762-2974.

Glossary

Accrual method When the cost of a resource occurs. This may be at the start of a task, prorated during the task, or at the end of the task.

Actual The facets of a task that have begun, including dates, cost, and work accomplished.

Base calendar The primary calendar for a project.

Baseline Called also the Baseline Plan or simply the Plan. The final copy of all project aspects before the project start date. The baseline is used as a point of reference after the project begins.

Calendar A list of the working time periods and nonworking time periods in a project.

Collapsed outline The outline of tasks where all or part of the subtasks are hidden under summary tasks.

Combination view A screen showing two views. The bottom view shows details of a highlighted feature in the upper view.

Consolidation A combining of projects.

Constraint A condition that limits the start or the finish of a task.

Critical path A sequence of tasks that must finish on or ahead of schedule for a project to be completed on time.

Critical Path Method (CPM) A procedure for setting the start and finish dates of tasks to ensure an on-time completion of a project.

Date line A dashed line running vertically in the Gantt chart to either indicate the computer's system date or a current date set in Files⇨Project Info.

Demoting To set a task as a subtask in a task outline structure.

Duration The units of time of a task or group of tasks. Duration units are minutes, hours, days, and weeks.

Expanded outline   An outline view in which all subtasks are visible.

Field   A data entry point in a table.

Filter   A condition or group of conditions that acts as the basis for an information search in a project.

Fixed cost   A cost, such as a contract agreement, that remains the same independent of the duration or the number of resources used.

Fixed-duration scheduling   A type of scheduling that sets a fixed length for a task. Numbers of resources have no affect on fixed duration tasks.

Gantt chart   A graphical depiction of a project. The length of Gantt bars in a Gantt chart represents duration. Lines between tasks represent task relationships.

Interactive filter   A filter that asks the user for information as the basis of a search of matching information in a project.

Lag time   A set length of time that is established between a task and its predecessor as the basis for the task to start.

Legend   Reference information on a chart explaining the relevance of graphic representations.

Leveling   A procedure of lengthening task durations to decrease demands on a resource or a group of resources.

Linked tasks   Tasks connected in some kind of relationship.

Master project   A project containing one or more subprojects.

Milestone   A task that indicates a beginning, a completion, or a significant event in a project. Milestones have a duration of 0d.

Node   The box in a PERT chart containing properties of a task.

Outline   A structured format in the Gantt Chart view containing higher-level summary tasks and lower-level subtasks.

Overallocation	The overassignment of tasks to a resource in a particular time period.
PERT chart	A network chart depicting relationships among tasks. Tasks appear as boxes, or nodes. Task relationships are illustrated by connecting lines.
Predecessor	A task that precedes another task.
Promote	In an outlined project, to move a subtask to a higher level. Promoting is performed by outdenting.
Recurring task	A task that repeats at regular intervals throughout all or a portion of a project.
Report	A compilation of project information that you print.
Resource	A person or equipment that does work.
Resource calendar	A designation of working and nonworking days and hours for a specific resource or a group of resources.
Resource-driven task	A task whose duration is directly affected by the number of resources assigned to it.
Resource pool	A list of resources compiled so that they are available to all tasks.
Resource view	A view that shows resources instead of tasks.
Schedule	The current status of a plan.
Slippage	How much a task is behind its baseline start date, finish date, or both.
Subproject	A project file shown as a single task in another project file.
Subtask	A task indented under a summary task.
Successor	A task that follows another task.
Summary task	A task that comprises a summary of the duration, cost, and work of a group of subtasks.

Task	One of the planned activities of a project.
Task view	A view of a project based on task information.
Template	A Microsoft Project file format that enables you to use an existing schedule as the basis for making a new schedule.
Timescale	Units of time used to depict a project schedule. The timescale has levels of measurement — the major timescale and the minor timescale.
Variance	The difference between baseline data and current data.
View	Any one of a large number of possible presentations of project information.
Work breakdown structure (WBS)	A hierarchical structure used to organize tasks for reporting schedules and tracking costs. With Microsoft Project, you can use the outline feature, use task IDs, or assign a WBS code to each task in the task detail form.
Workspace	A group of project files that can all be opened at one time. Workspace files are created by choosing File⇨Save Workspace.

Index

Notes

Notes

Notes

5. **Limited Warranty.**

   (a) IDGB warrants that the Software and disk(s)/CD-ROM are free from defects in materials and workmanship under normal use for a period of sixty (60) days from the date of purchase of this Book. If IDGB receives notification within the warranty period of defects in materials or workmanship, IDGB will replace the defective disk(s)/CD-ROM.

   (b) IDGB AND THE AUTHOR OF THE BOOK DISCLAIM ALL OTHER WARRANTIES, EXPRESS OR IMPLIED, INCLUDING WITHOUT LIMITATION IMPLIED WARRANTIES OF MERCHANTABILITY AND FITNESS FOR A PARTICULAR PURPOSE, WITH RESPECT TO THE SOFTWARE, THE PROGRAMS, THE SOURCE CODE CONTAINED THEREIN, AND/ OR THE TECHNIQUES DESCRIBED IN THIS BOOK. IDGB DOES NOT WARRANT THAT THE FUNCTIONS CONTAINED IN THE SOFTWARE WILL MEET YOUR REQUIREMENTS OR THAT THE OPERATION OF THE SOFTWARE WILL BE ERROR FREE.

   (c) This limited warranty gives you specific legal rights, and you may have other rights which vary from jurisdiction to jurisdiction.

6. **Remedies.**

   (a) IDGB's entire liability and your exclusive remedy for defects in materials and workmanship shall be limited to replacement of the Software, which may be returned to IDGB with a copy of your receipt at the following address: Disk Fulfillment Department, Attn: Microsoft Project For Dummies, IDG Books Worldwide, Inc., 7260 Shadeland Station, Ste. 100, Indianapolis, IN 46256, or call 1-800-762-2974. Please allow 3–4 weeks for delivery. This Limited Warranty is void if failure of the Software has resulted from accident, abuse, or misapplication. Any replacement Software will be warranted for the remainder of the original warranty period or thirty (30) days, whichever is longer.

   (b) In no event shall IDGB or the author be liable for any damages whatsoever (including without limitation damages for loss of business profits, business interruption, loss of business information, or any other pecuniary loss) arising from the use of or inability to use the Book or the Software, even if IDGB has been advised of the possibility of such damages.

   (c) Because some jurisdictions do not allow the exclusion or limitation of liability for consequential or incidental damages, the above limitation or exclusion may not apply to you.

7. **U.S. Government Restricted Rights.** Use, duplication, or disclosure of the Software by the U.S. Government is subject to restrictions stated in paragraph (c) (1) (ii) of the Rights in Technical Data and Computer Software clause of DFARS 252.227-7013, and in subparagraphs (a) through (d) of the Commercial Computer—Restricted Rights clause at FAR 52.227-19, and in similar clauses in the NASA FAR supplement, when applicable.

8. **General.** This Agreement constitutes the entire understanding of the parties and revokes and supersedes all prior agreements, oral or written, between them and may not be modified or amended except in a writing signed by both parties hereto which specifically refers to this Agreement. This Agreement shall take precedence over any other documents that may be in conflict herewith. If any one or more provisions contained in this Agreement are held by any court or tribunal to be invalid, illegal, or otherwise unenforceable, each and every other provision shall remain in full force and effect.

Installation Instructions

The project files on the accompanying disk are used as a reference throughout the book. Here's what you'll find on the *Microsoft Project For Dummies* disk:

- ✔ Sample Microsoft Project files you can use to master your project management skills
- ✔ Sample graphics to use with your projects

See Appendix C for complete installation instructions.

Don't worry about using the files. I tell you when you need to open the first file.